HURRICANE BILLY

BILLY
THE
STORMY LIFE
AND FILMS OF
WILLIAM FRIEDKIN

NAT SEGALOFF

William Morrow and Company, Inc.
NEW YORK

Excerpt from Vito Russo's *The Celluloid Closet: Homosexuality in the Movies* (New York: Harper and Row, 1987) reprinted by permission of the author.

Excerpt from "Bell Tells" by Arthur Bell appeared in *The Village Voice*, July 1, 1979. Reprinted by permission of *The Village Voice*.

Recognizing the importance of preserving what has been written, it is the policy of William Morrow and Company, Inc., and its imprints and affiliates to have the books it publishes printed on acid-free paper, and we exert our best efforts to that end.

Library of Congress Cataloging-in-Publication Data

Segaloff, Nat.
    Hurricane Billy : the stormy life and films of William Friedkin / by Nat Segaloff
        p. cm.
    Filmography: p.
    Includes bibliographical references.
    ISBN 0-688-07852-4
    1. Friedkin, William.   2. Motion picture producers and directors— United States—Biography.   I. Title.
PN1998.3.F75S4   1990
791.43′0233′092—dc20
[B]   89-12181
                                                                      CIP

Printed in the United States of America

First Edition

1 2 3 4 5 6 7 8 9 10

BOOK DESIGN BY MARSHA COHEN

To Robert S. Steele who validated my passion for film, and to Sally Hergrueter who shared it.

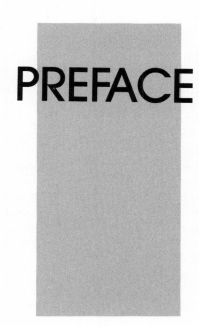

PREFACE

I've known Billy Friedkin since January of 1974 when I was doing publicity for a Boston movie theater chain that was showing *The Exorcist*. Some nutcase woman in Massachusetts had brought her child to see the film, then had gone straight to a judge to have us all indicted for "obscenity, blasphemy and corrupting the morals of a minor." The minor, of course, was the one she had bought the ticket for.

When Billy heard about it, he was under the gun to finish the foreign-dubbed versions of the film before leaving on a nation-wide lecture tour. Still, he telephoned his support.

"You've got to tell these people that they don't have any right to tell others what they can or cannot see," he said on the phone. Mind you, this is the hottest movie director in the country and he's calling a little twelve-screen theater chain to deliver a pep talk on the Constitution. I realized at that point that, aside from making some pictures I found exciting and intellectually invig-orating, William Friedkin—and, yes, I call him Billy most of the time—was also a detail man.

So, by the way, was the judge who heard our blasphemy case. He threw it, and the lady who brought it, out the door. As it turned out, it was on the first day of Lent. Make of that what you will.

Billy and I actually met a month or so later, during that lecture tour, when I was asked by Warner Bros. to make sure he and his companion, Jennifer Nairn-Smith, had transportation to the airport and otherwise to keep a studio presence. He was speaking at Clark University, Holy Cross College, and Worcester Polytechnic Institute in Worcester, Massachusetts, in the cold winter of February 1974. I quickly learned—studio-rented limousine idling nearby—that Billy was just as quick to hang out at a campus coffee shop as he was to dine formally with the president of the school. With either group he was completely at ease, boyishly enthusiastic and occasionally profane.

Not a lot of directors, I have since learned, are like that.

What continues to interest me about William Friedkin is that, unlike some directors I have met, he truly gets off on making movies. He possesses the raw energy of a kid playing with a toy thirty years after he discovered it under the tree. At the same time he is so serious about using that toy that you know it would be dangerous to use it on any terms but his.

This contributes to Billy's celebrated "moods." I've only sampled a few of them; others, as you'll read in this book, have felt the whole spectrum. He can be impatient, abusive, vulgar, goading, sarcastic and even physical. But he can also be encouraging, soothing, caring, supportive and unbelievably inspiring. And anybody who can't take it, go play somewhere else.

There is, as well, a storm of enigmas swirling around him. Billy loves to dismiss other people's work as "superficial" and deride his own achievements as "flawed" or outright failures, yet he has chosen to make commercial feature films in Hollywood—a community where superficiality is a given and his own flaws are seen as the efforts of a brilliant mind to try something new. It's a conundrum he just won't talk about. If he wanted to make a real statement, he would go back to making documentaries; yet he feels (probably correctly) that more people can be moved and affected by a commercial feature film. But then he goes and makes some that are so complex or confused that they don't reach an audience.

This is what fascinates me about the man, this web of contradictions. The fact that he is one of the best technicians in the business—everybody says so—means, to me, that he is fully capable of realizing whatever vision he has, as long as he knows what that vision is. He also (contractually and by sheer force of his personality) maintains total control of his films, so he answers to no one but himself in deciding what to put in them. He draws from the well of his experiences and his imagination

(I don't know which scares him more) and thus I believe it is safe to analyze his work as a clear window of his soul. Billy Friedkin is not some journeyman director who conveniently gripes that the studio or the producer or the star destroyed his vision. Even the movies that didn't work out he willingly admits are his responsibility.

For all the interviews over fifteen years that went into this biography, none was ever less than candid. At no time did he contradict or correct himself. When I would check facts with others, with very few exceptions they would jibe with those he had given me; some were, as William Peter Blatty calls them, a *Rashomon* of differing interpretations, but nothing beyond a simple matter of point of view.

Still, there was something I knew I was not able to get. While I have no reason to suspect that he would ever go out of his way to get even with anybody who talked with me, a number of people—people big enough that it shouldn't matter even if he did—refused to be interviewed for this book. In fairness, I'm not completely sure that publicists and agents always passed along word that I wanted to speak with them; thus do the politics of Hollywood affect its scholarship.

But beyond those ellipses, Billy himself was frequently aloof. He repeatedly swears that he cannot remember dates of certain events, yet easily recalls names and even license plate numbers from his distant past. He says he doesn't care about keeping records, but allowed me to prowl through his private storage garage where I found a pile of cardboard boxes full of old scripts, memos, folders and budgets. When I wanted to learn about projects he had abandoned he would get angry and ask, "What the hell good is it to talk about that?" as though what a man *doesn't* do couldn't be as revealing as what he *does* pursue.

Yet I believe I am the only one to get all of this information in one place. I don't know how many times I spoke with people who had known him for twenty years yet who said, when I asked for details, "I don't know anything about his background" or "I don't know about that part of his life." Friedkin has managed to construct an existence by parceling out pieces of himself to others. If they ever got together in the same room, he probably would not want to enter it. Then again, he might charge right straight in.

Billy craves perfection but is driven by the knowledge that he lacks it in himself. He is the sort of person who could stand on the rim of the Grand Canyon at sunset, see a candy bar wrapper fouling the ground, then go around saying, "The Grand

Canyon is ugly." In the end, it hardly matters what a film-maker thinks about himself. The work defines him. William Friedkin's work will live long after he does but, unlike most people who share his craft, he is completely responsible for what is there. I have hoped, in writing this book, to show why.

—Nat Segaloff
Cambridge, Massachusetts

ACKNOWLEDGMENTS

I once made the mistake of telling someone I was trying to interview for this book that William Friedkin had given me his permission to write it, but not his cooperation. This was during one period when I was waiting in Los Angeles for him to return my phone calls. When he did call me it was to hand me back, on as stern a vocal platter as I've ever received, my wisecrack that had been so dutifully (and accurately) reported to him by the person whom, if I recall, I never did wind up interviewing.

Now, I'm used to hearing from angry people; one does not report on movies without expecting to knock around a few egos. But Friedkin's reprimand wasn't an angry one. It was the sort of thing a parent or a teacher might offer as a means of prodding one to overcome perceived faults. In other words, exactly what a good director has to do.

Did Friedkin direct this book? Absolutely not. I know this because his friends and co-workers, while protective, are also possessed of distinctive personalities, as their stories within should reveal. He also has his detractors, to which the same evaluation applies. Those of either side who, for whatever their reason, requested anonymity have been granted it.

Among those whose contributions I would like to acknowledge are William Friedkin's staff—Adele Joseph Curcuruto and Larry Felix—who are both efficient and discreet and, despite my constant pestering, were never less than polite to me or loyal to their boss.

Pamela Perry, with her penchant for saving things and tracking down others, deserves immense praise and thanks for her support as my research associate. Liane Brandon, Gary Fleder, Daniel M. Kimmel and Diana Murray also provided considerable support and counsel when it was much needed. I would like to additionally note the gracious assistance, often in more ways than they realized, of the following:

The Academy of Motion Picture Arts and Sciences, Karen Allen, Atlantic Records, Arnold "Red" Auerbach, Noel Behn, Linda Blair, William Peter Blatty, Peter Bogdanovich, Bob Bosen, *The Boston Herald*, Peter Boyle, Doug Brode, Bill Butler, Terry Byrne, Sammy Cahn, Ed Carter, David Chapman, Cindy Chvatal, Cinema Center Films, CBS Music Video Enterprises, CBS-TV, Columbia Pictures, Sheldon Cooper, Donald H. Cragin, Mary Lou Crane, Curt Creager, Lock Crippen, John Cronin, Mart Crowley, Loretta Cubberly, Willem Dafoe, Philip DeGuere, Dino DeLaurentiis, DeLaurentiis Entertainment Group, Matthew Diebel, Kim Donlon.

Eddie Egan, Britt Ekland, Facets Multimedia Center, Tony Fantozzi, Films Incorporated, Four Star International, Susan Fraine, A. Alan Friedberg, G. G. Communications, Gerald Gardner, Allen Garfield, Elmer Gertz, Constance Gorfinkle, Walon Green, Alan Greenfield, Merrilee Griffin, Edgar Gross, Gary H. Grossman, Sonny Grosso, Phyllis Guarnaccia, Al Hall, Jane Badgers Harris, Jeff Hoyt, Paul Huntsman, Mark Johnson, Randy Jurgensen, Jim Kent, Jane Lanouette, Stan Levin, Toni St. Clair Lilly, David Majka, Leonard and Alice Maltin, John T. Martin, Alex McArthur, Malachy McCourt, Gregory Mcdonald, Patrick McGilligan, Eric McGrath, Myron Meisel, Terri Morris, Ned Nalle, NBC-TV, National General Pictures, Ken Nordine, Palomar Pictures International, Paramount Pictures, Ed Peltier, William L. Petersen, Gerald Petievich, Shelly Pierce, Richard Pillard, Sterling "Red" Quinlan, Arnie Reisman, Ralph Rosenblum, Joe Rotondo, Deac Rossell, Rick Russo, Vito Russo, Bernard Sahlins, David Salven, Auriel K. Sanderson, Jonathan Sanger, Nancy Seltzer, Bud Smith, Creighton Smith, Fred Spring, Nick Stevens, Patrick Stockstill, Jeffrey Sweet.

John Thompson, Sonia Turek, Twentieth Century-Fox, United Artists, UA/MGM, Universal Pictures, UCLA Film Archive, James Verniere, *The Village Voice*, Warner Bros., Bill Weber, Bob Weiner, Lois Solomon Weisberg, Wide World Photos, Billie Wayne Willsie, Michael Wimer, David L. Wolper, Ira Yerkes, Bud Yorkin.

My literary agent Helen Rees and her associate Cathy Mahar

deserve much thanks for their guidance, work and for actually returning phone calls. At William Morrow, James Landis, Adrian Zackheim and Pamela Altschul did the same, for which additional thanks.

The greatest appreciation, of course, goes to William Friedkin for taking part in a project over which he had no control.

CONTENTS

PROLOGUE

HEART ATTACK

William Friedkin demonstrates how he wants a shot framed.
COURTESY OF NBC PRODUCTIONS/WILLIAM FRIEDKIN PRODUCTIONS

WHEN THE PAIN started, William Friedkin did not know he was dying. The San Diego Freeway was no more or less crowded than usual as he drove himself to work. His bungalow offices at the Burbank Studios, where his personal assistant of seven years, Toni St. Clair Lilly, was probably already fielding his calls, were no more or less active than they were supposed to be. He was having no trouble getting meetings with Hollywood's power brokers to finance his films. The California sun was not shining any less brightly on him. And yet William Friedkin was having a heart attack.

It wasn't supposed to happen like this, he thought. Pain straight across. At first he thought maybe it was a muscle cramp, like when he played a little too much basketball. He wasn't overweight; in fact, he always knocked himself into pretty good shape between pictures. He didn't have high cholesterol and had cut down on eggs and stopped smoking so many of those cigars.

Maybe it was just a muscle cramp, he told himself. It can't be a heart attack. You don't know anybody who ever lived after one of those. Your mother didn't. You left the house feeling great and now a building fell across your chest.

Pull off the side of the road. Try to breathe. Try to open the car door. You can't do either. Try to sit up straight. It hurts. Shit, who's gonna notice you here? They'll think you're parked or drunk. A mile away, at the studio, everybody knows you. From the gate guard to the president, your movies pay their salaries. But here on a Burbank side street, you're nobody.

There's a sick joke in this town. It goes like this: A producer gets a call from a buddy in the film business.

"Have you heard?" the friend screams into the phone. "There's nuclear missiles headed right toward us. It's the end of the world!"

"It can't be," the producer tells him. "I just signed a three-picture deal at Paramount."

Bad things aren't supposed to happen to people on the A List. And William Friedkin was on the A List.

He started the car again and drove it with one hand to the gate of the Burbank Studios, made it just inside his office, and collapsed. The paramedics, summoned by Toni Lilly, were on him. They pounced, shoved an IV in his arm and a nitroglycerine pill under his tongue. Pumped on his heart. He couldn't open his eyes, couldn't see, couldn't feel anything. All he could do was hear.

One of the paramedics was taking his pulse. He was saying, "I'm not getting anything."

William Friedkin thought to himself, "My God, I'm dying. Jesus. I'm—I'm *dying*! I can't believe it."

He was terrified and scared and thought, "I have completely ruined my life and I have not put anything right and I'm gonna die now. That's it."

They took his body to St. Joseph's Hospital and in the emergency room the doctors tried to bring him back. Only he wasn't there.

"I was gone. I was moving toward a light, as though on an escalator. The light was very dim in the distance and I had no pain. I had a sense of anticipation but no anxiety. And the next thing that I remember was looking up into the lights, looking up into white-hot lights, and these guys were bringing me back to life and there was an oxygen mask over my mouth and I couldn't breathe and I thought I was in hell. Because the pain was back. Overwhelming and severe. And I was in pain, looking at these lights, hearing these voices. I couldn't breathe and I thought I'm condemned to purgatory forever."

But William Friedkin wasn't in hell. He was only in Hollywood.

In retrospect, the heart attack was probably unavoidable.

"I was born with a foreshortened twig in the circumflex artery," he now realizes.* "It was totally genetic. I was a time bomb from birth, as the doctor explained to me." He knocks wood. "I haven't had any recurrence." Nevertheless, he makes sure his tiny bottle of nitroglycerine pills stays fresh and he takes daily doses of vitamins. Lots of them.

"I would like to tell you that the heart attack made me a better person, but I don't know," he hedges. "I'll tell you, though, my faith is a little stronger, but I always had great faith. I didn't find religion, which is very disappointing. It's one of the sorrows of my life that it did not give me a clear, shining path to God. Because I'm a guy who is very much looking for faith in something and, not finding it, going on anyway. I'm still afraid to die, even though I feel there is a place to go. You're either ready or you're not, and I'm not."

Despite this brush with death, Friedkin professes no change in his art. On the personal level he reports an increased reverence for life and a heightened sense of his own frailty, but denies that these attitudes have affected the way in which he makes films. Now as always, he names but one nemesis:

---

* There is no exact heart condition so named, although a blockage in a circumflex artery *per se* would restrict blood flow enough to bring on a seizure such as Friedkin describes. It is congenital.

"Superficiality," he says, as if calling out a lifelong enemy. "That's my only fear in anything I do. Believe me, everything that I do at a certain point begins to be superficial. Nothing has ever come easy for me. Relationships have never been easy. My so-called ascent from the mail room was not easy; there were times when I thought I would never get out of the mail room, never get anywhere. I thought I was wasting my life on any number of occasions."

What Friedkin is describing, however, is impatience, not superficiality. To him the two are intertwined and result in an intolerable irony: not only can he not depend on others, but it takes so long to find out. That exquisite pairing of expectation and disappointment has planted in him a sense of betrayal that has found its way into all of his films and many of his friendships. It has inspired a combative manner, an abrasive style and a crassness in his dealings that polarize all around him. It also produces a highly charged creative atmosphere that few can resist, including those—and they range from secretaries to studio heads—who share equally the fallout from his mercurial temperament.

And it all seemed to come to a head on March 6, 1981, and made his heart stop.

In the nearly three months after that that it took him to recover, during which time therapists had to teach him how to move all over again, Friedkin could at last take the time to reflect on everything that had brought him to where he was.

Since hitting Hollywood in 1965 he had not stopped to catch his breath, reflecting a personal vigor that spilled over into his films. Driven and focused, both he and his movies took pride in ruffling feathers. Just why they did it, however, was not always clear.

Characteristically, then, when William Friedkin's life passed in front of him, it did not reveal the ending. The seven to twelve seconds he says he was clinically dead weren't enough for him to glimpse the future. But as he lay recovering in St. Joseph's Hospital in Burbank, around the corner from the studio, he wasn't being philosophical about his work. He just wanted to get on with it.

"I guess," he says, impatient with his divine intervention, "God didn't want the guy that directed *The Exorcist*."

CHAPTER 1

CHICAGO

William "Billy the Kid" Friedkin in the Senn High School
yearbook as a January 1953 graduate
COURTESY OF SENN METROPOLITAN ACADEMY

Rae and Louis Friedkin lived at 944 Montrose Avenue in Chicago when their only son, William, was born in 1935.
FROM THE AUTHOR'S PERSONAL COLLECTION

LIKE A MISTRESS, Chicago has always drawn William Friedkin back for visits but never—so far, anyway—to live or work. As his hometown it seems to hold loving memories and he returns with frequency to recharge his spirit. But he is married to Los Angeles, and to the movies, and so his reunions with Chicago remain like an interrupted love affair, separate and enticing.

They say that Chicagoans will always have two homes: wherever they are, and Chicago. The brash city is at once mother and father, teacher, lover, consort and foe, a moody enigma that is as addictive to others as it is to William Friedkin.

The list of paeans to the Windy City is almost obsessive: popular songs, the Second City comedy troupe, deep-dish pizza, a no-nonsense style of journalism, an elegant breed of jazz, and a peculiar political legacy that stretches from Al Capone to Richard J. Daley.

Movies have enjoyed a special relationship with Chicago, as well. Among the industry's first (and best) writers once the screen gained its voice were Chicagoans Ben Hecht, Charles MacArthur, Jules Furthman and Preston Sturges. Modern-day writers whose words continue that tradition include John Hughes, David Mamet, Michael Mann and Lawrence Kasdan, all of whom have also turned to directing to ensure the clarity of their speech.

William Friedkin shares that hypnotic fascination with Chicago. He was born there on August 29, 1935, although subsequent official biographies show the date as 1939, a glitch in history he felt little compulsion to correct (to do so would have jeopardized the *wunderkind* status the press had jubilantly conferred upon him when, in 1972 at age thirty-two, he won the directing Oscar for *The French Connection*. In reality he was thirty-six years and 225 days, coming well after Norman Taurog [in 1930/31 for *Skippy* at thirty-two years, 260 days] and Lewis Milestone [in 1927/28 for *Two Arabian Nights* at age thirty-three, 228 days], according to data for the latter two at the Academy of Motion Picture Arts and Sciences). Friedkin, when asked, now readily cites the 1935 date and expresses puzzlement that there could have been any other.

Louis Friedkin, forty-two, and Raechael Green Friedkin, thirty-five—he of Chicago and she from Kiev, Russia—brought their son, William David, home from Lake View Hospital to their small apartment at 944 Montrose Avenue.

"It was a fucking slum," William Friedkin declares coldly. "Now it's a war zone. But as I look at the world today, those days were pretty mild. There were no gang shootings in the streets. Most of it was in the area of mischief, just kids fighting.

There *were* areas you'd have to walk through carrying chains. But, on the other hand, I remember summer evenings—we had no air conditioning—sleeping in the park, my mother and father and me. Right in a public park along with thousands of other families, all right under the stars with no fear of getting ripped off or hassled or anything like that."

That may be because, contrary to his memory, the area of the city where the Friedkins lived was a comfortable, though hardly impressive, middle-class Jewish neighborhood. Street crime was nothing like it has become in the inner city, and in fact at the time the main threat to society came from kids like Friedkin and his playground cohorts—mostly shoplifting from Goldblatt's dime store or disturbing the peace between home and the basketball court at the Clarendon Field House a mile away.

Two blocks away from Montrose, on Kenmore Avenue, was the Graeme Stewart Grammar School where young William began developing his narrative talents by inventing stories to scare his female classmates. He also earned a reputation as "The Phantom of the School" by donning a mask and bursting into classrooms, tossing all the erasers from their blackboard shelf onto the floor—and sometimes at the teacher—and making a clean escape before anyone knew what was happening.

Friedkin's hoop sessions at Clarendon Field House were beginning to put dreams of professional basketball in his young mind. The only thing that threatened his career as what he refers to as a "playground rat" was a budding interest in girls.

"I was in love with this girl who sat in front of me in the first or second grade," he told interviewer Anthony Loeb. "Her name was Nancy Gates. She was quite beautiful and wore this enormous hat to class. She was all of seven years old. One day in class she turned around—I sat behind her—and she smiled at me. All my troubles sprang from that.

"We used to hold hands during the showing of the *Encyclopedia Britannica* movies. We used to kiss and get excited.

"One day she didn't show up. She wasn't in class. That one day stretched into a number of days, and a number more. They'd call the roll and she wasn't there. I began to realize that she wasn't coming back. I was too shy and embarrassed to ask where Nancy was. So I used to walk the streets of Chicago. I walked all over Chicago looking for this girl. It was in that way that I discovered the parameters of my world.

"It turned out, of course, that her parents had moved out of the neighborhood. I never saw that girl again."

But the seven-year-old boy did have something to show for his broken heart: he was a walking atlas of Chicago.

"I think that's probably what ultimately led me to want to go into media and reflect the city," he offers. "I came into television not wanting to reflect the world, but facets of the city that I cared about and understood."

With their son in school, Rae and Louis looked for a larger apartment. Louis, according to his son, "was sort of an itinerant guy" who "never earned more than fifty dollars a week in his life," a description revealing both the pity and contempt that will come to characterize the fathers that turn up in Friedkin's later film work.

His mother, however, was quite another matter. To supplement Louis's income, Rae resumed her profession as an operating room nurse in the various hospitals near 4826 N. Sheridan Avenue (at Gunnison) where the family moved. She would scrape together bus fare for her son, who would often pocket it, preferring to walk to school. His favorite route took him past a grisly location.

"There was a house on the way that had a tremendously profound influence on me," he says with relish. "It was the house where a little girl had been taken out of her upstairs bedroom and she'd been mutilated and her body parts would be found around the house and the block for days—an arm or a leg or something else. It was a famous case in Chicago: the Susan Degnan murder. They finally found the killer, William Heirens, and he later turned out to be the Drake Hotel murderer, the one who wrote in lipstick on the mirror, 'Catch me before I kill more.' It pretty much replaced the Leopold-Loeb murder as the crime of the century and, virtually every day, I passed that house going to school."*

Apparently Friedkin left his mind at the Degnan house, not in the classroom, because it was in high school that his academic performance started to drop dramatically. By the time

---

*The crimes occurred in 1946 when Friedkin was eleven. Heirens was convicted of murdering both Degnan and Frances Brown (in the Drake Hotel incident which earned him the nickname of the "Lipstick Killer"). Heirens used the insanity defense to escape Illinois' electric chair and eventually achieved a certain fame by earning a college degree while behind bars. Friedkin mined these memories for two subsequent films: in *The Exorcist* (1973) he authorized the advertising phrase, "Something almost beyond comprehension is happening to a girl on this street, in this house, etc." and more profoundly in 1987 with *Rampage*, a complex examination of the insanity plea. Elements also turn up in his 1989 film, *The Guardian*, about a murderous nanny who ritually kills infants.

he entered Nicholas Senn High School (now Senn Metropolitan Academy) his parents had once again moved—to a more comfortable high rise at 5200 N. Sheridan—it began to be apparent that the college prep program his fellow students were taking held little interest for him.

"I barely got out of high school," he confesses. "I *did* fail Latin. I mean, I didn't continue an extra term, I didn't have to do five years, I did four. But I still have recurring nightmares about failing school. I didn't know if I was going to graduate. In grammar school everything came very easy to me. In high school I was less motivated."

One of his distractions during school was the ever-present need to earn money for the family. He hawked sodas at nearby Wrigley Field, ran errands in the neighborhood, did duty in a cut-rate clothing store on South State Street owned by his uncle, Sid Green, and was barback in a tavern run by his other uncle, Harry Lang.

"Sid went crazy and wound up in Elgin Mental Hospital," Friedkin recalls of his uncle. "I was always disturbed around him. Not in awe of him, but deeply disturbed by what I could see was encroaching madness and weakness. He was a case. He wound up thinking that he was Christ."

Harry Lang, however, was different. Lang had married Rae's sister, Sara, and brought a sense of danger into the family that Friedkin instantly liked.

"Those two guys were polar, and a lot of what I'm about is polarity," he figures. "Some strength of character, some failure of character. Moments of courage, moments of cowardice."

Friedkin canonizes Lang and enjoys repeating the legend: how Lang was a Chicago policeman during the reign of Al Capone, how he and his partner Harry Miller were on the take from Frank Nitti (Capone's enforcer), and how the two cops were ordered by a new, anticorruption police commissioner to bring Nitti in.

"They went into Nitti's office," Friedkin describes, "where they used to go all the time, and this is how Nitti got caught, as opposed to all the fiction about it. Nitti had no weapon, but they did. My uncle shot Frank Nitti eight times. *And Nitti lived!* My uncle then shot himself in the left hand and claimed that Nitti had drawn on him first."

Nitti survived but Lang's career did not. He was busted off the force and got a job as bodyguard to Chicago Mayor Anton Cermak. Subsequently, at the 1932 Democratic Convention in Miami, an assassin's bullet missed party nominee Franklin

Roosevelt and killed the man Lang was supposed to be protecting. Lange thereafter retired from the bodyguard business, opened the Sip 'n' Bottle, and attracted the crowd of cons and cops that entranced Friedkin.

It also plugged him into the Democratic party machine that was running Chicago. Through them he learned about patronage, how to buy votes, and about the function of societal structures within structures that he would examine in his most successful films.

Not much of this had to do with Senn High School, of course. Neither did Friedkin. Although his yearbook *(The Forum)* lists him as a January 1953 graduate (at age eighteen, half a term behind his peers) with the nickname "Billy the Kid," his extracurricular activities dwindled in number by the time he made it to senior year. Although early on he took part in intramural sports, was a marshall (hall guard), a Red Cross representative and a member of the Grammar, Psychology and Biology Clubs, by the time he was ready to graduate the entirety of his efforts seems to have been given to just getting out. And basketball.

And even basketball was looking disappointing. When he stopped growing at six feet, the hoped-for athletic scholarships did not materialize. Thus, in the summer of 1953, with college out of the question, he did what every teenager did: he picked up the classified ads.

"I remember not knowing exactly what I wanted to do," he says. "I had no bent toward the arts or media or anything."

At some point he scanned the "Help Wanted: Male" column in one of the Chicago papers and came upon:

> Opportunities to start in the mail room of
> a television station and work your way up
> in television.

He bit.

Television had just begun its seduction of America in the early 1950s. Unlike radio, TV had not consolidated into networks and some cities maintained their independence long enough to develop separate identities. Chicago was adamantly the most independent. Far enough away from New York, in a different time zone, Chicago was blessed with visionary executives who felt their calling and their city were intertwined. Stations WBKB (now WLS), WBBM, WGN and educational station WTTW were fiercely separate from the power elite they saw dominating the East. Into that environment walked William Friedkin in 1953 clutching his copy of the *Chicago Tribune*'s classified ads.

At WGN in the Tribune Tower he met Ray Damalski, who ran the mail room, and asked for the job. The two men talked about the future of television. They got along. Damalski gave Friedkin the job.

There was just one problem: there had been no job. Friedkin had walked into the wrong building. He had meant to go to WBBM, not WGN. He had literally talked his way into a job that didn't exist. In any event, it paid thirty-five dollars a week and offered the Friedkins a reprieve from poverty. It also offered promise.

"I was just a guy delivering mail, you know?" Friedkin recalls. "That's how I learned everything I know—just watching in control rooms, hanging out, watching how they put programs together. I was a gofer: I would get coffee and sandwiches for these guys and they'd let me stand there, and occasionally I'd get up the nerve to ask a question and they would answer it. I think I was in the mail room for about a year, and then there was an opening for a floor manager, which is the equivalent of a stage manager in theater and an assistant director in films."

One of those whom Friedkin assisted was Sheldon Cooper (now president of Tribune Entertainment).

"Bill's quick rise came both from his skills and the fact that Chicago television was rapidly growing," Cooper explains. "People moved pretty quickly back then because there was not a pool of talent to choose from so every station developed its own people. But Bill was a quick learner."

By 1955, two years after graduation, he became a full director at WGN, moving from assignment to assignment with the assurance of a seasoned pro. His salary climbed to two hundred dollars a week.

Cooper noticed immediately that his protégé possessed the spark that separated him from other television directors.

"Everything we did in those days was live and you had to create the shows as you went along with whatever you had," Cooper says. "Bill used the camera to tell stories about the people he was shooting. He threw all of his senses and emotions into whatever was going on, and out would come a loud, emotional shouting of orders, but also a lot of flair."

That mixture of passion and pique earned Friedkin a reputation as a talented, if mercurial, craftsman.

"He was a smart-alecky guy," Cooper recalls, noting Friedkin's tendency to provoke as well as inspire. "He was a guy who felt he knew what he was doing, so therefore he had the right to come back with a smart answer.

"I recall one project that we had worked on, but that never came about. The Chicago Museum of Science and Industry wanted us to make a short film about a boy who gets locked in the museum at night after everybody else had been shown out. Everything that we had seen earlier in the museum that was fun and exciting and wonderful suddenly becomes ominous and eerie and frightening. Bill was going to direct it. We'd raised most of the money and the man who ran the museum was behind it. But as Bill developed the story more and more, it got so frightening that the museum wouldn't let us do it there and they threw us out!"

All childhood fantasies froze during the summer of 1955, however, when Louis Friedkin suddenly fell sick and died. His was an ignominious end.

"He died in the Cook County hospital," Friedkin recalls distantly. "In a bed in the hall. He was just deteriorating; everything was going. Here was a guy who'd basically never been sick a day in his life, and then everything started to break down: liver, heart, lungs. He was an incessant smoker, I remember, but never drank. And one day he just started to fail and was warehoused.

"I used to go see him. It was devastating. I would watch him disintegrate before my eyes. I have a feeling that it was cancer, but since there was no real treatment, no diagnosis, he was just warehoused. I remember going with my mother from time to time while he was dying, just slipping away. He was in a bed in the hall and he just laid there and he died."

The only person at home who mattered was Rae.

"She was a powerful influence on him," says Edgar Gross, Friedkin's business manager and friend. "She was a diminutive woman; I don't think she was over five feet tall. She was quiet but—" Gross pauses. "He sort of idolized his mother. He doesn't talk about his father."

After Louis's death Rae decided not to remarry and devoted her life to raising her twenty-year-old son, who was quickly entering the fast lane among Chicago's opinion makers. He was also gaining a reputation as a scrapper.

"He was directing a musical show featuring the Weavers, one of the first we did on videotape," reports Al Hall, a WGN producer. "The producer of the show, Jim McGinn, decided to cut one of their songs. [The Weavers' tenor, Pete Seeger, had been blacklisted by the networks in the wake of Joseph McCarthy and the quartet was considered controversial.] Bill and McGinn got into a big fight over it. It made news and got a lot of publicity for the show," Hall reports, "but I got the feeling that it was a staged occurrence to attract attention."

By 1959, however, Friedkin ran into opposition that no amount of brashness could intimidate.

"A new guy [Ward Quaal] came in and I was fired in a wave of cost-cutting," he remembers. "He fired all the guys who were single. It was literally because they had to cut staff and I was the youngest and the only single guy. Who knows; as I look back on it, it's really what got me going, because I was doing well and I probably would still be there."

Suddenly "at liberty," Friedkin offered his services around town as a free-lancer. WTTW, the local affiliate of the growing National Educational Television (NET) system, now PBS (Public Broadcasting Service), eventually hired him. It was a dream come true for the mechanically minded young director.

"That's where I really cut my teeth," he says, "because they had no unions there. I was directing and it was hands on the equipment. That's where I really learned." *

Some proof of his professional education can be glimpsed from *Beginnings*, a run-of-the-mill public affairs show directed for NET in the WTTW studios around 1960 and preserved on kinescope.

Introduced by announcer Ken Nordine and hosted by Northwestern University professor Don Federson, *Beginnings* is an interview with Detroit Public Library librarian Dr. Ralph Ulveling. It is an unremarkable example of perfunctory public service television except for director Friedkin's complete disinterest in the questions of Federson in favor of the replies of Dr. Ulveling. Possibly Friedkin is avoiding a distractingly gap-toothed Federson; whatever the reason, the show is a serious attempt to talk about censorship, library access and careers in library science.

"He was always looking for some way to better himself," Ken Nordine remembers of Friedkin in these early days. "He was eager, driving and opportunistic. His strength, outside of his energy, was his ability to size up situations and people that he could get the most out of and to learn to use in some way."

In the one year he worked for WTTW he also recalls creating a series of thirteen programs on the American Civil War entitled *Ordeal by Fire*, adapted from the Fletcher Pratt book by

---

* Friedkin's technical curiosity remains insatiable. He is widely praised for his vast knowledge of the most intimate details of filmmaking, and his inability to perform many of the jobs himself because of union jurisdiction may contribute to his impatience with those who are hired to do what he feels he can do better.

Chicago Tribune columnist Fran Coughlin. Coughlin and Friedkin had met in the WGN mailroom; both were ambitious mavericks eager to expand their influence. Today Friedkin considers Coughlin his mentor.

It was Coughlin who introduced Friedkin to Chicago's literati and instilled in him a love of literature that school had failed to inspire.

Mostly, there were evening soirees at the Scott Street home of Lois Solomon, editor/publisher of a progressive periodical called *The Paper* and a magnet for most of what was electric in mid-fifties Chicago. At her home gathered Miriam Romwell Selby of Chicago's *Time* bureau, broadcaster Studs Terkel, columnist Nelson Algren, lawyer Donald Page Moore, journalists John Justin Smith, Irv "Kup" Kupcinet (Solomon's brother-in-law) and Coughlin. Friedkin also remembers Lenny Bruce dropping in, as would anybody else in the arts or politics who craved this heady company.

"It was a salon in the sense that everybody who amounted to anything in literature or music would sooner or later be at Lois's home," says noted civil liberties lawyer Elmer Gertz, who was one of the core members of the group. "We plotted the battle against capital punishment there. People in general weren't aware of it, but there was a group of all of us of all ages who were. It was an inspiration for Billy."

It was here that Friedkin expanded his contacts. Coughlin led him to literature. Terkel showed him around Chicago's jazz clubs. There were Friday night poker games at Nelson Algren's Evergreen Street apartment and late night encounters with James Jones, a priest whose ministry included Chicago's prison and derelict population. Friedkin met Tony Fantozzi, a jazz drummer from the neighborhood. The future looked as broad-shouldered as the city.

In 1960 Friedkin got a call from, of all people, Ward Quaal: would he consider coming back to WGN as an all-purpose writer-producer-director to work on special projects, among them the Chicago Symphony broadcasts? Friedkin got the station to agree to bring Fran Coughlin along too, at last paying back his mentor, and the pair made a triumphant return.

At the same time, portable film technology in the form of the Arriflex "BL" synchronous sound camera was appearing in Chicago. No longer did documentary crews need to lug hundreds of pounds of equipment around the streets; a fully loaded Arri rig, its motors muffled to allow sound recording, weighed under twenty-three pounds. Friedkin grabbed studio cameraman

Wilmer "Bill" Butler, drove to Jack Behrend's equipment rental house, and learned how to use the equipment.*

Their first project was *A Walk Through the Valley*, a religious program for a Protestant group headed by Father Robert Serfling.

"That was probably the first film Butler or I ever did," Friedkin figures. "We were cutting our own negative and handling it with our hands and one day a station director named Ernie Lucas walked by and said, 'Is that *negative* you guys are handling?' I said, 'Yeah.'

" 'You *never* touch your negative.'

" 'What do you mean?'

" 'Your negative is your *original*. You make a copy which is called a *workprint* and you cut *that*!'

"That's how we started. We would sit there in the newsroom and we would use their equipment and sort of cannibalize it. And periodically we would reach into a barrel where they had outtakes they'd thrown away, and I'd find shit and say, 'Hey, this looks interesting,' and we'd cut it into our picture. That's how we started."

"We didn't know what we were doing, but some wonderful people lent us their time and taught us how, and slowly but surely we caught on to what was going on," says Bill Butler. "Where angels fear to tread, we jumped in."

Although he was slightly older and more experienced, Butler soon found himself in awe of the brash young Friedkin.

"Billy was very much a street person," he explains. "He knew the world from that side and had a lot of friends. We never used to pay to go to the movies because he could talk his way into any movie and never pay for a damn ticket. He loved that slight touch of the con artist; he would like to watch people just get floored by his ability to throw names on them."

Soon the con artist would be asked to play it straight. At Lois Solomon's house there was a *cause célèbre* brewing that would consume Friedkin and link his life inextricably with that of a man he had never met, but whose life he would soon hold in his hands.

On March 20, 1953, Paul O. Crump was involved in a robbery at the Libby, McNeil & Libby Co. in Chicago's stockyards and, in the course of the $20,000 robbery, Theodore Zukowski, a se-

---

* Now having dropped Wilmer, Bill Butler is one of Hollywood's most sought-after cinematographers whose credits include *Jaws, One Flew Over the Cuckoo's Nest, Biloxi Blues* and *Grease*.

curity guard in the food plant, was killed. On June 19 of that year twenty-two-year-old Crump was sentenced to die in the Illinois electric chair. His codefendants (David Taylor, Eugene Taylor, Harold Riggins and Hudson Tillman) were also convicted of murder but received prison sentences of from fifteen to 199 years.

Two years later the Illinois Supreme Court reversed Crump's conviction and remanded the case for a new trial; again he was convicted and given a death sentence.

There were a number of people who felt that Crump should not die. Many of them were those who gathered at Lois Solomon's house. One, in particular, was William Friedkin.

Friedkin had become increasingly bored with WGN and was seeking challenges elsewhere. A chance meeting with Sterling "Red" Quinlan, the affable general manager of competing WBKB–TV, sparked a proposition.

"You go out and put your career cap on and come back to me with a project, a single, one-time project," Quinlan told Friedkin. "If I like it, I'll find money in another account. We won't tell New York about it."

Quinlan didn't tell Friedkin, but he, too, was looking for a way out from under the thumb of the New York-based ABC network that was crimping his own ambitions. If Friedkin could come up with a world-beating show it might be worth the fight.

He did, and it was. Through Father Serfling at one of Solomon's gatherings, Friedkin heard about the case of Paul Crump. Lawyer Donald Page Moore was then representing Crump with Elmer Gertz and his associate Donald S. Rothschild. Their cause was aided by Fran Coughlin, reporter John Justin Smith and Irv Kupcinet who secured an unprecedented broadcast interview from the Cook County Jail where Crump was incarcerated. The man who made the arrangements was Warden Jack Johnson, an enlightened penologist who would later testify in Crump's behalf.

Illinois Governor Otto Kerner was already getting pressure to commute Crump's sentence to life imprisonment. The issue excited Friedkin and he brought it to Quinlan as a documentary film project.

"What kind of documentary?" Quinlan asked Friedkin. Friedkin said he didn't know, but that it was going to be defensive of Crump, kind of a personal statement. "That started to appeal to me," Quinlan recalls, "as long as it was clearly labeled."

Quinlan arranged a phantom budget of $7,000 for Friedkin, Butler, film editor Glen McGowean and an assistant, Jim Wagner, then waited out the summer of 1962 to see what footage came in.

"Word was out that he was on the South Side re-creating the crime," Quinlan recalls. Then he heard nothing. "When are you going to get something to put on the screen, Bill?" he began asking. "The guy will be electrocuted and it won't be news anymore."

But Friedkin was intentionally keeping a low profile; he had heard that documentarist Robert Drew was also making a film about the Crump case entitled *The Chair* (it was finished after Friedkin's). And there was another reason Friedkin didn't advertise his activities for WBKB: he was still working for WGN.

"We were on the WGN payroll all day," Bill Butler reveals, "and we were doing the film on weekends and nights. If it was a night shoot I can remember being out at four in the morning in the heart of a black area where no white man with common sense would be, and here we were, these two white guys with a camera. We'd walk into clubs and, Jesus, we got unbelievable, real stuff. I remember one woman who was chewing out some guy at the table with her. I'm sitting across the room with a long lens. You don't even have to hear it, you can just read it; the whole thing in a capsule tells you what they are. There are things like that in the whole film."

During this time Butler remembers the support that Rae Friedkin gave her son:

"We were sitting at her apartment till four in the morning and she'd be trying to sleep and we were hollering at one another over the cuts. She got pretty used to the two of us. She felt I was good for Billy; she wanted the best and she thought I was a good influence."

The People Versus Paul Crump, as the film was called, took the point of view that not only was Crump innocent, but that the Chicago police had beaten a confession out of him. In the hour-long program reporter John Justin Smith recounts the story: how Crump and four men* carried out the robbery that turned into murder, how Crump was identified solely by his voice, how he was named by a co-defendant but insisted he had an alibi, and how in nine years under Warden Johnson's supervision in jail he had, in fact, been rehabilitated.

Along with visceral dramatic images, Friedkin and Butler captured heart-rending interviews with Paul's mother, Lonnie, and some particularly revealing footage of Crump himself articulately narrating his own memoir.

---

* Actually, it was five men, but Friedkin's re-creation is convincing.

During the restaged prison beatings (which are graphic and impressionistic at the same time), Crump dissolves in tears. According to writer (now producer) Bob Ellison, who profiled Friedkin for *Today's Filmmaker* in 1973, Friedkin got the convicted murderer to cry by attacking him on camera.

"You lying SOB," Ellison quotes Friedkin as having told Crump during a filmed jailhouse interview. "Everything you've told us is shit! I want the truth—do you understand—the truth!"

"Crump broke down," Ellison writes, "because Friedkin's fury meant to the killer that he was losing a friend—his only friend—the man who was going to save his life. Billy's rage was a calculated risk, born of an alley-wise insight, not Psych 202. The kid took his chance, and won."

The actual footage, however, is not discernible in the finished program.

"We ran out of film," Friedkin explains, clarifying Ellison's account. "When Paul Crump first told me his story he got very emotional about it and broke down in tears as he told it to me. When he told it to me on film he was unable to bring back the emotion. By that time he had gotten to trust me a lot and I felt that [I could take] the chance and [do] that in order to get him into the emotional framework to be able to re-create the way he told me the story where he *did* break down in describing the police brutality that was used against him."

Friedkin admits hitting Crump.

"I did, but I didn't say, 'You're full of shit.' I did it as a calculated risk. He was not being interviewed by the press at that time; he was a forgotten person and he sat alone with me and he broke down telling the story. And I felt, How the hell am I going to get this guy into the same emotional bag? I'm going to have to make him feel as though I, who was his only friend, had betrayed him."

The portrait of Paul Crump that emerges as the hour unwinds is of an articulate, compelling, self-aware man with a sense of his own fate and his own dignity.

"I did some things that I was not caught for," Crump admits. "This proves that what goes around, comes around. But I never killed anybody."

"It was a stirring piece," Red Quinlan—now a consultant with IDC Services, a media accounting conglomerate—recalls of Friedkin's film. "I was delighted with it and was going to put it on the air when Don Moore [Crump's lawyer] called me and said, 'You can't run that!' "

Moore—who charges police brutality in his on-camera interview—was concerned that Chicago Mayor Richard J. Daley would be angered by the broadcast, and that an angry Daley was capable of anything, including dissuading Governor Kerner from commuting Crump's sentence.

"I said it for what was intended," Moore pleaded to Quinlan. "But now the climate's changed and you will kill this man. He will definitely be electrocuted."

Quinlan summoned Friedkin to his office and learned that the lawyer and the filmmaker had increasingly been at odds. Friedkin knew why.

"He was drunk the night of the interview," Friedkin says. "When Moore gave that statement to us, he had hit the bottom. He was much more concerned, in the cold sober light of day, I feel, about the impact of his own statement than the impact of the film. At that time for *anyone* to say that in any public medium in Richard Daley's Chicago would have been a bombshell."

Quinlan, seeking mediation, privately screened *The People Versus Paul Crump* for opinion makers, Warden Johnson, Moore and "everybody but Crump himself."

"I asked for a show of hands whether it should be run or not. My recollection is that it was sixty percent against showing it," Quinlan recounts. He deferred to the majority.

Friedkin was shattered. He had invested everything in the film. More than that, he had come to regard Red Quinlan as his second father. And then to have the film pulled off the air *because he made it too well* was devastating.

"I don't know if Bill has ever forgiven me," Quinlan says softly. "We don't talk about it."

Friedkin, in retrospect, distanced himself from the conflict and remains friends with Quinlan:

"I was disappointed, of course, that it did not go on the air, but I don't feel that the decision was made by Red out of anything other than Don Moore saying that if it airs, Crump will go to the chair. Which I thought was extreme."

On August 1, 1962—thirty-four hours before Paul Crump was scheduled to be executed—Illinois Governor Otto Kerner commuted his sentence to 199 years, but without parole.

There is only one problem: *Paul Crump is guilty.*

"He was asked if he killed the security guard and he said yes," reports Elmer Gertz, who represented Crump in 1965 at the first of many parole hearings. "That was the first time he publicly confessed his guilt. I was present. And it hadn't deterred anybody from feeling very strongly that he ought to be paroled."

Friedkin is not convinced of Crump's admission.

"It isn't even clear to me that he did commit the crime,"
Friedkin maintains. "A large part of his legal advice over the
years has been, 'Look, we've been getting nowhere saying you're
innocent. Why the hell not say you're guilty and throw yourself
on the mercy of these people?' A part of his problem was that
as long as you say you're innocent, they're just going to keep
you in there."

"If Billy thinks that he may be innocent, Billy's just deceiv-
ing himself," Gertz says patiently.

Does Friedkin—who pretended to betray Crump in order to
get an effective interview—now feel that Crump had, in turn,
betrayed him? No. Would he have made the film had he known?

"I've never really thought about it or been asked that question," he ponders. "God knows, that was the film that propelled my career as a filmmaker, and it was propelled by a very
strong desire to preserve life and seek the freedom of this individual."

That desire has become a commitment for Friedkin, who has
returned to Chicago numerous times to testify in Crump's behalf and has promised to underwrite a $15,000-a-year treat-
ment program at Illinois' Isaac Ray Center should Crump's
attorneys ever succeed in winning him a parole. As a practical
matter Crump—who has developed symptoms of schizophrenia
during his thirty-five-year incarceration—could never rejoin the
free world, although the four men convicted along with him
have long since been released.

"Our ways crossed in the past and fortune smiled on me and
frowned on Mr. Crump," Friedkin testified in 1985. "I have to
put myself in the place of that other human being whose path
crossed mine. Why does the state think it's proper to incarcer-
ate someone in a penal system that only deteriorates their humanity? What contribution is it to a society to keep someone
vegetating in a jail somewhere for the rest of their lives? Over
the years," he adds ironically, "I've come to believe that there
is a mercy in capital punishment."

Crump's continued appeals have raised civil rights issues and
stirred bitterness on all sides. Friedkin and Gertz feel that Illinois Governor James Thompson, whose career was enhanced
by prosecuting the original Crump case, sees Crump as a symbol for whom he does not wish to show compassion. Crump—
his initial talents toward poetry and prose (including the unpublished memoir *Burn, Killer, Burn*) now dulled by drug therapy—continues to reside in Illinois's Menard Center. It is a
psychiatric facility.

The People Versus Paul Crump has never been broadcast.

CHAPTER 2

LEAVING CHICAGO

Paul O. Crump, whose execution in the Illinois electric chair was prevented by Friedkin's first film, *The People vs. Paul Crump*

COURTESY OF WILLIAM FRIEDKIN, STERLING "RED" QUINLAN, AND FACETS MULTIMEDIA, INC.

AFTER THE CRUMP controversy William Friedkin was sure that his future lay in film, although he didn't yet know that Chicago was not the place to pursue it. Red Quinlan had kept his promise to bring the twenty-seven-year-old filmmaker aboard WBKB with his own "documentary unit," but in reality this consisted of nothing more than Friedkin, Bill Butler, a secretary and a budget that could buy lunch or film, but not both.

It wasn't Quinlan's dictum, it was just the facts of local television life: unless a program has appeal broad enough to get shown in other markets it must glean its entire income from the city of its origin, and such revenues being limited, this forces producers to severely cap their spending.

"You couldn't make a movie and sell it in Chicago," explains Tony Fantozzi, who had moved from playing clubs to booking acts from the Chicago office of the powerful William Morris Agency. "If you wanted to make films, you had to go to California."

Satisfied with his life in Chicago, however, Friedkin looked no farther west than the Mississippi River. Between 1962 and 1964 he continued to direct live television while seeking documentaries that would allow him the greater freedom of working in film.

One was an episode of *Home Again*, Red Quinlan's series profiling celebrated Chicagoans who had left town to make their marks on the world. Among subjects Quinlan assigned to staff directors were writer Ben Hecht, musician Benny Goodman and poet Archibald MacLeish. He saved Chicago Bears halfback Red Grange for Friedkin.

Titled *77—Grange of Illinois*, Friedkin's resulting half-hour portrait was produced late in 1962 to coincide with the "Galloping Ghost" 's election as a charter member of the Football Hall of Fame. Using newsreels, film clips, still photos and graphics intercut with new footage of the gridiron star, it sets Grange against the background of the rise of professional sports in America.

From Friedkin's and Butler's first shot it is clear that *Grange of Illinois* is not a standard documentary. Standard documentaries don't start with a helicopter view of a college scrimmage or continue with a high-angle crane shot which lowers to field level as the subject of the show enters the frame on cue. The sparse narration and dramatic staging make it clear that Friedkin is seeking neither cold objectivity nor cheap nostalgia. He is trying to portray Grange's inner conflict between being a man and a celebrity.

Every interview excerpt that follows Grange's "descent from Heaven" runs in counterpoint: the bigger the historical headlines, the more humble Grange sounds; the more others talk of him as a god, the more human and vulnerable Grange's remarks become. He talks about being broke and getting a call from Chicago businessman Jim Peterson to come to work with him (it's never clear doing exactly what). Grange lectures a team of high school athletes about "learning to give and also take a licking" while the camera dwells on the kids' scrubbed faces, not Grange, as if a Norman Rockwell painting is sitting in judgment.

The conflict comes to a head in a disturbing sequence which employs distorting wide-angle lenses as Grange recalls the time he thought he had the flu when, in fact, he was having a heart attack. His trip to the hospital, flat on his back, is mimicked by the camera from the stretcher as it is loaded into the ambulance.

Also notable in the portrait is that, despite Grange repeatedly mentioning his wife, neither she nor so much as a photo of her is ever shown. Either gods—even gods being humanized—live alone or it is a continuity lapse; probably the latter.

Grange of Illinois proved that *The People Versus Paul Crump* was no fluke. It also showed that Friedkin was interested in bringing a dramatic sensibility to the documentary form, not a documentary style to drama, as critics have repeatedly and conveniently insisted. His strength as a filmmaker is not just to make fiction look real but to make reality dramatic. Of course, this discovery was years away; for the present, Friedkin was just trying to shoot a show.

"I didn't know what a documentary was," he says. "Neither did Bill Butler. The challenge was only *How do you tell this story?*" And the answer was just to try everything and see if it worked.

As *Home Again* succeeded, other productions failed. There was an abortive attempt to create a series around Second City, Chicago's famed improvisational theater troupe.

"In 1962 he had been working with ABC [WBKB] as director and Red Quinlan was very high on Bill," recounts Bernie Sahlins, Second City's mercurial director. "He got him together with us to do a special called *Second City Reports.*"

Sahlins remembers that Friedkin directed a sequence from the show called *Lovers Day in America.*

"It was incredible. We went up to this small town [Richmond, Illinois], a redneck town near Chicago. We got the whole

school band out, the American Legion, a parade with floats—
and it was a put-on!

"Along about halfway through they began to smell a rat and
we got out of town in a hurry."

It didn't faze Friedkin in the least; his attitude was secure.

"He acted as though he had sprung full-blown from the head
of Zeus," offers Sahlins, who has also nurtured talents from
Mike Nichols and Elaine May to Barbara Harris and John Be-
lushi. "I mean that as a compliment. I don't notice a lot of
difference between the way he was then and the way he is now.
With our bunch where they really appreciated recklessness, he
fit right in, so there were no problems."

Second City Reports failed to become a regular feature on the
station because of disagreements over how the income—or lack
of it—would be shared within Second City. In the meantime
Friedkin's visibility increased not only around Chicago but across
the country as *The People Versus Paul Crump* hit the festival
circuit and began attracting attention.

One man whose attention it drew was David L. Wolper, then
the most powerful figure in American television documentary
at a time when the form was being redefined.

"Documentary, in spite of what people say, has some staging
in it," Wolper explains. "People know they're being photographed, so they move in certain ways. 'Documentary' has been
changed by the television networks to mean something else;
it's *their* concept. But Flaherty's [Robert Flaherty, the "Father
of American documentary"] original concept was always taking real people and staging them. Films that they honor as the
great documentaries of all time were not like the NBC news
shows. The definition of *documentary* is 'the creative *interpretation* of reality.' It didn't say *reality*."

When Wolper saw *Crump*, it had just beaten some of his own
productions by winning the Golden Gate Award at the 1962
San Francisco Film Festival where Red Quinlan had entered it.
He recognized Friedkin as a man who shared his vision.

Wolper came to documentary out of inspiration and frustration—the former after having seen an educational film when he
was in school and realizing that motion pictures could inform
as well as entertain, and the latter by trying to deal with the
networks. A string of refusals in the late 1950s led Wolper to
privately finance, then personally syndicate to 105 separate local stations, *The Race for Space* in April 1960. It was the first
time that a non-network documentary reached a national audience and its success allowed Wolper to start building his staff

by hiring young, talented, and—more important—unspoiled filmmakers.

Among those who joined him were Jack Haley, Jr., Mel Stuart, Arthur Swerdlow, Alan Landsburg and Walon Green.

It was the many honors bestowed on the 1963 airing of *The Making of the President: 1960* that helped Wolper negotiate a deal with the 3M Company to produce a series of specials that would be shown on ABC. Although his staff had already grown to two hundred people, he still needed directors.

"Wolper, at that time, was the most imaginative, aggressive guy, and he was looking for filmmakers," remembers Tony Fantozzi, who by now was representing Friedkin in Chicago. "It didn't take great genius to put Friedkin into the Wolper company."

Friedkin took some convincing.

"I didn't give a fuck about network or worldwide or anything," he says. "The stories in Chicago interested me. I was very happy there. My memory is that the first time Wolper wanted me to go to work, I wasn't interested in leaving Chicago and didn't know who the fuck David L. Wolper was. Then Fantozzi told me who he was and what he was trying to do. I only decided to work for Wolper after Red [Quinlan] had gotten fired and the whole thing fell apart.* I went out on a Monday and I was at work with him by Thursday. I drove out with my old Ford Fairlane which Sonny Bono used to call the Batmobile."

It was 1965 by the time Friedkin packed his gear in the back of the Ford, drove to Los Angeles, got a place at the Sunset Marquis residence hotel on Alta Loma, and entered Wolper's "absolute crucible of filmmaking," as he recalls the intensity of the experience. Wolper recalls it too.

"He was a wild young man," the producer says. "Cocky and wild. Wild and super-hyper. At times we didn't have that much money to do shows and we had a pretty tight rein on everybody. He was terrific, had a great eye, but he was a little weak on story at that time. He had a lot of flashes of great stuff but he didn't know quite how to assemble it."

Friedkin directed three hour-long shows for Wolper and 3M: *The Bold Men, Pro Football: Mayhem on a Sunday Afternoon* and *The Thin Blue Line.*† To ease the tyro filmmaker into the sys-

*Quinlan and the ABC brass in New York had had escalating territorial clashes before and after the *Crump* project. Quinlan eventually resigned in 1964.
†Not to be confused with the 1988 documentary of the same title by Erroll Morris.

tem, he was paired with staff film editor Bud Smith. The Fried-kin-Smith collaboration lasted twenty years.

"His whole career, from the time I first met him, is that he decides the film he wants to make and he proceeds to make it and very few outside influences can really change his mind," Smith explains. He completed *The Bold Men* and half of *Mayhem* before being assigned elsewhere in the company.

"He's a detail freak," says Smith who, as editor, compiled such things into seamless sequences. "Everything has to be just exactly detailed, whether you see it on screen or not. If somebody's reading a newspaper, it has to have the correct date, the correct writing inside; it can't be a phony newspaper."

Friedkin's mania for minutiae, Smith says, led him into dangerous waters for *The Bold Men*, his first Wolper documentary, which explored the people who performed death-defying exploits.

"He shot a guy who jumped out of an airplane without a parachute," Smith recounts. "On the way down he made contact with another person and put on his chute and went to the ground. I don't know if this had ever been filmed before, but it was a very bold thing the guy did. The FAA [Federal Aviation Administration] naturally heard about this particular thing—it's against the FAA to jump out of a plane without a parachute on—and I think they fined the guy five thousand dollars and his salary for jumping out of the plane was five thousand dollars, so he basically did it for nothing.

"Then Billy went down to Mexico and shot the guys that dive off the rocks in Acapulco, and bullfighting, lion-taming—all this stuff."

According to Smith, Friedkin led something of a charmed life. While covering the lion-tamer in Thousand Oaks, California, Friedkin became so captivated at the action that he grabbed the camera himself and went into the cage. A week later, that same tamer was almost killed by that same lion.

Friedkin's penchant for matching his subjects dare for dare was even more pronounced when he and his crew set up to film professional driver Art Arfons, who was trying to break the land speed record on the Bonneville salt flats in Utah. The goal was 526 mph and it was Friedkin's notion to sit in the cockpit and photograph Arfons at the moment of triumph. Space was tight, however; there was room for either the camera or Friedkin, but not both; naturally the camera won.

So, in a way, did Friedkin. During the first attempt, the enormous air resistance shattered the car's cockpit. Had Friedkin been sitting there, he would have been killed.

"Besides just operating a camera," Smith awards, "he would never ask anyone to do anything he wouldn't do. And he's proven that over the years I've known him."

In light of Friedkin's reputation for flamboyance, Smith's statement may seem forced, yet with the exception of the use of professional stuntmen (whose work for Friedkin is remarkably normal), his films are marked by none of the irresponsibility that has come to be represented in Hollywood by the *Twilight Zone—The Movie* tragedy. If anything, it reflects a compulsion to be the peer of anybody he works with, a need to belong to a team while still being its captain. Friedkin has never reacted well to authority, but at Wolper he had to accept it. The Chicago whiz kid, for the first time, found that he had competition.

His first taste was in the screening room when he and Smith presented their first cut of *The Bold Men* to Wolper. Nothing in those days was done in private; into the screening room strolled every staff director to view the footage and, if necessary, offer changes. The men they all watched were Mel Stuart, whose sense of pacing was legendary, and Wolper, whose philosophy to both entertain and inform sometimes made his films go for the phrase rather than the fact. *The Bold Men* was supposed to be a fifty-minute documentary. Friedkin's and Smith's first cut came in at over two hours. By the time the lights came up, Wolper was about to explode.

He stood up and took off one of his Gucci slippers and hurled it at the screen, then wheeled around to face his young director.

"There comes a day when the white hot light goes on and the bullshit falls away like bricks on the ground," he said to the stunned Friedkin. "You know what I mean?"

Friedkin did—he knew the film needed heavy cutting—and to hear Wolper demand it was the kind of guidance he had not been used to getting.

"What imagery, Dave," the thirty-year-old Friedkin offered in an effort to save face. "Only you could've said that."

"I didn't *request* it," Wolper explains of the dressing-down. "I think he knew we knew what we were talking about. He was cocky, but when he got into the screening of his footage in front of the whole group, he lost it *fast*. We were all a shop of documentary filmmakers, so you couldn't con anyone. You had to have a tough skin or you couldn't survive in our productions."

So Friedkin, Smith and Stuart went to work turning, as Walon

Green analyzes, "this two-hour piece of shit into a one-hour show."

Although its execution is vigorous, its concept is not particularly unusual: *The Bold Men* presents a series of scenes of thrill-seekers of the sort that always found popularity in weekly theatrical newsreels, on such TV shows as *You Asked for It* (and later *That's Incredible*) and even feature-length films like *Mondo Cane* and *Ecco*.

The genre exists because of the public's fascination with men and women who push human courage past the point where an ordinary person dares to follow. The impetus for such acts may come from a variety of sources—an inner quest, a dare, the competitive urge or a crass drive to find one's niche in the record books—and sometimes a combination of all of these. The interweaving of those motives is what Friedkin and writer Don Bresnahan grapple with in the hour-long program, at times more successfully than at others, but finally even they must admit that the need to test the laws of nature is essentially a private and enigmatic one.

"Fear is common," host Van Heflin explains as the hour begins. "The highest courage is rare." By the end, he intones, "Boundaries exist only to be crossed; the impossible is only a temporary barrier. Before a man can face others, he must face himself. These men have."

In fact, *The Bold Men* does little to actually explain the mystery of the courage that drives such men as Art Arfons, Chet Jessick, Rod Pack and the others to defy death. There is little interview material and few voice-overs, and nothing in what there is goes beyond the anecdotal: these men simply act, they don't waste time elaborating on why they do it. Moreover, their reasons are as elusive as courage itself, and perhaps to dissect one would be to destroy the other.

But *The Bold Men* does not anguish over this dilemma. Instead, in the best lurid style, it thrusts the viewer into a lions' den, jumps out of an airplane, swims beside a shark and balances on steel girders.

"He tried things editorially that I had never heard of," marvels Bud Smith, citing a sequence in which speed driver Art Arfons powers a car from a jet engine in an effort to break the land speed record. The setting was a fourteen-mile stretch of the unforgiving Bonneville salt flats; the dramatic objective was to suggest that Arfons was thinking about a friend of his who had died making a similar attempt.

"In the 1960s subliminal editing wasn't widely talked about,"

Smith explains, "or moving a camera all the way into some-body's face, into their eye, and calling it 'in their mind's eye' and cutting to what they were thinking about at the time. Like Art Arfons who was watching a friend of his doing this five-hundred-mile-per-hour run and had crashed and killed himself, and then pulling back out and you were right back where you left. Instead of just cutting to something and having the nar-rator say, 'Last year . . . ,' it was like a visual narrative. I was in awe and Friedkin was just trying things. He didn't know it either."

The Bold Men is an anthology of episodes loosely linked with a unifying theme, but it does not create the steady rise in dra-matic tension that could sustain a feature film. Immediately, Friedkin moved into another exercise that offered a smaller canvas but a more clearly defined subject.

Pro Football: Mayhem on a Sunday Afternoon (usually called simply *Mayhem on a Sunday Afternoon*) was the Wolper look at the National Football League's ascension to the forefront of American sports and how it reconciles (or fails to) its gladia-torial with its commercial attraction. It was a ripe topic: the year before (1964) the Cleveland Browns had earned first place among U.S. football franchises and, with that title, scrutiny by the mass media who reported that pro ball was becoming a business that (then) generated $50 million annually, $14 mil-lion of it from television. *Mayhem* would examine the effects of the change.

It does so in a strangely schizophrenic way. Although its de-tailed historical approach shows how football went from a money-losing operation into a money-making industry, the narration (this time written by Bernard "Bud" Wiser) con-stantly refers to the violence of the game. Everything on screen supports this, from scrimmages, workouts and actual game footage to moments in the locker room and players limping off the field. There is mention of the general dangers inherent in athletics, but no one on screen engages in any debate about it, giving the impression that it was an editorial decision not sup-ported in the field. In fact, David L. Wolper recalls that football commissioner Pete Rozelle had concern with the show, al-though nothing ever came of it; moreover, the on-screen credit to NFL Films belies any reservations that the organization might have had.

In *Mayhem*, Friedkin was again on familiar ground, specifi-cally the *Home Again* segment that he had made for Red Quin-lan in Chicago. He even brought in his old friend Red Grange.

Mayhem is not a pointed documentary, but it is an expressive one. It goes behind the scenes to state, in revealing detail, how a game that was once played by Roman soldiers in occupied England has become an industry in America. There are its specialists: "Doc" Shaughnessy, who is paid by teams to invent plays and find loopholes in the rulebook (he invented the T formation); Cleveland quarterback Frank Ryan, whose career rests on beating the Baltimore Colts (he does); Browns' owner Art Modell, who never made a team, so he bought one; Y. A. Tittle, returning to his old Giants to bring along its younger members. If baseball is known as a game of fathers and sons, football is seen as a tradition of armies and generals.

The statistics enforce such an interpretation and *Mayhem* cynically cites them. Each player, it notes, represents an investment of $750,000. Blockers are defined as being hired for their "guts, desire and total disregard for their own safety." The jargon of football passes quaintness to approach high tech. The value of the playbook is near that of classified government documents (and a two-hundred-dollar fine is levied for its loss). Each player consumes two thousand calories each meal, each day. And it all takes place at the Browns' practice camp located, of all places, at a convent where nuns share dining facilities with the players.

Pro Football: Mayhem on a Sunday Afternoon is straining at its own bit. While it achieves distinction for its factual portrayal of the growing importance of professional football in America, it also shows evidence that Friedkin is seeking human conflicts and is imposing a vision on reality that seeks to restructure it in affecting, dramatic ways. His third program for Wolper allowed him to do just that in ways that led directly to his emergence in the film industry: *The Thin Blue Line*.

It was *The Thin Blue Line* that first articulated the kind of film that has become most closely identified with William Friedkin. He even alludes to its title when, in interviews, he refers to "the thin line between the policeman and the criminal."

Walon Green also notes, "There are a couple of really remarkable scenes in *The Thin Blue Line;* there are a couple of cops playing pool, talking about what your partner means to you, and it's like a dramatic scene. I don't know exactly how he shot it—I never talked to him about it—but it is a remarkable scene for a documentary. Suddenly you feel you're in a feature film."

The Thin Blue Line is *The French Connection* in sketchbook form. It has the same elements: cops, partners, drugs, police routine and the conflict between protecting the peace in society and preserving the rights of the individual. It is tightly edited (by David Blewitt and Nicholas Clapp) and sometimes excruciatingly intense.

"No matter what color you are," a policeman says as the hour begins, "if you're a Negro policeman, if you're a white policeman, you've got a blue uniform. You've got to consider, we're all blue. We're not black or white, we're blue." Thus stated—that there is a brotherhood of policemen who see themselves in an "us vs. them" struggle with the public—*The Thin Blue Line* deftly marks its territory. As in all good melodrama, there will be good guys and bad. Though in later films he will begin blurring the boundaries and draw the sides closer, with this statement Friedkin comes down on the side of the policemen.

The police, he reminds, are needed. There are urban riots. There are assailants on the streets (and some extraordinary footage where a knife-wielding man is disarmed in front of the camera). There is traffic that chokes the cities. There is a civilization to protect.

"Hidden beneath the grandeur and affluence of American society," advises host Van Helfin, "there's an unparalleled epidemic of crime. One murder every hour. Three thousand burglaries every day. Three million Americans hopelessly addicted to narcotics. The cost of crime: twenty-four billion dollars a year. Never before has any country demanded so much of its police, and never before have the police been so criticized."

The irony of *The Thin Blue Line* is its sympathetic stance toward the police from a director who, three years earlier, had accused them of racism and brutality in *The People Versus Paul Crump*. The intervening years had seen the rise of the civil rights movement and the beginning of the end of institutionalized segregation, but it was still years before the Chicago Democratic Convention and the apex of Vietnam resistance riots shattered police respect in many Americans' eyes. Although it constantly hints at the Constitutional conundrum between the rights of the accused and the rights of society, *The Thin Blue Line* only gives the debate the briefest of airings.

Rather than get mired in such heady philosophical issues (which he will do to his disadvantage twenty-two years later with *Rampage*) Friedkin goes straight for the gut. Regardless of where one stands, he asserts, the fact remains that the police are caught in the bind between society's decay and the ideals that must be addressed in rebuilding it. He is less interested in the *why* than the *how* (a continuing fascination, critics have noted) and the *how* is what the documentary captures with cauterizing effectiveness.

Police procedure offers the means to do this without becoming judgmental. An evening behind the switchboard of the Chicago Police Department's communication room is the setting. Uniformed operators handle a routine night's calls: ambulance requests, accident reports, etc. A woman calling to say an invisible man is being beaten outside her window by an invisible attacker is told, "We'll have our special unit get right on it," and is diplomatically dismissed. Unlike law enforcement as seen on TV cop shows, this is the nuts-and-bolts of reality, a reality that handles nine thousand calls every twenty-four hours.

Then the night is torn by a woman's frantic voice: "There's someone in the house!" she screams into her phone. "Please! I've got a baby here! Hurry!"

The operator gets the woman to tell him her address and a squad car is dispatched. Then he hears, "Please, please God, don't go down."

"Your husband's still upstairs, isn't he?"

"No he isn't."

"He went downstairs?"

"Yes!"

"The police are there now. *Tell him!*"

The woman calls out, "The police are here . . ."

Suddenly there is a gunshot. The woman screams, becomes hysterical.

"Hello? Ma'am? Who fired the shot?"

"I don't know."

"Keep your child there. Hello?"

The arriving officer picks up the phone and tells the operator (and the viewer) that no one has been hurt. The woman is still sobbing in the background.

The power of the sequence is intense and is made more so because it is presented only as sound. The terrifying audio, juxtaposed with the calmness of the communication room, is both frustrating and evocative and is frightening because of what it does *not* show.

Having established the grim reality of police work, Friedkin now shows how a policeman is made. At the police academy, recruits go through training: how to drive a car in a chase, how to disarm suspects, how to make arrests and how to keep order in a city that seems bent on losing it. Some secrets emerge: it is useless to fire a warning shot during a car chase, for it cannot be heard over the noise of the engine; it is better to treat an innocent person like a criminal than risk treating a criminal like an innocent person.

"If you think you may be dealing with a felon," the instructor urges, "run the risk of offending a good citizen and apologize later. You're no good with a hole in you."

Soon the program is back on the streets. A hidden camera dogs a small-time pusher in the hope of finding his supplier; from June to August of 1965 investigators buy from, observe and try to trap a service station attendant. It is a low-key display of tedium with little drama, yet it is edited, scored, and narrated as though to presage similar sequences in *The French Connection*. When the bust finally goes down ten screen minutes later it is followed anticlimactically by maddeningly unproductive stationhouse interrogation. It is only then that the viewer realizes that he has been excited by anticipation, not payoff. *The Thin Blue Line* thereby succeeds in creating interest out of pure illusion.

Friedkin is at his best when setting the environment and then standing back to reap what he has sown. As Walon Green noted, a poolroom conversation between two Rochester, New York policemen about job pressure and the importance of partnership has an air of bonhomie that dramatic films would envy. The casual rapport links these off-duty lawmen with "Popeye" Doyle and "Cloudy" Russo in *The French Connection* six years later.

The major flaw in *The Thin Blue Line* is a heavy-handed narration common to many similar shows when the footage doesn't meet the need for storytelling. Van Heflin does not have a light touch, and his tour of duty—he pops up to bridge continuity gaps—is distracting, if understandable.

The final third of the hour chronicles a typical lobster shift for a typical patrolman. Officer Tom Day works at night (an obvious pun the show bravely ignores) and deals with an epileptic seizure, a wino needing an ambulance, a family argument (potentially the most dangerous situation), a suicide attempt, the apprehension of two thieves and miles of driving through the urban nighttown.

The Thin Blue Line concludes by admitting that, despite the loss of respect for police in the eyes of their countrymen, America still needs them. Yet there is no reconciling this conflict: each cop must do it for himself.

Friedkin's sympathies throughout the show are clear: he has become infatuated with the police, not the law. Here is the first statement of the man-against-institution theme that weaves through all of his work. He identifies with the police, but more notably with their darker side, the side that lurks just below their uniformed, bureaucratic façade. It will appear briefly in his next project but will otherwise remain submerged until he hits the streets in 1970.

While he was working for Wolper, Friedkin's agents were working for him. Tony Fantozzi had alerted Joe Wizan, an agent at MCA (and later the producer of *The Guardian*), about the *Crump* film and suggested Friedkin as a choice to direct one of the television shows then being churned out by MCA's studio subsidiary, Universal.

The men agreed that Friedkin's first major film company assignment would be an episode of *The Alfred Hitchcock Hour* called *Off Season*, produced by Hitchcock's longtime friend, Norman Lloyd. As fate would have it, *Off Season* was to be the final show of the series, a lame duck situation that carried a tinge of bitterness for the thirty-year-old director.

"Norman Lloyd saw the Paul Crump documentary," Friedkin explained, "and he said he felt it had more suspense in the first five minutes than anything they had done all season on the *Hitchcock Hour*. He had one final show that was open, and said, 'I wish I could make you a staff director here, but I have one show left and here's the script.'"

It was written by Robert Bloch, who also wrote *Psycho*, and concerned a violence-prone policeman (played by John Gavin) named Johnny Kendall who is fired from the city police force and must take a job as the security guard in a small resort town where his boring duties include making sure the tourist cabins are locked at night. Indus Arthur is Sandy, his girl-friend, who finds work as a waitress in the same community.

He learns from the sheriff (Tom Drake) that he is replacing a deputy who had been fired for carrying on an affair with a woman in one of the vacant cottages. When Johnny sees the deputy (Richard Jaeckel) paying attention to Sandy, he suspects that another liaison is about to take place. One night he visits a shuttered cottage in which he hears the sound of two people making love. Inside the darkened room Johnny recognizes the deputy, who tries to shoot him. Johnny disarms the deputy and kills him, then kills the woman. It is only then that he discovers that the woman is not Sandy but the sheriff's wife.

"I had never done anything on a soundstage, but I leapt at

the opportunity," remembers Friedkin with obvious under-statement. There was just one problem that stood in the way of doing *Off Season:* he was still under contract to David L. Wolper.

"He asked to be let out of his contract," Wolper says, a grin starting across his face. "So I did. He signed [another] contract that he would owe me one movie for ten thousand dollars. I still have the contract and he still owes me the movie. I haven't called him for it yet. I could call him tomorrow and call it in, as long as he's not doing a picture!"

Friedkin regarded his first day on a soundstage, directing professional actors, as one more step on the way to some vague goal.

"I wasn't afraid," he says. "I only thought of the challenge of it. It was a *hell* of a challenge. I must say I thought of all of those things in those days as a learning experience. I always felt I was going to go farther than what I was doing and all of these were just temporary sidebar excursions to learn the craft."

As a filmmaker whose reputation was a willingness to break rules, Friedkin made an attempt to learn the Hollywood ropes. He visited the MGM studios where James Goldstone was di-recting a *Man From U.N.C.L.E.* episode and tried to see how assembly line television was produced. The most important thing, he noted, was to get the show to come in on schedule.

The man he had to ultimately please, however, was Alfred Hitchcock, the legendary figure not known for paying compli-ments and who, according to his biographer, Donald Spoto, was concerned with the TV series that bore his name only to the extent that it earned him royalties.

A few days into the filming of Friedkin's episode, Norman Lloyd brought the Master of Suspense to the soundstage to for-mally meet Friedkin.

"He was with an entourage," Friedkin remembers, "and he put out his hand, which was kind of limp, and he said, 'Ah, Mr. Friedkin, I see you're not wearing a tie.' I thought he was kid-ding and I said, 'No, that's right, I'm not wearing a tie.'

" 'Usually our directors wear ties.' "

Whereupon Hitchcock turned and left the soundstage.

In subsequent interviews when he has told that story, Fried-kin—whose film work is routinely compared with Hitch-cock's—would add, "So I've used that advice in all of my suspense films." In fact, there is a postscript that is even more telling.

"Five or six years later, I hadn't seen him," Friedkin relates.

"It was the evening of the Directors Guild award for *The French Connection*. I was just coming down off the stage with the award and I had a tuxedo with one of those ties that snap. I walked right in front of Hitchcock's table and I snapped my bow tie at him and I said, 'How do you like the tie, Hitch?' He didn't remember, but I did. Revenge is a dish that is best served cold."

The incident is illustrative for two important reasons. One is Friedkin's glee at tweaking one of Hollywood's most respected noses only moments after being confirmed as one of his peers. The other is that he would even recall the necktie comment at all. Both demonstrate Friedkin's ability to act like an outsider even while he is invited inside.

Something that had happened on the *Off Season* set served to make Friedkin sickeningly aware of Hollywood politics in a way he has never forgotten. Producer Norman Lloyd had help-fully advised him to start by shooting an easy scene as quickly as possible to establish an authoritative pace.

"That advice hit me just the wrong way," Friedkin says. "What I did, instead, was to work out a scene that was three or four pages of dialogue, which was a lot. A very complicated scene for the first shot. It didn't come easy. But now the guys in the black suits from Universal start to appear on the set.

"Finally we get a take, but now they think I'm making trouble because 'This isn't what we do.' I was a first-time director, first time I'd done *anything*, let alone a *Hitchcock Hour*, so word was around that I could be trouble."

The next day, however, the same executives visited the set after they had inspected Friedkin's footage. They liked what they saw in dailies and immediately, according to the director, one of the crew members who had fought his doing the shot the day before suddenly tried to take credit for it.

"I was absolutely stunned," Friedkin reports. "Here's this guy, and he was taking credit for this funky, *nothing* little shot that I had made, that he basically resisted. It was a lesson that I carried with me through the years that is rather typical of the way these things work, and that is that people do things behind your back and people try to usurp credit where none is due. If you have to say it's your idea in the first place, you're in trouble."

Off Season is a disinterested show, and not only for Friedkin; even Alfred Hitchcock, whose sarcastic introductions were filmed separately, invites viewers back for next week's show when, in fact, he knew that this was the end of the run.

Its only value is in demonstrating that Friedkin could work

within the Hollywood studio structure. He acted like any seasoned professional but, inside, seethed at the kind of formulaic
mentality that was rampant within the film business.

The mid-sixties were the era when Doris Day movies were
waning in popularity, when James Bond was poking fun at the
myth of the screen hero, when John Wayne was misreading
American sentiment about the Vietnam War, and the Beatles
had revolutionized popular music. Against such impending
culture shock the last thing a boy wonder would be expected
to do was make movies for grown-ups.

So Friedkin's agents decided to put all their youthful eggs in
one countercultural package. The result was a feature film that
one star remembers, one star forgets, and its director casually
dismisses: *Good Times*.

CHAPTER 3

FIRST TIMES

Pizza the Chimp, Cher, and Sonny in *Good Times*
COURTESY OF THE MUSEUM OF MODERN ART FILM STILLS ARCHIVES
AND COLUMBIA PICTURES; COPYRIGHT © 1967

SALVATORE BONO and Cherilyn LaPiere Sarkisian could not have
been farther from what the American music industry in the
early 1960s would have called stars. He was a scrawny, thin-
voiced man with sad eyes and a haircut borrowed from Moe of
the Three Stooges. She was a lanky, too-young girl with a throaty
voice that often cracked in midphrase. Together their mismatched images and, worse, differing ages courted the cops,
not fame.

Yet Sonny and Cher were rapidly becoming the country's
hottest singing duo. Their single, "I Got You, Babe" was an
upbeat love ballad that could not be easily co-opted by the traditional popular singers who appealed to adults (Vic Damone,
Rosemary Clooney, etc.). At the same time they were a respectable distance from rock and roll performers who had domi-
nated teenage airwaves in the fifties. They would eventually
come to represent the quintessential flower children in all their
innocence, yet in 1966 both they and the youth movement were
held in bemused fear by the Establishment they would soon
rebel against.

But that was a safe distance away. What made Sonny and
Cher important at that moment was their immense visibility
and, thus, in Hollywood terms, their movie potential.

Such a formula was clearly in keeping with the film industry
penchant for packaging current pop stars in quickly produced
films designed to exploit their celebrity before it faded. It is a
tradition with a lengthy body count. Chubby Checker, Her-
man's Hermits, the Dave Clark Five, Bobby Vee, Fabian, Cliff
Richard, Roger Williams, Johnny Ray, Peter Frampton, the Bee
Gees, Neil Diamond, Lulu, Petula Clark, and Olivia Newton-
John, among others, all enjoyed a fling at movies. Although a
few young performers managed to survive the "quickie" genre
and even flourish—Elvis Presley and Ann-Margret are the most
notable—most did better for their producers than for themselves.

Sonny and Cher made their screen debut in *Good Times* in
1966, five years before they confirmed their pop stardom with
their television series, *The Sonny and Cher Hour*, in 1971. It's
hard to remember, long after Cher has become an Oscar-winning actress and Sonny has become Mayor Bono of Palm Springs,
California, that the pair's image during their career together
was offbeat, even radical. Much of that image and chemistry
came out of *Good Times*, a pseudobiography that pokes fun at
the duo's age disparity, diverse romantic images, and separate
perceptions of talent. Moreover, the comedy sketch format of
the film was eventually developed into their six-year television

run (broken only by a 1974 interruption for a well-publicized divorce). Sonny wisely knew that Sonny and Cher's biggest-selling point was Sonny and Cher.

So did producer Steve Broidy, who had secured an agreement from Sonny (who then ran Cher's affairs) to put the two into a film in keeping with the ritual of pop stardom. Scouting around for a young, "hot" director, he heard Friedkin's name.

Momentum may be Newton's first law of physics, but it is also Hollywood's first rule of success; in other words, a career in motion tends to remain in motion. Hollywood's second rule similarly quotes Newtonian physics: a career in motion continues in a straight line unless deflected by some kind of force, such as a flop. But in 1966—with Friedkin's name being widely circulated as a comer—the perception that he was a success was more powerful than the limited television track record he had actually compiled. Hollywood worked on dreams, and Friedkin and Sonny shared them.

"Sonny wanted a young director that he could relate to because at the time he was a freak," Friedkin recalls. "Middle-age people were literally afraid of the whole movement. He started to tell me some of his ideas, I liked him a lot and we liked each other.

"He had total control over Cher in those days. She was just a pawn in his life. She doesn't talk about those days at all and I understand why. She felt bossed around by Sonny, and she was. I would never have thought that she would transform herself into what she has become. [She] was not a smart kid; she had no great ambition then, at least none that showed. But she really loved Sonny. He was a pleasure to work with; the crew and I all thought *she* was a drag. I got to know her a lot better since," he allows. "She's very complex."

As far as *Good Times* was concerned, however, complexity had nothing to do with it; the story was straight out of the Judy Garland-Mickey Rooney "let's put on a show" school of drama.

The plot borrows from Sonny's and Cher's public/private images to show them being offered a film career by a mysterious Mr. Mordicus (George Sanders), a droll megalomaniac who dabbles in other people's lives.

Cher is suspicious and would rather shop for clothes. Sonny, however, is game for a meeting. Mordicus lays his cards on the table: I'll make you stars, he promises, trust me. The instant Sonny leaves the office, however, Mordicus begins his machinations against them.

Good Times becomes a series of fantasy films-within-the-film

in which mostly Sonny, but also Cher, try to visualize the sort
of vehicle that could meet Mordicus's dictum and not sell them
out. One fantasy is subtitled *The Saga of Irving Ringo*, a western spoof that allows Sonny and Cher to perform a zesty dance
hall number. The tune changes, however, when Knife McBlade
(George Sanders) comes to town and blasts Sonny back into
reality with his six-guns.

Regardless of whether the western motif will work, Sonny is
told by Mordicus that production will start on *Rags to Riches*
in ten days with or without their input. "For a genius, ten days
is an eternity," sneers Mordicus at his would-be stars. "The
world was created in seven. You have three extra days and all
of this." He sweeps his arms toward a soundstage full of props.
"Make of it what you will."

They try. Sonny browses through the objects while Cher heads
to the clothes racks. Singing "Trust Me," Sonny tries to convince Cher that he has been making the right decisions for them,
despite this snag. His next story idea is *Morry, King of the Jungle*, a Tarzan spoof.

This ersatz epic is built on Sonny's apparent lack of talent;
as a bush-league Tarzan he can't even yell right. Even their pet
chimp, Pizza, beats Sonny at checkers in their tree hut.

Soon white hunters (George Sanders again) invade Morry's
jungle in an attempt to raid the ivory in the elephants' sacred
graveyard. Morry tries to thwart them but the animals, tired
of his abrasive yell, refuse to come to his rescue. Eventually he
eludes Sanders but accidentally drowns in quicksand.

Awakened from the jungle reverie, Sonny is still mired in the
bind he has put Cher and himself in with Mordicus. A domestic
spat sends him off on his motorcycle while Cher sings for his
deliverance in "Don't Talk to Strangers." On Sonny's safe return, she suggests a private eye spoof that might solve their
identity crisis.

Cher's choice is the most interesting in the film. As *Johnny
Pizzacatto, Private Eye*, Sonny continues to be a klutz but this
time his world is equally maladroit. A clever takeoff on 1940s
film noir, this third satirical sequence includes an homage to
James Cagney's grapefruit from *Public Enemy*, suitably rainy
nights, fast dialogue, acerbic voice-overs, period clothes, chintzy
decor and actors with scars. Cher appears twice—first as a
blond femme fatale who gets it in the back, later as another
blonde who runs a club called Samantha's where plots are
hatched.

For the third time George Sanders is cast as their killjoy;

here he's the brutal gangster, Zeruthian, who hypnotizes Pizzacatto into blowing up the city's police commissioner with a planted bomb. Needless to say, it backfires and Zeruthian is blasted along with his henchmen. Pizzacatto, however, also gets killed and now Sonny—once again awake—must approach Mordicus with yet another dry well for alternative plot ideas.

Mordicus is unforgiving. He refuses to allow Sonny to buy his and Cher's release from *Rags to Riches* and threatens to crush the team's careers if they fail to show up next morning to start production: "We will make this picture," he says. "It will make money. And that, my boy, is what it's all about."

Cher feels that Sonny has betrayed her. When he once more storms out of the house, she sings "I'm Gonna Love You" about him. At the same time, Sonny wanders through the night-lit city singing "Just a Name" and the two miraculously find each other and apologize.

The next morning Mordicus is ready to begin when Sonny arrives on time but without Cher. He tells Mordicus unequivocally that they will not do his hillbilly picture even if it means that they will never work again. He hands back the *Rags to Riches* screenplay and leaves.

Mordicus takes the situation pragmatically. Deciding it isn't worth his effort to blackball the duo, he tosses the script into the trashcan himself.

Outside the studio, Sonny—resolutely expecting Mordicus's wrath—shares a simple ice cream cone with Cher.

"Still want to make the movie?" she taunts. Sonny smiles and they wander through nature singing their hit single, "I Got You, Babe," once again at peace with themselves.

"I did *Good Times* because it was a chance to do a feature film," Friedkin told a group of Fellows at the American Film Institute in a 1974 *Dialogue on Film* seminar. "I got very close to Sonny and Cher, and we're good friends to this day. But I didn't do that project because there was a belief in Sonny and Cher. I would have *paid* them to be able to direct a feature film at that time."

The years since *Good Times* have taken the edge off Friedkin's cynicism and he almost seems to pine for the mood of innocence in which he and the Bonos worked.

"We were all shaped by those days, and even if we try to get away from what we were, we cannot escape our past," he avers. "I think perhaps Cher would like to forget those beginnings a lot more than Sonny would. She's come light years from that and I guess Sonny didn't.

"I was at the recording sessions [where Sonny produced the songs]. Sonny was amazing. He couldn't read or write music, but he would go into a studio and he would write some things down and get musicians together. He would tell the horns what to play, the piano what to play, and there would be a guy there like an arranger who would try and write down the music that was in Sonny's head. No conductor. Sonny would then go into the control room and say, 'Hit it,' and they would start to play and he would say, 'Drums, lay back a little' or 'Horns, play faster' and he would literally go out and make action paintings with music. After he got a track, he would sit down with a brown bag that had contained lunch and he would write out, for the first time, the lyric that was in his head. This would be about seven or eight at night. He would then send a car to his house to pick up Cher and bring her to the studio and take her into a tiny booth and they would stand there holding this paper and rehearse it. Then they would sing it together.

"And that's how 'I Got You Babe' and 'Bang Bang' and 'The Beat Goes On' were done. I was at those recording sessions. Sonny was an absolute genius and I never thought Cher would be that big. I was very happy for her, and I must say it made me think about those days [when], wow, here's Cher getting the Academy Award. I was very, very pleased for her. I also thought a lot about Sonny."

During the frantic preproduction period when they were scrambling to get *Good Times* ready for the Columbia Pictures cameras, Friedkin and Sonny became friends, further isolating Cher from the collaboration. Ensconced in the Bonos' Encino, California house for a marathon weekend of rewrites, the guys hired a typist to decipher their handwritten scratches on yellow tablets and put it into proper screenplay form.

"I was acting mostly as story editor for Sonny," Friedkin admits. "He was really the only person who could write for Sonny and Cher."

After four or five hours of a Saturday morning during which the filmmakers were passing scraps of yellow paper to the typist in the kitchen, they suddenly stopped and listened to what sounded like a frenzy of activity, far more work than they had composed.

"What the hell is going on?" Sonny said. "We haven't written that much and she's typing *War and Peace* in there."

Sonny entered the kitchen and returned to Friedkin moments later, a sheath of pages in his hand, shaking his head in confusion.

"You're not gonna believe this," he moaned, handing over the manuscript.

Friedkin smiles slightly at the memory. "What this girl had done is, from the pages we gave her, she had tripped out on her own fantasy and started to type a whole other story about a girl who's being called as a secretary for Sonny and Cher, and she put that into the script. Whatever the hell we had given her was now completely usurped into a script that Sonny had to pry loose from her. We laughed our asses off and then he had to go in and let her go."

As befits a personality vehicle, *Good Times* tries to be a musical in the "mod" style of the successful Beatles movies, *A Hard Day's Night* (1964) and *Help!* (1965), made by American expatriate director Richard Lester. Their themes are even similar: musical celebrities are pursued by various exploitive forces (fans and villains being interchangeable) but constantly take time to sing and show off their winning charms.

"The plot is funny and far out," Friedkin told *Variety* when the film opened in 1967, "but it really is about a guy who nearly sells himself to the Devil. It was a chance to present a parable in popular comedy form."

Given the casting of George Sanders, the Faustian analogy is appropriate, although the filmmakers—mindful, no doubt, of the persistent whammy against movies about movies in Hollywood—do their best to portray Mordicus as an industry interloper along the lines of a Howard Hughes or a Joseph P. Kennedy. In truth, Friedkin and Bono *were* selling their souls to the Devil in exchange for a feature film, although producer Steve Broidy seems to have had little more interest in the project he was financing than putting his name on it. In fact, Friedkin even agreed to do another film for Broidy after *Good Times: The Hundred Dollar Misunderstanding*, which never materialized.

Good Times almost didn't, either. Broidy's budget bought his youthful filmmakers twenty days of shooting with a union crew, about half of what any respectable musical film needs.

"He started the picture at Paramount and he spent all the money," says Bill Butler, who became listed as "Photographic Consultant" on the production after a rescue mission. "He hired a DP [director of photography; Robert Wyckoff is credited with the dramatic photography] from the union, shot on a stage and then one day I got a call [in Chicago] and he says, 'Hey, they've cut me off, I've spent all the money. The film doesn't have our creative look—all the imaginative stuff we used to come up with right off our fingertips.' I said, 'I'm there.' "

The problem was that Butler was not yet a union member, which explains his unusual credit and the adventurous manner in which the two old friends literally stole the shots they needed.

"There we were," Butler confesses, "out on the streets running up and down, shooting all over the place—on the freeway, illegally—I mean, the things we've done in our day we should be arrested for and thrown in jail. But we finished the film."

One of the Butler-Friedkin gambits was shot on the western street of the Paramount back lot from which they had been evicted.

"We'd drive on that lot with the station wagon loaded with camera gear and Billy wouldn't think twice about it," Butler says. "We'd park in front of the office and if we'd gotten caught they'd have sued the studio [Columbia] and who knows what they would've done. But he's that kind of con artist. He wouldn't hide; he'd do it right under their noses and nobody ever caught us. The film was over and done before anybody knew what we were doing."

On the whole, *Good Times* is a lot of energy bottled up in a container too small to hold it. When it does manage to break loose it is in those moments when it hovers tantalizingly close to reality, such as when Johnny Pizzacatto (Sonny) and a shadowy femme fatale (Cher) encounter each other in a nightclub:

> Cher: Johnny, have you ever thought about getting into some other kind of work?
> Sonny: A man's gotta stick to what he knows best.
> Cher: That's what I mean. This private eye stuff is getting us nowhere.
> Sonny: Look, Sam, I told you a hundred times, next case I solve, bang, we get married.
> Cher: That's what I mean. You told me a hundred times.
> Sonny: What's your hurry, Sam? You're only nineteen.
> Cher: Yeah, but we've been engaged seven years. People are beginning to talk.
> Sonny: Not as much as they talked when we first got engaged.

Despite such allusions to Sonny's and Cher's private lives, *Good Times* did not excite their fans to buy tickets in the droves for which Columbia Pictures had hoped. Released in April of

1967 it was something of a cinematic contradiction—too staid to be a rock musical yet too hip to fit the Hollywood formula.

"The picture came out too square," Friedkin assessed after it dropped dead in a commercial marketplace that also included two Elvis Presley movies, the breezy *Thoroughly Modern Millie* and the somnambulent *Camelot*. "They held up the release date for almost a year and it might have done better if it had been released right away [at the end of 1966]. But the ethics and morality the picture represented are out of date. The kids weren't interested."

Friedkin found himself in a career bind. Although his agents were still selling him as a hot young director whose vision would rejuvenate a slumping Hollywood, he was being offered only those old-fashioned projects that traditional industry thinking deemed commercial. The whiz kid who infused documentaries with more drama than current dramas held couldn't find a way to show it.

"The plotted film is on the way out and is no longer of interest to a serious director," he groused to Bill Ornstein of *Variety* on *Good Times*'s release. "A new theater audience, I'm told, is under thirty and largely interested in abstract experience." He cited Michelangelo Antonioni, Alain Resnais, Claude Lelouche, and Federico Fellini as "prophets of this new expression. I defy anyone to tell me what *Blow-Up, Juliet of the Spirits, La Guerre Est Fini* and the Beatle films are about," he challenged. Moreover, he chastised the very economic system of filmmaking which, he held, was driving production budgets far too high (an accusation that proved both prescient and ironic, given his own flagrant financial excess within less than ten years):

"If the films I'm going to do have budgets over one million dollars, I'll cut 'em down to size," he said, citing *A Man and a Woman*, Lelouche's hot film, which had cost a mere $175,000 but was nearing a $900,000 domestic gross.

It's always easy to throw rocks from the outside, and Friedkin—despite having made a Hollywood feature—was still on the outside. It's a perspective he found convenient intellectually but awkward commercially. To appear more acceptable despite a stated penchant for abstract cinema (a safe goal to pursue in an industry which would never compete to achieve it), he announced a slate of future commitments guaranteed to make even the most rebellious of directors appear establishment.

He planned to do *The Hundred Dollar Misunderstanding* (later retitled *The Hostages*) for Steve Broidy, then would reteam with

Sonny and Cher for *Ignac,* then announced a three-picture deal with the powerful Mirisch Productions followed by the film version of Harold Pinter's *The Birthday Party* with David Hemmings, the hot young star of *Blow-Up.*

He also pitched writer William F. Nolan *(Burnt Offerings)* on Nolan's script, *DePompa,* about a brooding young man who forms a kinky sexual liaison with an older woman.

"Billy got nervous and hopped away to New York to direct another picture," Nolan reported, but not before the two men had survived an adventure in a storm-tossed airplane flown by Steve Broidy's son, Art. While Nolan was sweating to match the storm, Friedkin was curled up in the plane's backseat. "Wake me when we land," he told Broidy and Nolan, daring Nature to defy him.

Friedkin's apparent nonchalance extended into his professional life as well. By Hollywood standards a hot young director is routinely sent every script available, even those for which he is clearly unsuited, in the off chance that whatever talent has made him "hot" will just as arbitrarily cause him to find something of interest in a strange producer's pet project. Thus, while Friedkin's agents were considering which big-budget motion picture their young client should accept to further his career, he shocked them by choosing the most improbable item making the rounds.

The Pickle Brothers was a pilot for a half-hour television situation comedy being produced by Four Star Productions for the ABC network. Shamelessly patterned after the Marx Brothers, the Pickles were a trio of male siblings of enormous ambition but minimal ability who each week (if the series was greenlighted, that is) would become involved in a different line of work only to predictably destroy an entire profession.

Baxter Pickle (Ron Prince) was the conniving brother, a Groucho clone who looks like a cross between Monty Hall and Milton Berle (and is, in fact, Berle's nephew); Buddy Pickle (Mike Mislove) is the bespectacled Jerry Lewis ripoff who might be the spirit of Chico Marx; and Bobo Pickle (Peter Lee) is Harpo right down to his girl-chasing and facial contortions, although he also speaks a few lines.

The premise of the first episode is that the brothers decide to become movie producers and check into the posh Manor House Hotel to hold auditions. By the end of the pilot they've made everything but a movie, posed as publicists, helped a princess, and wrecked the building before deciding what to do next.

The one-profession-per-week format provided a forum for

satire (not unlike Chicago's Second City) and the kind of co-
medic edge that television did not routinely attempt in early
1967 when it was produced. That edge comes in large part from
the show's writers-producers Dee Caruso and Gerald Gardner.

"When Four Star sent the script over to Friedkin it was not
with any great expectation that we would get him," recalls
Gerald Gardner. "But Billy found the script extremely funny
and called us and we welcomed him with open arms. We never
dreamed we'd be able to get a director of Billy's eminence because there's a certain stratum in Hollywood where certain directors direct television and others direct motion pictures. He
was being represented by agents at the highest level of the William Morris office and they had a stellar career mapped out for
him—in motion pictures."

Friedkin not only confounded his counselors, he pleased his
producers.

"I must say, he got every laugh that was in the script and
built in a great many more that were not. He made the thing
move like a house afire, and the only thing that Tom Moore of
ABC said after seeing the pilot was, 'You can't make me believe
that it's possible to turn out something as fast and funny as
that each week!' And of course that was a tribute to Billy."

Friedkin shared their enthusiasm to the extent of promising
to direct every one of the twenty-six yearly episodes if *The Pickle
Brothers* was approved as a series.

"It was part of the irony of the situation," Gardner adds, "that
Four Star was wary of committing themselves to one director
all season. But they never faced that problem because it never
went on the air."

To prepare for the shoot Friedkin, Gardner, *frères* Pickle and
a photographer were sent to stay at New York's Plaza Hotel to
steal publicity shots that would match the show's fictional Manor
House, a set that was yet to be built. Gardner remembers
Friedkin commandeering a chambermaid's housekeeping cart
and riding it around the Plaza's carpeted corridors with Prince,
Mislove, and Lee aboard.

"Billy can be quite charming," Gardner says, chuckling. "He
just went up to this woman and said, 'Madam, we're going to
need your cart' and took it from her while she was swept up in
this whole adventure. I have recollections of Billy directing this
frantic chase down the hallways of the Plaza."

Gardner remembers Friedkin's patience with actress Carol
Veazie, the Pickles' Margaret Dumont-like antagonist, who was
having trouble with her lines during studio shooting.

"We watched with fascination while Carol kept blowing her lines," Gardner reports. "Here was this lady costing us so much time but you would never know it from Billy's manner, which was very gracious. When he finally got a good take out of her, I praised him for it, and he said, 'Gerry, when people see this up on the screen they will never know all of the effort that went to get this performance on that line. They'll just see it and laugh.'"

When Four Star's film editor assembled the footage, however, Friedkin was not laughing.

"The pilot is still in the can" he whispered to Gardner, meaning that the first editor had not used the scenes that Friedkin considered the effective ones. He then summoned Bud Smith from Wolper to recut the show.

"The distinction between the two pilots was the difference between night and day," writer-producer Gardner says. "The reason ABC did not put it on the air was their fear that we could never replicate it each week. But it is still a tradition that they show that pilot to people who are undertaking farce comedies for the network: This is what we're aspiring to."

Like its obvious inspiration, the Marx Brothers, *The Pickle Brothers* is an anarchic comedy pitting the existential forces of pure chaos against the Establishment. But the literate, fine-tuned scripts crafted for the Marxes by such luminaries as George S. Kaufman, Morrie Ryskind and S. J. Perelman could never be generated on a weekly basis for network television. Moreover, ABC just wasn't ready for three derivative, obnoxious vaudeville-style comedians.

"It was considered funny, too savage at the time," Friedkin observes. "I remember liking those guys, especially the middle one (Mike Mislove). I don't think there's anything like it now. I don't know. Maybe there shouldn't be."

Although it is possible that in future episodes the Pickles might have moved farther away from the Marxes and become better defined, the show's concentration on sheer farcical energy rather than logic makes *The Pickle Brothers* seem adrift, literally rebels without a cause. By 1967, however, American television did get its comedy about lovable farçeurs: *The Monkees*, the trendsetting musical comedy show for which Gerald Gardner became story editor.

"*The Monkees* was a success," Gardner says, "but I don't think it ever achieved the level of farce that Billy managed to get out of the three young men on *The Pickle Brothers*."

The Pickle Brothers was finished and forgotten even before

Good Times quietly came out. ("It died, had a short happy life. I think it was seen by eleven people in Topanga Canyon," Friedkin notes, adding knowingly, "I'd like to have the rights to it now, though.") Sonny's and Cher's residual feelings, however, are more emotional. In 1969, buoyed by the filming experience, Sonny sank a considerable amount of his own money into the film *Chastity*, in which he directed Cher using the fake name Alessio de Paola. It cast her as a teenage runaway seeking her own identity on the road. Cher received encouraging notices but the film did not; its only legacy is in inspiring the name of their daughter.

Cher has an even more abrupt way of dealing with both of her early films: she has purged them completely from her prepared publicity biography.

For Friedkin, however, the memories are more positive. It got him out of television and onto the meeting circuit. It also fueled him with a scene he later used in real life.

In *Good Times*, Sonny rejects Mordicus's *Rags to Riches* script with a firm refusal: "There's no way we're making this picture." Friedkin handled his own subsequent job interview the same way.

He was summoned to Paramount by Blake Edwards to direct the film version of Edwards's popular TV series, *Peter Gunn*. Handed the script of *Gunn* Friedkin was excited at the prospect of getting his big break. When he sat down to read it, however, his elation dissolved.

"I hated it," he says. "I didn't really know what to say to Blake because I really wanted to do the picture, but not *that* picture. So I went back to see Blake and I said, 'Blake, I really hate this script. As a matter of fact, I think it's the worst piece of shit I ever read in my life.' "

Edwards listened patiently to Friedkin's objections and then pressed a button on his desk.

"Well, I'd like you to tell that to the fellow who wrote the script," he said. "He's sitting in the outer office."

The writer entered, shook Friedkin's hand, and took a seat.

"He has read your script," Edwards told the writer, nodding toward Friedkin. "Tell him what you told me."

Friedkin did.

"I didn't temper my comments too much," he says. "But after I said it [the writer] broke into hysterical laughter and said, 'You know, you're absolutely right. It really is a rotten script and nobody here has had the guts to say it.' "

Needless to say, Friedkin didn't get the job. Blake Edwards

went on to direct the film himself and it was released in 1967 only to share the same fate as *Good Times*.

Friedkin made an impression on the writer, however, who, far from being slighted, came to respect the young director for his honesty. The writer was William Peter Blatty.

"Billy was definitively rejected," Blatty concurs, "and the reason for his being rejected made me a Billy Friedkin admirer from that moment.

"I had co-written *Gunn* with Blake and part of my contribution was a dream sequence which Blake liked very much. Billy raised one objection to the script: the dream sequence.

"Now, you must set this into context," Blatty adds in the teaching manner born of Jesuit education and discipline. "Billy had, at that time, only done one film. I'm sure Billy will agree that it was not an auspicious beginning. This interview was extremely important. I sat back and reached for another cigarette and thought, Well, now he's going to give way and like the dream sequence when he sees how much Blake likes the dream sequence.

"*Billy did not back off*, knowing full well that he was not going to get this important job. He stuck to his guns and he didn't get the assignment. I never forgot that. That is why, when it came time to find a director for *The Exorcist*, I threatened Warner Brothers with a lawsuit because of their refusal to consider Billy."

Having shot himself with *Gunn*, Friedkin was sent by his well-connected business manager, Ed Gross, to see Bud Yorkin and Norman Lear, the team that had closed a production deal with United Artists and needed a director for their nostalgic look at the last days of vaudeville, *The Night They Raided Minsky's*.

It seemed like a perfect match. At the time, UA was known for allowing its filmmakers a free hand. They were also closely identified with such risk-taking directors as Norman Jewison (*The Russians Are Coming, The Russians Are Coming*), Billy Wilder (*Some Like It Hot, Kiss Me Stupid*) and Blake Edwards (*The Pink Panther*) and were enriched by the phenomenal worldwide grosses of the James Bond series that they had released.

Their most acclaimed young stylist, however, was Richard Lester, the Philadelphia-born filmmaker who struck gold in England with his jump-cut, breezy, frenetic *A Hard Day's Night, Help!* and *A Funny Thing Happened on the Way to the Forum*. Lester's movies borrowed from TV commercials, the French New Wave and the syntax of America's burgeoning experimental film movement. He was inventing, in the 1960s, the devices that would later become institutionalized by music videos in the 1980s, and United Artists craved more of the same.

The style was called the New Look, a technique easier seen than done.

"Had anyone dared to acknowledge that the New Look we hoped to achieve in *Minsky's* was essentially a Lester look, we all might have been saved some anguish," says Ralph Rosenblum, the film's editor. "But such an acknowledgment would have been considered inappropriate, if not blasphemous, and so it barely crossed our minds."

The upshot of this unspoken homage would be sixteen weeks of wild production, three weeks of manic editing and nearly a year of desperate reediting on a movie that not only chronicled the end of an era but very nearly the demise of the careers of the people who made it.

CHAPTER 4

MINSKY
AND
PINTER

Britt Ekland is flanked by Norman Wisdom (left), who wants and respects her, and Jason Robards (right), who just wants her, in *The Night They Raided Minsky's.*
COURTESY OF UNITED ARTISTS TANDEM PRODUCTIONS

AT A COST of $5 million, *The Night They Raided Minsky's* was, in 1967, one of the most expensive motion pictures ever filmed in New York City. It was also four times what William Friedkin had proclaimed should be the top budget for any of his future films only a few months earlier in *Variety*.

An affectionate valedictory to vaudeville, it boasted an ensemble cast of veteran character actors that included Joseph Wiseman, Harry Andrews, Bert Lahr, Jason Robards, Denholm Elliott, Norman Wisdom, Forrest Tucker and newcomers Britt Ekland and Elliott Gould. Also in the cast were Jack Burns (formerly of Second City), Eddie "The Old Philosopher" Lawrence and Richard Libertini, later to become one of the screen's most popular and eccentric comic actors.

The script (by Arnold Schulman, Sidney Michaels and Norman Lear) was based on an actual raid on the famed Minsky's Burlesque on New York's Lower East Side in 1925 which, for the purposes of the film, was presumed to have symbolized the imminent changing of burlesque as a forum for low comedy into an arena for strippers.

Authenticity would be the hallmark of this musical comedy. Producers Bud Yorkin and Norman Lear (who would soon reshape television comedy with *All in the Family*) had originally planned to shoot their film on a Hollywood back lot, but moved it to New York when Mayor John Lindsay revamped the city's Film Commission to encourage location work.

"The Lower East Side is just like it was fifty years ago," pronounced Friedkin to *Variety* before the film's September 11, 1967 start date. "All you have to do is rip out the parking meters, conceal the air conditioners and put some old cars on the streets."

Friedkin and Lear also decided to revamp the script to reflect a change in cast. Originally hired to play the straight man and his top banana who would feud over the same girl, Tony Curtis and Joel Grey were parted when Curtis won the starring role of *The Boston Strangler* and bowed out—the day after a big farewell party in Los Angeles in his honor. Next, Yorkin and Lear wanted to team Alan Alda and Joel Grey, but Broadway show commitments made scheduling impossible. Finally they prevailed upon Jason Robards (fresh off *A Thousand Clowns*) to join the British comic Norman Wisdom, and *Minsky's* was back in place.

Sixteen weeks of location filming were planned involving sets as diverse as a sleazy hotel, the National Wintergarden Theatre, the old elevated subway and an atmospheric Lower East

Side strewn with pushcarts and costumed extras recalling an immigrant past.

As eager as Yorkin, Lear and United Artists were to make the film look authentic, they were also looking for it for the next summer's release schedule. To both ends they engaged Friedkin.

"UA was in a rush to get it going and we just couldn't swing time," says Bud Yorkin, who would, under most circumstances, have directed the picture himself. "I was in Europe shooting *Start the Revolution Without Me* and that was a problem." Yorkin met Friedkin and they hit it off.

"I loved his mind and thought he was an excellent picture maker. I had seen his documentary (*Crump*) and thought that he was the perfect guy to give a break to."

Yorkin's absence during *Minsky's* filming spared him the woes that fell to his partner, Norman Lear—all from this spritely musical that was supposed to be a story about, to quote narrator Rudy Vallee's introduction, "This real religious girl [who] by accident invented the striptease."

It is 1925. Wholesome and stunningly attractive Rachel Schpitendavel (Britt Ekland) arrives on New York's Lower East Side from Smoketown, Pennsylvania, bent on dancing stories from the Bible as befits her devout upbringing. Brought backstage of the National Wintergarden Theatre, home of Minsky's Burlesque, by former top banana Professor Spats (Bert Lahr), she is captivated by the excitement and color.

Less capitivated by it, however, is Louis Minsky (Joseph Wiseman), who owns the building and the show. He is so revolted at the parade of skin that his son Billy (Elliott Gould) is putting on that he issues him an ultimatum: either buy the theater or prepare to be evicted in a week when the lease runs out.

To raise the $200,000 his father wants (well, $190,000 as a favor) Billy seeks gangster Trim Houlihan (Forrest Tucker). The only thing that can stop the deal, however, is if Vance Fowler (Denholm Elliott), a local censor, raids the show first.

This is when the Burlesque's two comic headliners, Raymond Paine (Jason Robards) and Chick Williams (Norman Wisdom), hatch an idea: why not hire Rachel with the fake name of Madame Fifi ("She Drove a Million Frenchmen Wild"), dare Fowler to raid the show, then clean up at the box office and embarrass the censor into oblivion when Rachel/Fifi dances from the Bible instead of hootchy kootchy?

Billy buys the idea, but matters cloud up when Rachel's stern father Jacob (Harry Andrews) arrives in search of his wayward daughter. This occurs just as Chick is falling in love with Rachel and Chick's lecherous partner, Raymond, is conspiring to steal the girl away from his friend. Chick discovers Raymond's duplicity after a fight in a delicatessen and interrupts the seduction in Raymond's hotel room. Raymond later gets even during their stage performance by bashing Chick in front of the audience who thinks it's part of the routine.

Several doublecrosses later, the house is packed for the midnight show. Rachel's father arrives, Vance Fowler and the cops are standing by, and Rachel begins her "bawdy" dance to the obvious outrage of the audience. When her father tries to pull her off stage, he instead rips her costume away, and the joint is raided.

With the troupe's departure for jail, burlesque, too, is gone. Inside the now empty theater Professor Spats carefully picks up a seltzer bottle, vaudeville's greatest icon, and sets it gently on a stepladder as the house lights go out forever and the credits roll.

"I bullshitted my way into making *The Night They Raided Minsky's*," Friedkin confesses, still stinging from the experience. "I hated Norman Lear's script, which he thought was gold, which he thought was *Citizen Kane*, I thought was totally superficial, had nothing to do with the real feeling of burlesque or any of the people who practiced it. But I didn't say any of that to Norman Lear at the time. I wasn't candid with Norman because it was an opportunity to direct a major feature film for United Artists. My goal was to direct a major film for a major studio. Tony Fantozzi and I discussed this; it was Fantozzi who convinced me that a) I should do this picture because it's a golden opportunity, and b) I could fix it in the course of production. So my relationship with Norman and Bud was, up to a very deep point, bullshit."

However Friedkin may have felt at the time, he kept it to himself and plunged into *Minsky's* with energy and a growing level of directorial skill. The countless hours he had spent directing local television shows were paying off: he handled the pressure of time, he was not intimidated by the older, more experienced actors, and he demonstrated a mature sense of blocking and movement.

Gerald Gardner visited Friedkin at the National Wintergarden location in New York, which was actually a theater used on the old Jewish stage circuit that had been rented for the film.

"They were on a break and Billy was looking very chagrined

and very much appalled by some particular circumstance," Gardner remembers. "I asked how things were going and he said, and I'm not quoting verbatim, 'My God, I never realized all of these things went on and it's all on my shoulders.'"

If Friedkin had any personal doubts he kept them to himself during the film's lengthy sixteen-week production schedule. Ralph Rosenblum, the film's editor, however, remembers that something was coloring the young filmmaker's approach and he did not feel comfortable around it on the set.

"Here was Friedkin getting a major opportunity," recalls Rosenblum (who has also collaborated with Mel Brooks, Sidney Lumet, and was Woody Allen's editor through *Annie Hall*), "and I kept staring at him while we were shooting the movie and I said to myself, Where does this man get the arrogance and the swagger and all those other accoutrements that go with the stereotype of a movie director? I found Bill in terms of personality, purely in terms of personality, a little distasteful.

"I'm always thrown by arrogance," explains Rosenblum, who was hired by Norman Lear because of his reputation for saving films in the editing room. "He was dealing with well-known actors, old pros—Harry Andrews, Jason Robards, Denholm Elliott, and Joe Wiseman. These were terrific character actors and they were always making snotty remarks about him behind his back."

Britt Ekland, who at twenty-four was closer to Friedkin's age then her more seasoned costars, understood her director's arrogance.

"Billy was only twenty-seven at the time," she says. "He came up to me and said, 'I'm going to be gentle with you, but I'm going to be tough as nails with them because that's the only way I can keep them from intimidating me.' So he just charged right in with Jason and the others."

Pressured by the studio to compile a rough cut of the film while it was still being shot, Friedkin saw all schedules suddenly made useless when Bert Lahr, who was playing a major role, died halfway through production.

"We were shooting in the old Minsky's theater and one morning they gathered us all together and told us that he had died," Ekland recalls. "They weren't sure whether they were going to continue with the film, but they decided to go ahead."

"He was the reason for the whole picture, in a strange way," Bud Yorkin muses about Lahr's presence in the picture as a former "top banana" whose day has passed yet who yearns for the spotlight.

Lahr's part was eliminated where possible or was given to

other characters; for those few shots where he was needed to preserve visual continuity his double, comedian Joey Faye, was photographed from behind. These shots occur early in the film and include Professor Spats showing Rachel into the theater upon her arrival in New York.

Then, less than a month after the completion of principal photography, Friedkin left the film. Ralph Rosenblum, who had hurried with the director to finish a first cut of the footage, was shocked.

"He had a contract to do *The Birthday Party*," Rosenblum says. "The whole thing surprised me because usually studio heads, when they're dealing with a very expensive picture, don't allow a director to sign up for another picture that quickly. First of all, most directors wouldn't do it because they want some editing time. They wouldn't take another picture for three to six months. For some reason—I didn't ask why—Bill was off in three and a half weeks."

"Billy was close to Norman and me at that time," Yorkin explains, "and I think he kind of trusted that whatever we would do would be okay. I think he felt there were some things lacking that would have made the picture better if someone had had the time to spend on it."

According to other sources, however, Friedkin's leaving *Minsky's* was not mourned. There had been increasing tension during the four-month shoot and by the time the picture's first cut was screened, "We were as far apart as three collaborators could be," Rosenblum writes in his book, *When the Shooting Stops . . . The Cutting Begins*, with Robert Karen.

He recalls that when he, Friedkin and Lear sat in United Artists' Seventh Avenue screening room in the fall of 1967 they had "some of the least compelling footage any of us had ever seen. There was no pace, no suspense, and not a moment of believable dialogue." At that point it was decided to wait a few days, take a new look and see what could be done. Friedkin packed for England. The producers took the precaution of striking a rough print of his cut.

The question, of course, was really why Rosenblum, Friedkin and Lear hadn't noticed the problems with the film while they were working together and could still address them.

"I had a sense when I read the script," Rosenblum insists. "Not that the script was terrible, but that it was just hackneyed. I should've realized when I read the script that unless there was some technique involved here, it would be just an ordinary movie. It didn't occur to me then and it didn't occur to me when I saw the dailies we'd shot, and I saw them with Norman Lear. Weeks—four months—looking at dailies, it didn't occur to me. Not until much later on."

The solution became what Rosenblum calls the New Look.

According to Rosenblum, he and Lear painstakingly achieved it by a combination of fast-paced cutting, stock footage, black-and-white intercuts with Friedkin's color footage and a meticulously built subtext of sound and image that, in effect, creates a cinematic juggling act that holds the viewer's attention, if not his logic.

"But to give him a great deal of credit," Rosenblum offers, "on the professional side, he shot a lot of film. He used that [sixteen-week production] schedule well. And I can say quite honestly and factually that if he hadn't shot all the film he did we never would've been able to make out of it the picture we did."

Friedkin fumes at Rosenblum's assertions and adds some of his own:

"There have been editors who have contributed to films that I've made. Rosenblum is not one of them. His account is fraudulent. Norman Lear wanted to try everything. And Norman Lear did a lot of things in *Minsky's* in order to save the picture, and I believe the picture was unsalvageable from the script. I think the film is a total failure on every level. I'm completely divorced from it."

He also comments on the film's most noted device of combining black-and-white and color footage to suggest a newsreel approach to its yesteryear setting. The black-and-white footage was created in the lab by removing the color from what had been shot, then switching back and forth between the two on screen to suggest nostalgia.

"It was in the original—Lear's basic notion," Friedkin insists, "filtered through me. I mean, I went out and shot all those scenes to look like newsreel footage. A part of what attracted Lear to me was that I could fake documentary, and that's what I did. All of those shots were always meant to look like newsreels, Norman never said to bleed them to black-and-white but he said those shots should look like newsreel footage, and I loved the idea. Who knew till you went looking for the stuff that all the newsreel footage was in black-and-white? So the obvious choice was to bleed the film."

In the end, they still needed more. Lear and Pablo Ferro (a stylish editor, designer and director known for superb title work) shot an additional six days of crowds laughing, atmosphere and the smoky speakeasy sequence at Houlihan's hideaway. Bit by bit, the film was tweaked into something that reflected, if not the script, then the original intent of the project from its producers' standpoint.

"Now, this is very important—it isn't faulting Bill," adds Rosenblum (who left the project himself before the year-long process was finished). "Whatever the people wanted out of this movie, the only way they could get the movie they wanted was in the cutting room. And if I didn't know that going in, there was something wrong with me. I knew it when I was ass-deep in film—with Friedkin or without Friedkin. Every trick had to be used, every optical effect had to be used."

And that's the New Look.

But Friedkin, who remains close friends with Bud Yorkin (and asked him to produce *Deal of the Century* fifteen years later), seemed more interested in his next project. According to Rosenblum in his book, two months into the intense reediting process (long after Friedkin's departure) Norman Lear called him into his office and showed him a transcript of a guest appearance Friedkin had made on a British talk show as *The Birthday Party* was being shot. The host asked the director about his most recent project before leaving the States.

"The biggest piece of crap I ever worked on," Rosenblum quotes from the transcript. "Something called *The Night They Raided Minsky's.*"

Laments a source close to the production, "It was a labor of love, but not for Billy. It was not his finest hour."

Characteristically, Friedkin summarizes it even more brutally.

"I should have never directed the film. I unfortunately have to confess that that terrible piece of shit was directed by me, and shot by me, badly, and I did not help the actors much because I didn't know what to tell them, because I didn't get a clue from Lear other than to tell them it was supposed to be a joke, everything they said to each other off the stage was supposed to be part of a shtick, and I didn't agree with that. But I did the picture anyway. That horrible, twisted, demented demon is mine and the final cut is not all that far from what I delivered other than touches that I tried to bring to it that would give it more depth. But if [Ralph Rosenblum] wants to take credit for *The Night They Raided Minsky's*—over the years I've never discussed any of this—as the Jews say, *lezine!* [He can have it]"

The public felt much the same way, although certain critics found an exuberance in the pace and lightness of the picture.

In cinematic terms, however, *The Night They Raided Minsky's* can be seen as two films, both of them highly spirited but each at odds with the other. For all its life, *Minsky's* is a film about the end of an era, an historical importance that dwarfs the concern for the individual characters. That case is best stated in the final scene in which Bert Lahr—himself resonating with history—leaves the stage for what we know will be the last time. Originally, Rosenblum and Friedkin had accompanied this symbolic exit with a temporary music track of the Chico Hamilton jazz tune "Thoughts," a downbeat piece in a minor key.

"My God, it's absolutely beautiful, it's what the movie is about," Friedkin told Rosenblum. "Whatever you do, don't cut that piece of music."

Unfortunately, "Thoughts" was deemed *too* downbeat and was replaced by a brassier number that changes the tone of the film from one of lost innocence to a more upbeat, things-will-be-okay attitude, which is patently false.

This schizophrenia pervades the entire film. Just when it seems that two characters (Chick and Rachel, Raymond and Chick, Spats and Billy, etc.) will relate to each other, music breaks out. In a traditional musical such interludes would be ballads in which two people deepen their relationship; in *Minsky's* it's usually comic distraction.

Yet in *The Night They Raided Minsky's* can be seen the first stirrings of a mixture of moods that will come to dominate Friedkin's films: you can have fun but you'll pay a price. Friedkin's characters are skilled in their profession and then find themselves compelled to use those skills in ways that ultimately jeopardize their own happiness. It is a duality, a sense of Fate that at once entertains and chastises. And the next time he made a film Friedkin would bring that duality into the realm of literature.

The Birthday Party was the film for which Friedkin had left *Minsky's*. It is easy to see what attracted the young American filmmaker to the young English playwright whom he calls "one of the greatest living writers." Like Friedkin, Harold Pinter writes about societies within societies with broader implications than the immediate frame of the drama.

When it was first produced in 1958 *The Birthday Party* was booed off the stage of Cambridge's Arts Theatre—hardly an encouraging, though certainly an auspicious, debut for its author. The day after it closed (having run only a week), *The Sunday Times* drama critic Harold Hobson pronounced it "One of the major plays of our time," yet not until 1964 did it enjoy a second London production. By then it was greeted with kudos and was a triumph.

William Friedkin had seen *The Birthday Party* at a San Francisco workshop production in 1962 while he was in town to accept the Golden Gate award for *The People Versus Paul Crump*.

"It changed my life," he said later, and vowed to direct it on screen. There was just one problem, of course: in 1962 few people knew Harold Pinter and even fewer knew William Friedkin. Nevertheless, Friedkin and Pinter met in New York and the two men agreed to form a company to make the film. When, just before starting *Minsky's*, Friedkin found financing from independent producer Max Rosenberg of Palomar Pictures International, *The Birthday Party* started to look possible.

As eager as Pinter was to have his play filmed, he had one unalterable condition: his play must be shot in its entirety without deletions. Friedkin agreed.

The movie marketplace was changing in 1968 when *The Birthday Party* was made. The old Hollywood censorship office was being replaced with what has become the current MPAA movie ratings and audiences were seeing more adult fare on the screen. Among films released that same year that reflected a new morality were *The Killing of Sister George*, *The Fox*, *Rachel, Rachel* and *Rosemary's Baby*. Into that crowded arena quietly came *The Birthday Party*, about a broken concert pianist (Stanley) whose retreat to a seaside boarding house is invaded by two mysterious strangers who goad him into a mental breakdown.

Friedkin's casting coup in attracting David Hemmings to play the pianist melted before the start of spring filming and he was replaced by Robert Shaw, a curious choice given the macho image he had created in 1963 with *From Russia with Love*. The cast also included Patrick Magee as McCann and Sydney Tafler as Goldberg, Stanley's tormentors; Dandy Nichols as Meg, the housemistress; Moultrie Kelsall as her husband, Petey; and Helen Fraser as Lulu, a young neighbor who is the play's only symbol of hope, ineffectual though she may be.

In every way *The Birthday Party* was a departure for Friedkin. It was confining where his previous work had been unrestrained. It was a tight drama of rising emotions with only the darkest of humor. And under no circumstances could it be *ad-libbed*.

Friedkin had arranged to present two complete performances of the play—one in the morning and the other in the afternoon—for Pinter's approval before any film could be shot. When the day of the run-throughs arrived, Pinter sat stoically in his seat and watched in silence as his work was put on before him. He then gave Friedkin and the actors his notes.

"Well, certainly some very interesting work is going on here," Pinter offered, according to Friedkin. "Of course, you're not doing my play."

"And we all died," Friedkin says. "Then he read from his notes and his notes consisted of six words that were wrong in the course of the two-hour-and-fifteen-minute play. He cited the words and what they were to be and we laughed. 'Is that all, Harold?' And he said, 'Yes, that's all, but they have to be right. That's it. If you want to do my stuff, that's it. It's got to be verbatim.' "

The plan was to shoot the play in its entirety inside a soundstage at Shepperton Studios with a few days' exterior work in Worthing by the Sea. The film's budget of $500,000 ("I think most film budgets are loaded with sloth and waste," Friedkin as now saying) included minimal salaries for everybody and a mandate to protect the dramatic property. Pinter was to be inviolate.

"That seems like a very consistent position," Friedkin later recalled for an American Film Institute seminar. "During the course of shooting, we came to the celebrated interrogation scene where these two guys, an Irishman and a Jew [McCann and Goldberg], browbeat [Stanley]. It's a kind of elaborate . . . inquisition, if you will, about things for which there are no answers.

"There were two lines that Patrick Magee . . . remembered that when Pinter first wrote the play . . . the Lord Chamberlain in effect ruled the British theater. You could make no reference to the Queen of England or to the crucifixion. And so there were two lines in the play that were deleted, Magee remembered, by the Lord Chamberlain. They were lines in which one of the questions was, 'Who hammered the nails?' and the other line was, 'Who drove in the screws?' which were two lines referring to the crucifixion and this man's and mankind's guilt in the crucifixion of Christ. Magee told me about these lines right in the middle of shooting and I said, 'Jesus, where the hell are these lines in the scene? They're great!' They weren't in the film script.

"So I called Harold, woke him up, and I said, 'Harold, those lines! Magee told me about those lines that you had to cut.' He said, 'What? What are you talking about?'

"I said, 'Who hammered the nails? Who drove in the screws?'

"He said, 'I never heard those lines.'

"I said, 'Oh, come on.' I told him that they were in the original version.

"He said, 'Wait a minute. I've got an original play script. Let me find it.' He went back and left the phone for about fifteen minutes. He came back and he said, 'I've got the damn scene here and those lines aren't in it.'

"I said, 'Oh, shit.'

"He said, 'Wait a minute, do you really like those lines? You think they work?'

"I said, 'Work? They're fantastic. They're the best lines in the scene.'

"He said, 'Keep it.' Now they're in the film and I've read critical nonsense about that scene and these lines from here to kingdom come about what he meant and what his intention was. That's how they got in there."

Friedkin's glee at baiting his critics while playfully courting them is a continuation of his "Phantom of the School" escapades—in effect, daring others to catch him at the game. It has asserted itself in several of his films (such as *A Walk Through the Valley*) where he will arbitrarily make decisions and then sit back to await their interpretation. Depending on his mood, he will either acknowledge or ridicule them, sometimes both.

Besides, the obscurities and stylization of *The Birthday Party* invite such speculation.

Described as a comedy of menace, *The Birthday Party* takes place at the boarding house run by Meg and Petey Boles—she an uncomplicated British housewife, he an old-age pensioner who operates the deck chair concession at the nearby beach. Their only boarder is Stanley Webber, a moody and lethargic man in his midthirties who has lived there for a year in apparent retreat from a promising career as a pianist. The Boleses are childless but Meg considers Stanley her own; in fact, her concern is both maternal and incestuous, since they make allusion to "those afternoons" in their banter. The only other person to share their world is Lulu, a neighbor whose flirtatious presence is apparent to everyone but Meg. Into their communal existence come two strangers: the wiry McCann and the garrulous Goldberg. Their arrival threatens Stanley, who harbors a fear of discovery, although specifics are elusive.

It is apparently a matter of some urgency that has brought McCann and Goldberg to Stanley's hideaway. At first they are polite to him but their insistent courtesy soon becomes interrogatory. When Meg reveals that today is Stanley's birthday,

McCann and Goldberg insist on throwing him a party. Before the festivities, Meg privately presents Stanley with a child's toy drum which he beats to excess. Later, when McCann and Goldberg return bearing liquor, the night of drinking—and Lulu's allure—bring about Stanley's complete breakdown. The next morning the two men presumably lead Stanley away to a doctor.

Despite Pinter's insistence on completeness, he deleted considerable material when adapting his play to the screen. Gone from his revised draft is any clear reason for Stanley's retreat to the Boleses' boarding house, the suggestion of a prior relationship among the three men (possibly involving Irish politics) and Stanley's sexual interplay with Lulu. That's quite a bundle to leave out, and the effect of the void is to make the film even more enigmatic than Pinter usually is. Devoid of the back story, Stanley's victimization is seen as an act of pure persecution with the even darker presumption of guilt. In this sense, the play is about mankind's ultimate responsibility and desire to escape from its consequences.

Nothing harvests this guilt more effectively than McCann's and Goldberg's abrasive, random and confusing hammering at Stanley, an exchange that soon develops its own rhythm and logic as well as perverse humor. It is one of *The Birthday Party*'s most memorable set pieces and Friedkin would later apply its techniques to *The French Connection*.*

Pinter's play is redolent with textures that Friedkin's film suppresses. By pruning the script of specifics, Friedkin turns it less into a mystery than a brooding essay in pure paranoia. Stanley's journey embodies that of a man's mental and emotional lifespan: he goes from whining child carping about cornflakes to an adolescent playing with toys to a libidinous teenager toying with sex to a senile old man descending into trancelike oblivion.

His oppressors, McCann and Goldberg (ironically an Irishman and a Jew, two of history's most victimized cultures), merely move in and out of Stanley's life like demonic forces. They never explain their pasts, their presence, or their exact relationship; they may, in fact, be homosexual lovers (supported by McCann's ire when Goldberg makes a pass at the ever-present Lulu).

* Primarily in the scene in which Gene Hackman and Roy Scheider badger the truth out of a suspect by assaulting his sense of sanity, alternating questions about a dope deal with the abstract, "Did you ever pick your feet in Poughkeepsie?"

Surrounded by such forces, Lulu is a comparative innocent. In the play she and Stanley have developed an ongoing friendship; she is his confidante and his virtual rape of her at the end of the second act—a debasing move that signals his abandonment of control and with it his sanity—is an omission the film suffers.

Through it all, Meg remains overly doting. Her jovial ignorance of the malice lurking just beneath the surface of her world may be comical in the film but it serves a larger purpose in the play: as she repeats (incorrectly) things she has heard (such as the reason Stanley has retired there) she adds drama to the exposition.

Petey is even more peripheral. His one flash of paternal concern is to challenge Goldberg's taking Stanley to the doctor at the end of his ordeal. The instant Goldberg (uncharacteristically) sharply resists his action, Petey drops it. Back to status quo.

Friedkin's cinematic treatment (with Denys Coop, B.S.C.) is meticulously varied within the single-room set. The Boleses' home may be a traditional English terrace house but it seems to have a surfeit of bedrooms; the only one shown is Stanley's for a brief shot as Meg awakens him as a mother would a child for school. Meg's kitchen is briefly shown for some sight gags early on (tea leaves and fried bread are easily made to look vile and unappetizing). There are a few exterior angles that establish the seaside location, and one particularly portentious shot through the front window of the sedan carrying Goldberg and McCann to the Boleses' house. Appearing during the titles, that sequence is accompanied by the unnerving sound of paper being torn—a noise later to be identified with McCann's compulsive shredding of his newspaper into five equal strips, an action from which *The Birthday Party* has derived some of its celebrity.

At times the claustrophobic setting is used to drive the characters against one another; one overhead shot during the second act blind man's buff sequence is both self-conscious and effectively distancing.

Other shots verge on the acrobatic: Friedkin's hand-held, wide-angle and point-of-view perspectives occasionally interrupt the narrative. This is as much an example of filmmaking in the 1960s as his own directorial cheekiness. Along with intercut black-and-white footage (whenever the screen goes dark and the staging calls for flashlights), there is continued experimentation with varying the camera coverage. To expand the confines of the one-room set, Friedkin moves the camera completely around the location, sometimes gratuitously but always in the service of objectifying the story.

In refusing to play Pinter's dialogue at traditional, respectful distance, Friedkin is calling attention to nuance while minimizing the inherent mystery plot of the play. Other Pinter works have been filmed—most notably by Joseph Losey and Bryan Forbes—that focus on character interplay to fine effect. But Friedkin is more bent on generating a palpable sense of dread that exceeds Pinter's parable. In embracing the absence of detail in *The Birthday Party* he realizes its profundity.

Unfortunately, few people saw it. As an independent release, *The Birthday Party* enjoyed few bookings in 1968 and even today is available only on cable television. Critics at the time found it too talky, too realistic, too dissipated in its tension. They also found it well acted and well staged and ultimately pronounced it a credible job, but of course Pinter is meant for the stage. And some noticed that there had, indeed, been cuts in the text.

Still, Friedkin had tried Pinter and it gave him the credentials to attempt another adaptation of a stage work—one last detour from the action films that would later solidify his reputation. Ironically, this next picture would give him quite another reputation, one that he has never been able to shake. He followed *The Birthday Party* with *The Boys in the Band*, a milestone in screen frankness about homosexuality and a millstone around Friedkin's ability to address the subject.

CHAPTER 5

FAIRY TALES

Mart Crowley (left) and Friedkin on the set of *The Boys in the Band* in 1969
PHOTO BY MUKY, COURTESY OF MART CROWLEY

THE SUREST WAY to anger the gay community is to cry "Friedkin" in a crowded theater. More than any other American director, William Friedkin has made it a practice to needle
homosexuals in almost every film he has made. It may be as
minor as a "sissy" gag in one of the *Minsky's* vaudeville numbers (in which Norman Wisdom gravitates toward a tall,
swishing man instead of a nubile chorus girl) or as rabid as Al
Pacino assuming the identity of a killer of gay men in *Cruising*.
Both Friedkin and the cohesive gay movement have become
mutual antagonists over the years and the first shot in the continuing skirmish was *The Boys in the Band*.

Mart Crowley's bitchy, groundbreaking play had its New York
premiere in January 1968 at the Vandam Theatre before moving uptown to Theatre Four in April to be directed by Robert
Moore. Set in a Manhattan loft apartment on a rainy summer
night, it presents a birthday party among nine men, one of whom
may be heterosexual. Praised at the time (mostly by straight
theater critics who, as gay activist writer Vito Russo observed
in *The Celluloid Closet*, termed every attempt at portraying gays
or the gay world as definitive) for its bold discussion of attitudes and stereotypes, the play (and film) have since come to
be regarded as a wallow in those images of homosexuality that
are ultimately self-defeating. It is concerned with the gay male's
obsession with appearing "masculine" and trots out a virtual
bomber crew of gay "types" and antitypes (butch schoolteacher, effeminate decorator, bookstore clerk, fashion photographer, dumb hustler, menial janitor, etc.) while doting on the
ever-present specter of age, blackmail, balding, ridicule, discovery and violence as gauntlets through which the gay male
must pass on a daily basis.

As a play, *The Boys in the Band* is a document of attitudes
toward homosexuality as of when it was written and, although
it offers hope, it is hope at the expense of its characters' straight
dreams; you'll be happy, Crowley teaches, but only if you're
happy being gay. Many audiences—depending on how willing
they are to accept the idea of gayness—are uncomfortable with
that position.

As a work of drama, *The Boys in the Band* needs no defense.
Any achievement that is so much a part of its era should not
be viewed out of its context.

Stage productions, of course, can be updated. Were *The Boys
in the Band* to be revived today it would have to deal with
AIDS, a shadow that hangs over any contemporary consideration of the text or viewing of the film.

The 1969 release date of the film is most evident in its hair-styles and costumes, although some flamboyance seems in line with the characters' theatricality. What targets it for criticism is its weepy presentation of a brand of homosexual angst and an omnipresent promise of lurid revelation that lurks behind every bedroom door and personal closet.

Nevertheless, in a 1970 interview, Friedkin declared, "*The Boys in the Band* is not about homosexuality," which is like saying that *Rocky* isn't about boxing. Certainly the two films address themes that reach beyond their specific settings, but there is still no denying who the players are.

Despite what would develop, over the years, into an ongoing feud with gays (culminating with *Cruising* in 1980), Friedkin was the first choice for director by writer-producer Mart Crowley. Crowley based his decision upon a coincidence.

"When I was writing the play Harold Pinter was writing what became known as *The Birthday Party*," he recalls. "At one point I had thought about calling *The Boys in the Band The Birthday Party* until suddenly there appeared at the same time a play called *The Birthday Party*, so therefore that title was out. But I was intrigued by it and I love Pinter's work, so I went to see the film. And I saw this man named William Friedkin."

Both Crowley and Friedkin had worked at Four Star at the same time four years earlier, Friedkin making *The Pickle Brothers* and Crowley as a contract writer.

"After I saw *The Birthday Party*," Crowley recalls, "I thought, well, anybody who has this gift of imagery within such enormous confines of a play with so much verbiage, and can still make some film imagery and get some movement and action out of it, then this is it. I went to Billy and asked him if he would direct it."

In hindsight, Crowley sees no irony in his choice.

"I felt that Billy was a very liberal and sympathetic person which certainly we needed. At that time we were very friendly. But, you know, working on any kind of theatrical project people become very close and obsessive about things; you have something in common. And when it's over you don't see each other anymore."

Having sold an unproduced screenplay some years before, Crowley had had experience with the savaging a work can suffer at the hands of a Hollywood studio—even newly formed Cinema Center Films where Dominick Dunne (another Four Star alumnus) had set up the project. Fearful that his groundbreaking play would be sanitized and randomly cast with whatever stars were dominating the late-sixties box office, Crowley demanded that the film be made with the same actors who had drawn praise on the stage.

Friedkin was not thrilled with having his cast dictated to him but told *Variety* in August of 1969 that, while he would have preferred to put his own choices in the roles, he used his three-week rehearsal period to discover "deeper roots and for the first time [explore] the real possibilities of their roles. *Boys*," he insisted, "is not about the gay world but about human problems. We don't want individual lines to be funny or outrageous. There'll be no pregnant pauses as there were on the stage. These are witty people who have quite proper things to say to one another." He also observed that, although the play concerns nine men, he hoped that audiences would consider themselves the tenth guest at the birthday party that forms the centerpiece of the action.

Despite the impasse over casting, Friedkin and Crowley reached an agreement on protocol.

"Both of us were very wary of each other to begin with," says Crowley, "and yet, for our youth, we were very professional. I remember we had a talk—I lived at the Algonquin Hotel then— and very early before the picture began we made a pact, so to speak, that whatever gripes and complaints we had with each other, we would never voice them in front of the crew or the cast no matter how wild with rage we could become. We would reserve it and speak to each other in private and we both held to the agreement. Although I think he had his difficulties with other people, I don't recall him ever having any trouble with me and certainly no public display of temperament."

Even when it came to firings—the initial cinematographer and art director were both replaced within a week of starting— director Friedkin and producer Crowley remained friends. It was Crowley who introduced Friedkin to Howard Hawks's daughter Kitty, a sometime model, and the three of them became inseparable during production.

"We would spend the weekends together," Crowley says. "I remember sometimes I'd get a little annoyed because he kept on talking about *The French Connection* [which Cinema Center was then considering] all the time.

"Kitty and he and I would go to the country together. Billy was always driving us around Brooklyn or someplace under all those els [elevated subway tracks]. Sometimes I thought, 'I wish you would stop thinking about this *next* movie and think about the one we're doing *now*.' But he was always amusing. He and

I got along well together; we talked about doing other things."
Crowley even sent new play manuscripts to Friedkin for what
he knew would be honest appraisal. In return, Friedkin sent
Crowley a copy of Gerald Walker's novel *Cruising*, which did
not interest the playwright in the least. They also made trips
to California to try to revive Crowley's dormant screenplay.
Nothing developed.

But *The Boys in the Band* did. Working with Friedkin, Crowley made the same kind of deletions from his play that Pinter
had made from *The Birthday Party;* particular points that were
cut were many that explained the characters' pasts. Reduced
were apologia for their homosexuality, arcane movie refer-
ences, and specific mention of certain brand name pharma-
ceuticals.

Surprisingly, the play's strong language remains and continues to provoke passionate debate among people who hold varying perceptions of gays within and without the so-called "gay
lifestyle." As luck would have it, the film was on the cutting
edge of a revolution.

On June 27, 1969, barely weeks before *The Boys in the Band*
went in front of the cameras in New York, patrons at Stonewall, a Greenwich Village gay bar, had fought against city police making a harassment raid. A week of demonstrations and
more riots followed as America's gay liberation movement was
born.

When released in the spring of 1970 *The Boys in the Band*
would earn an R rating from the Motion Picture Association of
America because of its use of language. In a sense, the MPAA
had grown up; the previous year it had slapped both *Midnight
Cowboy* and *The Killing of Sister George* with an X rating (no
one under seventeen admitted) merely for being *about* homosexuality.

Even with an R rating, it still carried the hex of an "adult"
film in an era when Woodstock and the youth movement were
causing apoplexy among stern American moralists. The newly
created movie rating system had been instituted to prevent
government censorship, but even the R brand could not mollify
those who felt "such things" shouldn't be filmed in the first
place.

The Boys in the Band lives up to its pedigree.

As "Anything Goes" plays on the soundtrack—first in a
scratchy old rehearsal recording made by Cole Porter himself
and then a glossier studio chorus—the seven principals of the
story prepare for an evening of merriment. Tonight is Harold's

(Leonard Frey) birthday and Michael (Kenneth Nelson) is throwing him a party. Michael is a spendthrift midwesterner who cannot come to terms with his gayness and has been carrying on a semi-relationship with his equally uncommitted lover Donald (Frederick Combs), who works as a janitor. Bernard (Reuben Greene) works as a clerk in Doubleday's book store and faces dual rejection from society both as a homosexual and as a black. Larry (Keith Prentice), a fashion photographer, shows up with Hank (Laurence Luckinbill), a schoolteacher, although he and Donald may have met before, a suggestion that sparks jealousy in both Hank and Michael. The least conforming member of the soiree is Emory (Cliff Gorman), an effeminate decorator, who is the subject of ribbing from his equally gay (but less flamboyant) peers.

Michael, in particular, is having a bad night. Although he has given up drinking and intends to curtail his profligate ways, he is alarmed when he gets a phone call from Alan (Peter White), a college chum who is unaware that he has come out of his closet. Alan, a lawyer, is happily married and has children but breaks down in tears on the phone with Michael, begging to come over and talk. Michael cautions his gay friends to expect a visit from a straight WASP, but Alan then cancels just as mysteriously.

Then he shows up.

Michael is caught between his two worlds—the one of family and friends who think of him as heterosexual and the other society, his new gay friends, who see him hypocritically play-acting against the truth.

Soon a hustler, Cowboy (Robert LaTourneaux), arrives—Emory has "bought" him as a gift for Harold, who has yet to show.

Alan is confused by everything he sees; he detests the fey Emory, is puzzled by Hank's presence, and wonders what Michael is doing here. Then Harold eventually shows up—a jumble of neuroses in a clenched, unattractive form.

The evening wears on, and wears thin. Michael falls off the wagon. Harold goads everyone. The easy glibness of the cracked crab appetizers turns into drunken confessions by the main course.

The game of Telephone is the Rubicon for the boys in the band. Its rules are simple and devastating: a player must phone the person he loves most, get him on the line, identify himself and say, "I love you." The winner gets ten points—and also an irrevocable commitment to his new way of life.

Bernard calls a white playmate he hasn't seen for years and gets the now-grown friend's mother; Emory calls a dentist on whom he once had a crush and who had humiliated him for it. Larry and Hank phone each other, declaring their commitment to one another (more or less), a move that appalls Alan, who had been telling himself that Hank was straight, like him.

This infuriates Michael, who accuses Alan of having carried on a homosexual affair in school with Justin Stuart, a gay mutual friend who used to tell Michael all about Alan. Alan vehemently denies it and, moreover, adds that once he learned that Justin was gay, he never spoke to him again.

Michael is shattered—not only was he apparently misled by Justin, whom he still knows, but he can see his own rejection by Alan, his last link with the straight life, lurking in the wings. He challenges Alan to play the telephone game and phone the person he loves most: Justin Stuart. Alan picks up the receiver and, to Michael's horror, calls his wife, Fran.

As the party breaks up Harold—taking his gift Cowboy in tow—gleefully delivers Michael the coup de grâce:

"You are a sad and pathetic man. You're a homosexual and you don't want to be. But there is nothing you can do to change it. Not all your prayers to your God, not all the analysis you can buy in all the years you've got left to live. You may very well one day be able to know a heterosexual life if you want it desperately enough—if you pursue it with the fervor with which you annihilate—but you will always be homosexual as well. Always, Michael. Always. Until the day you die."

Michael and Donald are alone. It is still a mystery to them why Alan had called in the first place—was he breaking up with Fran before this display of loneliness drove him back to her? They will never know. Michael leaves his apartment to walk off the booze. Donald tells him that he will visit him again next weekend, but that he will be gone when Michael gets back. The credits roll.

The Boys in the Band offers little hope for those who will not face the truth in their own lives. It need not be a sexual truth, but it must be Truth. In Crowley's play, the truth is not merely the self-declaration of being "different"—after all, "difference" was the most celebrated commodity in the hip 1960s, even though the so-called "Summer of Love" in 1967 should have been more appropriately called the "Summer of Heterosexual Love." The kind of truth Crowley seeks in his drama carries the price tag of ostracism from society. What makes it even pricier is not only that Michael can never return to his previous life, but that he is probably stuck with the self-destructive people he's just spent the evening with. As such *The Boys in the Band* paints a bleak portrait of the options offered by a homosexual lifestyle, especially one which is presented as being so separate from the mainstream of civilization.

The pronouncement that gays are tragic, lonely figures doomed to eternal ostracism raised a battle cry from the gay community.

"The internalized guilt of eight gay men at a Manhattan birthday party formed the best and most potent argument for gay liberation ever offered in a popular art form," wrote Vito Russo in *The Celluloid Closet*, his exhaustive examination of homosexuality in the movies. "It supplied concrete and personalized examples of the negative effects of what homosexuals learn about themselves from the distortions of the media. And the film caused the first public reaction by a burgeoning gay rights movement to the accepted stereotypes of Crowley's play."

Russo indicates that the images of gays in *Boys* weren't false but they were incomplete.

"It was a homosexual period piece just as *Green Pastures* was a Negro period piece. But blacks are visible and gays are not, and Hollywood was not moved to change a whit by all this hysteria in the gay drawing rooms of Manhattan."

The most threatening figure (to straights) in both the play and the film, Russo reminds, is not the limp-wristed Emory but the "normal" Hank. The fact that an athletic, beer-drinking, pipe-smoking macho man—and a *schoolteacher*, no less—could have left his wife and children for another man bothered the audience as much as it threatened Alan. Are there really queers among us? is what Crowley wants people to ask, Russo maintains, saying that despite Friedkin's apparent hipness, he is in reality quite reactionary, even square.

"Oh, well, you must consider all sides of it," Crowley rebuts. "Russo is an entrenched person himself with his own attitudes and is rather inflexible. I don't know; I don't think Billy is all that square at all."

Nevertheless, Friedkin denied any world-beating intentions at the time: "The film is not about homosexuality, it's about human problems," he insisted. "I hope there *are* happy homosexuals. They just don't happen to be in my film."

"*Boys in the Band* is a really fine script," he now says. "I didn't then and don't now have any strong feelings about doing any sort of film about the gay community.* It's hard for people who, let's say, are gay and have violent feelings about *The Boys in the Band* to believe that all that is to me is a marvelous story, a very good play with wonderful humor and pathos and drama and it's one of the best love stories I'd read in a long time.

"I don't feel it works as cinema because it works so well as a play and the two media just do not get together. A good play like *The Boys in the Band* relies for its effect essentially on good dialogue, verbal effects, the verbal interplay between characters, whereas my concept of a good film is not really that at all." †

Friedkin's addition to the work was to "visualize it" and to add "a few interpretive things during the party. I concentrated on emphases, to get across the story better." A comparison reveals that he did a great deal more. Some changes are merely the fine tuning that any film director would address in adapting a work from another medium; others suggest an almost cynical reading of public taste.

In collaboration with Mart Crowley, Friedkin dropped several elements of the play, sometimes to streamline the action and sometimes not. Excised is Michael's long monologue to Donald explaining why he is is gay (his mother, naturally) and Donald's equally expository speech to Michael about his breakthrough in psychotherapy. Gone, too, is Emory's rambling and extraneous explanation of finding Cowboy not on a Times Square meat rack but as a referral from a campy lounge singer named Rae Clark. A final significant cut is the removal of an early discussion between Hank and Larry to the effect that they had made a deal prior to the party regarding Larry's promiscuity. It becomes important later in the play and its absence from the first act undercuts some of the tension in their relationship.

The Boys in the Band is less flashy visually than *The Birthday Party*—no sudden cuts to airborne cameras—yet it is built of carefully chosen and enormously varied angles that keep the action lively despite the enclosed setting. There is also the emergence of a deliberate, reasoned pacing: Friedkin and director of photography Arthur J. Ornitz shoot the first half with

---

*His comments on *Cruising* (1980), his second film with a gay subject, are consistent.

†This thinking also kept Friedkin away from accepting an offer to direct the film version of the gay-themed play *Bent* in 1980, acknowledging, "It would be something next to suicidal for a studio to get a gay-oriented subject and give it to me."

a restless camera and energetic staging, all in strict service of the expository material. Just as a real party expands to fill the number of rooms allotted to it, so *Boys* explores Michael's apartment. The breadth of staging allows background action that would have been distracting on the stage yet takes its appropriate place in the film.

By the time Michael's relentless game-playing tightens like a noose around the throats of his sodden guests, the film settles into static close-ups and relies on editing to create an almost disembodied sense of tension. No zooms or elaborate dolly shots complicate the rising drama.

Of course, some changes were needed to "open up" the one-set play; these are the sorts of things critics usually complain about but *The Boys in the Band* is aided tremendously in character development by actually seeing what everybody is doing before their arrival at Michael's. Some changes are perfunctory—Alan and Michael in the film intercut their phone calls with no loss of effect. Other changes are more profound, even controversial.

They have to do with men touching men—who does it, and how, and when. In the published play's stage directions, Michael and Donald—the two most tentative lovers—share loving embraces before the party and in the final scene. The film keeps them. Emory also gets to hug his costars in the film just as he did on the stage, and Cowboy delivers two kisses—for money.

Dancing is less permissive; in the play Harold danced with the Cowboy, and Larry with Michael. In the film the Cowboy stays stag while Harold joins with Larry, Emory with Leonard, and another couple (too much in darkness to identify) move with the music. All of them are photographed, however, through a sheet of red cellophane that the stoned Cowboy holds in front of his eyes. The effect suggests a drug high but, more practically, helpfully obscures any clear look at the contact the men are having as they dance. Friedkin seems aware that guys can hug each other in robust male bonding style, but close dancing is a taboo, especially where mainstream audiences are concerned.*

Meaningful glances comprise the rest of the film's commentary and form powerful reminders of the rejection waiting for the celebrants when they venture outside Michael's door.

---

* This thinking is not unique. Even the presumably more enlightened *La Cage Aux Folles* in 1978, a comedy about married gay men, showed precious little actual contact. Not until *Torch Song Trilogy* in 1988 did two gay characters actually get along the way heterosexual couples had been pictured on screen since the early 1900s.

Although Donald cruises a parking lot attendant and Emory picks Cowboy off a street hustlers' meat rack, the rest of the clues are offered by "straights": a cab driver, a delivery boy and a woman waiting for a bus all shake their heads in disapproval, while the audience notes the prejudice, and all to signify that these boys are not exactly the ones next door (or maybe they are).

Cuts in the text in favor of subtlety are overpowered by the emphatic nature of the performances which preserve more than a tinge of their stage origins. Combined with the assertive colors of the costumes and the soundtrack whose source music is loaded with double entendres ("The Look of Love," "Love Is Not a Heat Wave," "Good Lovin' Ain't Easy to Come By" and, of course, "Anything Goes"), *The Boys in the Band* is far from a naturalistic drama.

It was also, unfortunately, far from a commercial success. Against such competition as *M*A*S*H, Patton, Woodstock, A Man Called Horse, Willard, Cactus Flower, Beneath the Planet of the Apes* and *Airport* (all of which opposed it in the marketplace), a downbeat, adult drama about New York gay men did not attract the public's attention. It drew critical respect but little passion.

But it did attract Hollywood's notice. Where others had demurred, Friedkin had tackled a tough project. Despite a soft box office, *The Boys in the Band* inspired a dozen other films about homosexual life over the next year. It also led to an unusual typecasting for Friedkin.

"When I finished *Boys in the Band* I had firmly established myself as a director of homosexual films," Friedkin told newspaper writer Fran Weil. "I even got my picture in the *Fire Island Times.*"

It also began the ongoing controversy over Friedkin's attitude toward homosexuality in his films—at once he is fascinated with the lifestyle while he has also been accused of being homophobic. In meeting the demands of publicity he admits, "In those days it was easier to get through an interview by reaching for a snappy quote than by telling the truth because nobody wanted to listen to it." Now, however, hardened by two decades of battle, he throws up his hands.

"I don't know what I was known as or how I'm even perceived," he confesses with a sigh. "Or if people think I'm gay. No one's ever told me they did but there've been a lot of articles about my homophobia; principally I refer you to Arthur Bell, late of the *Village Voice.*"

Bell—as persistent and articulate a critic as Friedkin has ever had—codified the movement against Friedkin's filming of *Cruising* in New York during the summer of 1979. In particular, he reported on Friedkin's appearance in July of 1975 at the New School as a guest speaker.

Writing derisively, Bell told how Friedkin had recalled his research for *The Boys in the Band* in which he house-guested on Fire Island with Mart Crowley and sought a homosexual experience at one of the island's gay bars. He fled, however, when an opportunity presented itself.

"No wonder your movie was so lousy," Bell shouted from the audience.

Privately, Friedkin confirms the anecdote and elaborates on it.

"I can understand somebody going into the privacy of his own home, putting on leather, getting fucked in the ass, in the mouth, in the ear, going down on somebody. I can understand all of that in the privacy [of your own home]. But I can't understand it in a bar with two hundred other guys around you. Which is what I saw in the Mine Shaft [*Cruising*] and what I saw on Fire Island when I went there with Mart Crowley and saw the Meat Rack. I was stunned not by the act of homosexuality or the desire for a number of different partners; that doesn't in any way shock or surprise me—I understand all of it. What I don't understand is why people want to do it in the company of two hundred others.

"I've never had a homosexual experience. I tried one on Fire Island but I chickened out. I thought it might be good to go through this and experience it. I was seeing the gay lifestyle firsthand with Mart, as a kind of observer. And then I thought I'd get physical and I just couldn't, I just couldn't. But I didn't declaim it. I have no condemnation or criticism or fear of gayness. I'm not homophobic. Where I stand is that I don't want to know someone's sexual choice, or tell them mine. I will, casually, 'cause I'm not concerned about it or ashamed of it, but I really don't want to know."

During *The Boys in the Band* (and for two years afterward) Friedkin lived with Kitty Hawks. One day her father, whom she had not seen for several years, saw her on a magazine cover and called.

"It was like he hadn't seen her since Saturday," says Friedkin, repeating Hawks's casual conversation on the phone: "Hi, how ya doin'? Good to see ya—nice picture. Love to see ya. Would you like to come out?"

Friedkin and Kitty Hawks met the great director, as he designated, at the Chianti Ristorante & Cucina on Melrose Avenue.

"At that time he was in his seventies and he had, like, this baby face," the younger filmmaker recalls hauntingly. "Not a line on it. He got up and sort of greeted her, she gave him a hug, then he greeted me and picked up a brown paper bag which was like a grocery bag he had. He handed it to her and said, 'I brought you a present.' She was very touched and opened it and it was two men's shirts—they were not wrapped in any way, bought off a counter somewhere and thrown into this paper bag. She didn't know what to make of it. When we got home later and analyzed it, she broke up in tears and I wound up with the shirts."

During the course of the dinner Hawks asked Friedkin to explain what *The Boys in the Band* was about; the director of *Red River, Rio Bravo* and other classic John Wayne films was, to say the least, unimpressed.

"I don't think you ought to make pictures like that," Hawks told Friedkin.

"No sir?" the young man asked.

"Nah, people don't care about that stuff. What you wanna make is some kind of adventure pictures. Every time I made a film that went into some social problem or something else, it just fell right on its hind end. But when you make a film that's just an action picture that's exciting and has a lotta good guys against bad guys, it has a lotta success, if that matters to you."

Friedkin, who admits to preferring the films of John Ford over those of Howard Hawks, recalls the exchange as being "kind of superficial, just making conversation. But the words did stick in my brain. It's like somebody gives you a key and you didn't even know there was a lock; that's what that conversation was. It was a key that opened up and led to *The French Connection*."*

---

*Although Friedkin finds Hawks's choice of escapism over social concern to be opposite from his own taste in films, his work shares with that of Hawks many of the same themes: intense male bonding, pursuit of duty over one's personal safety, and a ruggedness that is particularly male and peculiarly Hollywood.

The two also share superb skill in staging action sequences as well as a love of violent stories that strained the tolerance of their times. Hawks's *Scarface*, for example, did as much to challenge the censors in 1932 as Friedkin's *The Exorcist* did forty-one years later.

Additionally, both Hawks and Friedkin regard their female characters in ways that are distinctly un-Hollywood. Hawks shapes his screen heroines according to male molds, granting them more respect the more they compete with men in their own professions: Rosalind Russell in *His Girl Friday*, Carole Lombard

*   *   *

Friedkin had moved his mother to Los Angeles from Chicago two years earlier, in 1967, and had rented her Mickey Rooney's old house on Walden Drive. He enjoyed living with Kitty Hawks while still being near his mother.

"Those were happy times for Rae and Billy," Ed Gross recalls. "She sort of solidified life for him because he was very cocky around her and she was the one person that I've ever seen on whom he couldn't pull all those mind games. He wouldn't dare to try that around her. They didn't have these little intellectual contests.

"Rae didn't raise her voice too often, but when she did she only had to do it once. He was a very obedient son, which he is not with anyone else and never has been. Including with me."

The weekend that her son was finishing the editing of *The Boys in the Band* in New York, Rae Friedkin collapsed on the street in Los Angeles and died. He was shattered.

"Ed Gross called me at four in the morning," Friedkin says. "I came back. Ed made all the arrangements. I just came back, put her stuff in storage and closed the house." He then grows silent.

"It's difficult for somebody who wasn't there before he became who he is to have anywhere near the imprimatur on Billy as his mother had on him while she was alive," Gross explains. "There will never be another person like her."

"She was lovely, she was brilliant," offers Bill Butler. "I was with her the week before she died. Billy was out of town, so there's a fondness there from Billy. She wasn't sick at all; she was a very bright person, one of those people you just like a whole lot. She was very much in love with her son and wanted the best for him."

The influence that Rae Friedkin had on her son remains intense and private. Her picture is the one memento he takes with him from film to film to place in front of him on his office desk.

It was at this point that Friedkin stepped off the Hollywood treadmill and spent a year on the streets. He did not go into retreat, however; he was totally immersing himself in a partic-

---

in *The Twentieth Century*, Barbara Stanwyck in *Ball of Fire*, etc. Friedkin, too, shows his regard for women in proportion to their survival skills in a man's world: Ellen Burstyn in *The Exorcist*, Patricia Charbonneau in *The C.A.T. Squad*, Sigourney Weaver in *Deal of the Century*. Neither director considers a passive woman an interesting one.

ular lifestyle he hoped to capture for his next film, a motion picture that would differ radically from his previous features but would summon the vitality of his earlier documentary work, notably *The Thin Blue Line.*

The French Connection would focus Friedkin's vision of cinema and consolidate his power as a director. It would allow him to suggest the way of life that had mesmerized him ever since hearing its legends through Harry Lang and his friends back in Chicago. He took to the streets with New York's undercover policemen and this insider's experience galvanized his interest in the Byzantine, often indefinable code of behavior and morality within the professional law enforcement community. He began to see that the law keepers and the law breakers were closer in temperament than he had ever thought.

"They don't meet *people* every day, they meet *criminals*," he said of Eddie "Popeye" Egan and Sonny "Cloudy" Grosso. After a while in their company he began to meet them too.

"I came back to clarity of presentation," he says of *The French Connection* and its direct form of storytelling. "Its impetus was in the thirties and forties films. American films of the thirties and forties had clear story lines and strong characters. Then the New Wave of European filmmakers took over and we all went out and copied Godard and Fellini, forgetting where our roots were and trying to emulate something with which we had very little connection."

The result of this "back to basics" approach to filmmaking was not a conservative, slick action film. It was a lightning-fast exercise in pure moviemaking that stood Hollywood on its Oscar.

CHAPTER 6

OSCAR AND BILLY

Gene Hackman and Roy Scheider eavesdrop on suspected drug dealers in *The French Connection*.

"IT HAS BEEN reported to police," Robin Moore writes in his book, *The French Connection*, "that even today the international dope-smuggling ring, whose operation was damaged so badly, refuses to believe that one of their own, a 'stool pigeon,' was not responsible for leading authorities to the unraveling of the massive conspiracy. The truth is that the New York City police alone, aided by Federal agents, pursued the case to the end without the help of a single betrayer."

Moore's meticulous account, written in 1968, followed the record drug bust involving 112 pounds of near-pure heroin and the crime figures on both sides of the Atlantic responsible for importing it. The investigation lasted the four months from October 7, 1961—the night that off-duty detectives Eddie Egan and Sonny Grosso happened to spot one Pasquale Fuca in the Copacabana nightclub—until January 27, 1962, when Fuca and five others were arrested on trafficking charges. The actual French "connection," supplier Jean Jehan, was never brought to justice.

The book attracted attention because of its subject but Moore's narrative—as specific as a police report and even aided by a diary kept by one of the suspects (not identified)—threatened to obscure the excitement of the story in a mist of detail. The truth of the matter was that there was no momentous incident that suddenly resolved the case; it was the result of relentless, consummate yet routine police work—hardly the stuff of movie melodrama.

In fact, Friedkin insists that he never read Moore's book but, instead, had gone right to detectives Egan and Grosso to seek their experience. At the same time, he and producer Philip D'Antoni were hiring a succession of screenwriters to shape a formal script to offer to various studios with increasingly frustrating results.

"Every studio in the business turned the picture down, some twice," Friedkin wrote in an essay in *Action*, the magazine of the Directors Guild of America. For ten long months D'Antoni and Friedkin persisted.

"Occasionally we would get a glimmer of hope and during one such glimmer we contacted Ernest Tidyman, who had been a criminal reporter for *The New York Times* and had written a book called *Shaft*, the galleys of which D'Antoni had read and passed on to me. Tidyman had not written a screenplay before. But we felt, because of what we read in *Shaft*, that he had a good ear for the kind of New York street dialogue we wanted for *The French Connection*.

"Phil paid him five thousand dollars and he came in for two

weeks. We gave him all kinds of material and he wrote something that was unusable but that is what got the project started: that script which I never ever shot."*

Richard Zanuck and David Brown, who were then in charge of production at Twentieth Century-Fox, decided to give the project a green light for reasons Friedkin to this day professes not to know.

His research on the feel of New York's streets took him from the crime-infested 81st Precinct with Egan to the equally troubled 26th Precinct with Grosso; the two detectives had been separated and reassigned following the 1965 verdicts in the case they broke.†

No sooner had Fox announced the picture and Friedkin begun preproduction then a man presented himself to the company with evidence that he, not D'Antoni, held the rights to the French Connection story. G. David Schine, who had been a staffer for the notorious Senator Joseph McCarthy during America's blacklist era, had supposedly been drinking with author Robin Moore at a point when D'Antoni, unable to raise financing, had allowed his option to lapse. Moore had assigned the rights to Schine on a cocktail napkin, which was now being dangled in front of the filmmakers, demanding a piece of the movie. To avoid litigation, Fox bought the napkin from Schine for five thousand dollars, made him executive producer, and gave him profit participation points in a movie whose set he was then barred from visiting.

Schine's name, and his association with McCarthy, have misled some observers to exaggerate his influence and force a right-wing spin on the film. Friedkin rejects such an interpretation, holding that *The French Connection* purposely confuses political, moral, and social notions in order to keep the audience continually reevaluating their own positions.

"These cops are doing a job they can't function in," he believes. "Everything they do is useless. But, given the fact that society at the moment wants the job done, the way Doyle and Russo in the picture—and Egan and Grosso in real life—do it is the only way possible. You've got to have the instincts of the people you're dealing with."

The French Connection not only portrays those instincts, it

---

*The typed April 26, 1971, script shows both Tidyman and Friedkin as screenwriters, as opposed to Tidyman's sole credit on screen. Friedkin: "If there should be a script credit, and there shouldn't be, it should be me."
†Egan remains upset at the film's implication that he and Grosso were reassigned because of the French Connection. In fact, he reports, the reassignment came six years and two equally large cases later.

embodies them. The film begins in Marseilles, where Pierre Nicoli (Marcel Bozzuffi) shoots the detective* who has been tailing the dapper businessman, Alain Charnier (Fernando Rey). It then cuts to Brooklyn, New York, where "Santa Claus" (a disguised Gene Hackman playing Jimmy "Popeye" Doyle) is collecting money from Christmas shoppers. His ringing bell alerts a nearby hot dog vendor, Buddy "Cloudy" Russo (Roy Scheider), who joins his partner Santa in chasing a suspect running out of a corner tavern known to be a "junk" house. The pusher (Alan Weeks) is beaten by Popeye and Cloudy, then confusingly interrogated. He is clean of heroin.

It is soon evident why the man is clean: more drugs are only now being shipped from Marseilles by Charnier and his people.

That night, back in New York City, Popeye and Cloudy† come off duty and try to relax in a nightclub before heading to their homes. While a singing trio makes music, Doyle's concentration is drawn to a rear table where Sal Boca (Tony Lo Bianco) is holding court with his wife, Angie (Arlene Farba), and some guests.

"I make at least two junk connections at that table," Popeye tells his partner. Just for the hell of it, the off-duty detectives throw a signal hat in the back window of their car and tail Boca all night. They watch as he makes his drops and then as he switches his elegant town car for a beat-up sedan before opening the small neighborhood luncheonette he and his wife apparently use as cover. They wonder how a guy who owns a two-bit deli can dine at the Copacabana.

Meanwhile, in France, Charnier and Nicoli ask TV star Henri Devereaux to do them a favor on his upcoming visit to America.

New York is starved for drugs. When Popeye and Russo bust a low-life bar they learn from an informant that a shipment is due. Their supervisor, Simonson (Eddie Egan), reluctantly authorizes a phone tap on Boca and soon the duo are merrily eavesdropping on their suspect's personal life.

Devereaux arrives in America to research a documentary; he brings with him the "favor" he promised Charnier: a Lincoln

---

*There is no indication in the film that the man is a detective. The notation appears in the screenplay.
†Robin Moore says that the nicknames come from Salvatore (Sonny) "Cloudy" Grosso's brooding strength and Edward (Eddie) "Popeye" Egan's penchant for girl-watching. Egan insists that his nickname really comes from a night court magistrate whose social life was being delayed by Egan's numerous collars. "Plenty Of People Enhance Your Evening" was glimpsed on the judge's scratch pad. "It's ruinin' his night but it's makin' my arrest record," Egan jokes.

Continental shipped in his name. Charnier and Nicoli have already arrived in the U.S.

The FBI has now become involved in the case. Agent Mulderig (Bill Hickman) already hates Popeye from a previous case, and Russo stands up for his partner.

But Popeye is not there; he is awakening in a drunken stupor in a neighborhood bar. On the way home he picks up a girl riding a bicycle. Later, when Russo comes to fetch him, he must first unlock Popeye, who has been fastened to the bed with his own handcuffs. Russo then breaks the news that Mulderig will work with them.

At an auto graveyard Sal Boca's brother Lou (Benny Marino) buys a scrap car while Charnier approves. Eventually Charnier calls Sal Boca to arrange a twelve o'clock meeting. Doyle and Russo, eavesdropping, dub the Frenchman "Frog One" and prepare to shadow Boca to the assignation. They lose him in traffic, however. Boca begins to get nervous when he spots Detective Klein (Sonny Grosso) but does not see Popeye or Mulderig.

The rest is just waiting: Charnier and Nicoli enjoy a gourmet feast while Popeye and Russo freeze across the street. Despite Popeye's objections, Mulderig and Russo feel that nothing is going on.

Well, something is. The twelve o'clock meeting wasn't for noon, it was for midnight, and Boca has brought a sample of Charnier's junk to his financial partner, lawyer Joel Weinstock (Harold Gary), for testing. It is deemed nearly pure, but Weinstock is reluctant to fork over the $500,000 the Frenchman is demanding from Boca, informing his novice partner that his phone is tapped.

The next day Doyle encounters Charnier, who has eluded the other detectives, but loses him in the subway after the Frenchman waves goodbye. Popeye is furious that he has been "made" by Frog One.

Boca flies to Washington, D.C., to meet Charnier and ask for more time to raise the money. Charnier is angry at the delay and also that Popeye is following them. On the plane back, he tells Nicoli to kill Popeye. He does not know that, following a fight with FBI agent Mulderig, Simonson has pulled Popeye off the case.

Not knowing that Popeye is no longer a threat, Nicoli tries to shoot him when he returns to his apartment. Popeye chases the fleeing Nicoli, who commandeers an elevated subway train. When the nervous motorman faints and falls over the throttle, the train crashes and Popeye—who has been pursuing in a car—kills Nicoli.

Doyle and Russo are now back on the case. They trail Boca, watch him again switch cars, and this time decide to stay with the Lincoln Continental. It is parked on a side street and, when a band of thieves tries to strip it, the Lincoln is towed to police headquarters and searched as "evidence." Nothing is found.

By then Devereaux, who had signed for the car, and his translator (Andre Ernotte) arrive to demand the return of the vehicle. It is still being reassembled in the back of the police garage. Russo happens to notice in the owner's manual that the car should weigh 4,675 pounds while the U.S. Customs form shows it at 4,795. That's a difference of 120 pounds, enough for sixty kilos of heroin. On a hunch, the police examine the car's rocker panels (running boards inside the side doors) and find the stash. They replace the rocker panels, return the car to Devereaux, and begin waiting.

Shaken but apparently ignorant of the subterfuge, Devereaux informs Charnier that his favor-giving days are over.

The next day an unidentified driver takes the Lincoln to the meeting spot—a crematorium—where dealers and buyers are set to finish their connection. Charnier places the $500,000 in the rocker panels of the junk car he had Lou Boca buy for him. Boca and his henchmen stash the heroin in a wall in the crematorium building, and then, when they try to drive away, the cops arrive.

Sal Boca is killed trying to escape. Others scramble like chickens. Popeye chases Charnier into the crematorium. He fires at him and, instead, hits Mulderig, killing him. Russo sees the fire in his partner's eyes and insists that Frog One is gone.

"The sonofabitch is here—I saw him—I'm gonna get him," Doyle hisses. Gun drawn, he walks away into a back room, disappears from sight, and fires a shot. The screen goes black.

Over photographs of the people named, the following words appear:

"Joel Weinstock was indicted by a Grand Jury. Case dismissed for 'lack of proper evidence';

"Angie Boca, guilty of a misdemeanor. Sentence suspended;

"Lou Boca, guilty of conspiracy and possession of narcotics. Sentence reduced;

"Henri Devereaux, guilty of conspiracy. Served four years in a Federal Penitentiary;

"Alan Charnier was never caught. He is believed to be living in France;

"Detectives Doyle and Russo were transferred out of the Narcotics Bureau and reassigned."*

Despite its cops-and-robbers setting, *The French Connection* is a less traditional film in terms of its technique. Its documentary style also convinces people that it is an absolute retelling of the events of the case when, in fact, it is largely fiction. But it is the little touches that imbue it with authenticity.

After the shock of watching Nicoli shoot the Marseilles detective in the face, the audience watches him blithely break off a piece of the bread the man was carrying: arrogance or playfulness? The film's mood courts both.

Even Santa Claus is a set-up. In truth, as Egan and Grosso worked it, one of them would dress up as St. Nicholas and stand in front of a barroom they suspected of being a drug emporium. They would use neighborhood children as their lookouts.

"They'd be singing 'Rudolph the Red-Nosed Reindeer' when a guy had bought something," Eddie Egan recalls. "When a guy was selling, the kids would sing 'White Christmas' and I would touch the guy when he went past me. I'd say, 'ho ho ho,' and that'd be the signal for the cops to bust him."

For the famous, if enigmatic, scene in which Popeye and Cloudy shake down a suspected drug dealer by asking him if he picks his feet in Poughkeepsie, the audience is asked to wonder whether Popeye is crazy, driven or merely a brilliant cop. By the end of the movie they may still be wondering.†

---

* In actuality Pasquale Fuca (Sal Boca) got seven and a half to fifteen years, as did his brother Tony (Lou Boca). Joe, their father, drew a suspended sentence.
  Jacques Angelvin (Henri Devereaux) was sentenced to three to six years in Sing-Sing as a knowing participant who may have previously smuggled in another car full of drugs that had gone undetected. François Scaglia (Nicoli) was not killed; a former Resistance fighter in World War Two, he was handed twenty-two years by Judge Liebowitz. Jean Jehan (Charnier) was caught in France, whose government refused to agree to his extradition to America.
  Detectives Egan and Grosso have enjoyed success as TV and movie technical advisors, actors and producers since retiring from the NYPD. Egan is particularly disenchanted with the events surrounding the denial of his pension—he asserts it was a film publicity scheme that ensnared him—and plans to produce *An Internal Affair* to show the real outcome of the French Connection case. A fictionalized sequel, *French Connection II*, was made in 1975 and fantasizes that Popeye Doyle tracked Charnier to France and killed him.
† The exchange in the film is a Pinteresque display of the "good cop/bad cop" routine. In reality, Detective Egan used it in the police station while questioning a suspect and typing up his arrest forms. "The guy'd say, 'I never been in Poughkeepsie,' " Egan recalls. "And I'd say that I had a fourteen-year-old girl who says she was in the next room and you sat on the bed and picked your feet, and I'm gonna bring her in and she'll say she was with you in Poughkeepsie! You see, they'd think I had something on them and they'd start talking. It was never played right in the movie." In the film one can also see a grinning

That lunatic tinge colors Popeye's obsession with the case. Its first demonstration comes in the nightclub scene where Popeye spots Boca. As he concentrates on Boca, the club ambience fades away and we hear only the sound of Boca's guests clinking their cocktail glasses. It is exactly the kind of exclusion that people do in their minds, but that Friedkin (and his sound mixing crew) fabricate as a film counterpart to real life.

It is an indication that Popeye's work propels his entire existence. Indeed, in describing Popeye to *Film Quarterly* writer Michael Shedlin in 1972, Friedkin repeated how he had used Eddie Egan for inspiration: "The first week I met Egan, he said to me, 'No matter how long you stay with me or how well you get to know me, you'll find there's only three things about me that you need to know: I drink beer, I fuck broads, and I break heads.' He was right. There's very little else to the guy. He's a kind of superpatriot. He really believes in what he's doing."

As personified by Hackman, Popeye Doyle is a rounder who cheerfully spouts racial epithets, loves watching people squirm (to him, the Miranda rights are something you read a guy *after* you've beaten him up) and enjoys throwing around his authority.

Nowhere is this more electrically portrayed than in Popeye's ebullient invasion of a predominantly black Brooklyn barroom junk house. He and Cloudy enter, gleefully announce themselves, and proceed to collect drugs as though it was trick-or-treat. He threatens men twice his size, pulls "dropsy" (tries to plant a substance on someone who wasn't carrying it) and violates the Fourth Amendment (search and seizure) knowing that none of these scumbags will dare protest. In the end, the whole raid has been staged so that Popeye can debrief an undercover informant (Al Fann). The ruse has worked, but Popeye has time for one more kick: "Where do you want it?" he asks his colleague, and—to make it look good—slugs him in the face. The informant is black.

"We're going now," Popeye announces cheerfully as he leaves. "We'll be back in an hour."

Scheider and Hackman rode with Egan and Grosso to research their roles and on at least one occasion found themselves in unexpected jeopardy.

"We would go in and bust a bar as you see in the film," Scheider recalled on the TV show *Cop Talk*. "We would shake

---

Roy Scheider turn away from costar Hackman, who he is afraid will again blow his lines.

them down and have everybody throw their stuff on the bar. It would take half an hour to clean the place out and then when it was over one of the cops would come walking out and show Gene and me all the pistols that had been thrown up on top of the phone booths in back of the bar. That means that all these guys were carrying weapons when we walked in! I can remember telling my wife these stories and she wasn't very happy."

Hackman, too, had reservations about his role and related them to writer Bob Thomas.

"On the first day I had to do the scene in the bar where I slap around a lot of tough-looking characters," Hackman said. "These guys looked like the real thing, and I was scared shitless."

Later Hackman was introduced to the extras and learned that they were all off-duty cops. Such tricks did not get Hackman and Friedkin off to a good start. The next day went even worse.

"On the second day of shooting I had a scene in a squad car in which I had to slap one of the guys we picked up," he continues. "Somehow it wasn't working; it was all too *Dragnet* or *Adam 12*—it didn't have the feel of a two-and-a-half-million-dollar production.

"Also, Billy and I weren't getting along and we were staring daggers at each other. He didn't like the scene, either, and we both wanted to shoot it again if Fox would let us."

Now a more secure actor, Hackman reveals the difficulty he had with the scene.

"I personally find it difficult to be brutal," he says shyly. "It takes a lot out of you, regardless of how easy it looks to an audience. And not only while you're doing it, but knowing you *have* to do it: a month down the line you have this scene coming up where you have to trash somebody. I'm not trying to make myself out to be this big, sensitive guy, but certain people can do certain things and I just couldn't do it very well. [Friedkin] told me we were going to have to reshoot it and I asked him to replace me. He didn't, thank goodness; we got through it."

Friedkin was also upset with Hackman's uneasiness in the role but recognized that he could harvest the emotion for the good of the film.

"He hated the guy he was playing, he hated Eddie Egan, he didn't identify with him and he didn't know he was doing great work. We had a number of arguments throughout the picture; most of them were petty. Very few of them enriched the work, although they created a tension on the set that worked."

"I tried to give the scene the Pinteresque flavor of the interrogation in *The Birthday Party*," he added in an AFI seminar. "And thirty-two takes later the scene was stiff, didn't work, couldn't get it to happen. Scheider would be pretty good, then Hackman would blow. Alan Weeks was getting slapped around. Real blood was coming out of his face because they were slapping him up.

"And he was saying, 'No, man, it's okay. Hit me. Go ahead. Hit me.' Then by take twenty-seven he was saying. 'It's okay, you can still hit me.' Lumps in his face. Hackman and I had given each other long looks. Boom. Thirty-two takes. The scene's no good. We lost the light. We got no shot. The scene was pathetic. Went home. I thought, 'Jesus, I'm through. I'm going to be fired off this picture. I can't direct scene one.' The whole crew is looking at each other: 'What's going on?' "

Friedkin didn't know either. It wasn't until later that night, after wrapping a disastrous day, that the light came on.

"This is not Harold Pinter," he told himself. "This is a street show. And these guys know what they have to do. I've got to let them improvise that scene."

Accordingly, time was found toward the end of the shooting schedule to restage it more freely and without pressure. Two cameras shot it at once to allow matching of action and the scene now appears in the finished film.

By that time Friedkin had also come to admire Hackman.

"He had tremendous desire," the director recalls. "He wanted every moment of every take to be the best that he could do. It was also true of Roy Scheider. Fortunately, we found each other at a moment when everybody had that desire."

Hackman, however, was not Friedkin's first choice for the Doyle role. The first was newspaper columnist Jimmy Breslin.[*]

"He was the vision I had of this cop," Friedkin explains. "A big, fat, slobbering guy, looked like that, and had a big gut and he was trying to run down the street, tripping over himself. Fox approved Jimmy Breslin, I rehearsed with Jimmy Breslin and Scheider for a couple of weeks in New York. It was clear that he couldn't sustain from one day to the next, which is what an actor can do. He also couldn't drive a car—it was one of those deathbed promises to his mother that he'd never drive. So that became an overriding factor."

Breslin did, however, have a unique talent: his mouth.

---

[*] Peter Boyle, Paul Newman, Robert Mitchum and Jackie Gleason were also considered and Friedkin, faced with losing Fox's interest, finally (and reluctantly) went with Hackman as "my last choice."

"He ad-libbed a line [during rehearsal] that I was dying to use in the film: 'Now either you're going to give me the name or you're going to be a memory in this town.' I mean, it just wiped me out."

The line was incorporated into the script but never appears in any of the film's improvisational dialogue.

Also removed from the final film was anything of a sexual nature, some of it alluding to sadomasochism.

"There's a scene where Popeye picks up a black hooker and fucks her in his car," Friedkin says (in the *Film Quarterly* interview). "There's a scene with Frog Two (Nicoli), the killer, and an actual one-hundred-dollar-an-hour sadomasochist. She does a full leather-and-whips number on him."

Casting director Robert Weiner recalls the shooting of that scene, for which he had hired a working New York City *maîtresse*.

"I brought her into the office at Twentieth Century-Fox," Weiner says. "She had never done anything in film. She had long hair. He [Friedkin] asked her to read from the script. So she started reading from the script. He asked her to take her top off, which she was not the slightest bit hesitant to do. She started reading the script and whipping her long hair on the floor and her nipples were getting hard and he was going crazy. He was going totally crazy, getting aroused, just going wild.

"She was hired, of course. It was supposed to be half a day's shooting and instead he went so crazy that not only did he shoot it over eight hours, but [Marcel] Bozzuffi's back was just all sliced up and Bozzuffi said, 'I'll never work for this guy again.' "

"It's one of the best things I ever put on film," Friedkin acknowledges. "At the end of the scene he [Nicoli] gives her fifty dollars, not knowing the currency. She comes on heavy with him. He grabs her by the throat and literally holds her life in his hands. It's a complete reversal of roles in an instant."

After being, as the script describes it, "caught in an ecstasy of pain and pleasure," Nicoli exits the woman's room while she calls after him, "You filthy faggot sonofabitch." The scene was later deleted.

"It was beautifully shot," Friedkin says. "I took it out because I didn't think it played.

"What I finally took out of *The French Connection*," he now confesses, "were all the scenes that would have added to the characters, not the story, but would have made the characters more complex."

In one instance that complexity was achieved anyway through an accident of casting.

The character of the dealer, Alain Charnier, (played by Fernando Rey as a fictionalized Jean Jehan), is not the coarse thug that Egan and Grosso might have found on their beats.

"I was obviously trying to make the audience identify with Charnier," Friedkin explains. "I felt the only way to get into the story was not to regard Charnier as a prick but to see him as a businessman, a man with charm and taste, devoted to his woman in France, etc. Then you have Doyle, who has no taste, no charm, he's a brutalizer of women, he lives out of his car. Charnier embodies almost all the qualities that people are brought up to think are important. The intention was to mix up those elements; it's not about black and white."

In fact, Friedkin got lucky when he hired actor Fernando Rey. He had confused him with another actor, Francisco Rabal;[*] both men had appeared in films by Luis Buñuel and Friedkin told casting director Bob Weiner to summon the wrong one to America. Under pressure to start shooting, Friedkin went with Rey.

Regardless of any director's misgivings about his most celebrated film, it is not the characters for which *The French Connection* is best remembered, but its chase. The chase is the one element that both D'Antoni and Friedkin agreed had to be present, even though it did not appear in Tidyman's script. D'Antoni, whose previous film, *Bullitt*, had received unanimous praise for its vertiginous chase staged by stunt driver Bill Hickman on the streets of San Francisco, wanted another such event as the centerpiece of *The French Connection* and rehired Hickman to make sure of it. The problem became where to put it in the story.

"One day D'Antoni and I decided to force ourselves to spend an afternoon talking with the hope that we could crack this whole idea of the chase wide open," Friedkin recounted in his *Action* piece. "We took a walk up Lexington Avenue in New York City. The walk lasted for about fifty blocks. Somewhere during the course of it the inspiration began to strike us both, magically, at the same time. It's impossible for either one of us to recall who first sparked it but the sparks were fast and unrelenting.

" 'What about a chase where a guy is in a car, running after a subway train?'

---

* The considerably rougher-looking Rabal appears in *Sorcerer*.

" 'Fantastic. Who's in the car?'

" 'Well, it would have to be Doyle.'

" 'Who's he chasing?'

" 'Well, that would have to be Nicoli, Frog Number One's heavy-duty man.'

" 'How does the thing start?'

" 'Listen, what would happen if Doyle is coming home after having been taken off the case and Nicoli is on top of Doyle's building and he tries to kill him?'

" '. . . and in running away, Nicoli can't get to his car.'

" 'Doyle can't get to his.'

" 'Nicoli jumps on board an elevated train and the only way Doyle can follow is commandeering a car.'

" 'Terrific.' "

The resultant chase lasts just over ten minutes on the screen. That was the easy part. The hard part was convincing the disparate authorities in New York City to allow the most reckless use of their streets in the sound picture era.

The plan was to use the Stillwell Avenue line in Brooklyn that runs from Coney Island into Manhattan. In particular, Friedkin and D'Antoni—working with associate producer Kenneth Utt and unit production manager Paul Ganapoler—settled on a stretch of the line from Bay 50th Street to 62nd Street. The Marlboro housing project, where Doyle lived, was nearby, helping the logic of the chase. The three elements of the sequence would be the car, the subway train and a number of shots which included them both. As is the practice with most films, the shooting would take place out of sequence over a period of five weeks during the winter of 1970–71.

For the record, the car commandeered by Hackman (who drove in more than half the footage used in the edited sequence, per Friedkin) was a brown 1970 Pontiac four-door sedan equipped with a four-speed gearshift. There were two cars used—one that Hackman would drive and which would be used for exterior views and another with its back seat removed to allow for the cameraman to shoot past the driver. At times Friedkin handled the 35mm Arriflex camera himself with Bill Hickman driving. Other cameras were mounted in front facing Hackman and on the front bumper to glean point-of-view footage through speed-exaggerating wide-angle lenses.

"Because we were using real pedestrians and traffic at all times, it was impossible to undercrank," Friedkin reveals. "The car was going at speeds of seventy and ninety miles an hour."

"We put a police light and a siren on top of the car," he told
Stephen Farber and Marc Green as recently as 1987 for *Outrageous Conduct: Art, Ego and the Twilight Zone Case.* "We went
twenty-six blocks through a lot of traffic, jumping lights. I handled the camera myself. I wouldn't let the cameraman do it
because he had a family, and at that time I didn't. Anything
could have happened. It was against every law. Thank God no
one got hurt. I was very fortunate. I would never do that shot
today."

Randy Jurgensen agrees, but for different reasons. Jurgensen,
who appears in the film briefly, was a real NYC detective who
accompanied Friedkin on some of his street research prior to
filming. He was in the Pontiac with Friedkin and Hickman, riding shotgun.

"To my knowledge there was no siren on the car," Jurgensen
maintains. "Bill Hickman did the driving and Billy operated
the camera. Billy and Bill Hickman got so charged up about
what we were going to do that I noticed there was a lit cigarette in the ashtray of the car and Bill Hickman lit up another
one. That was an indication of things to come.

"It was a hairy ride. It's not speeded up at all. When we got
to where we felt was the end, Hickman did a vicious U-turn
under the El and now we start back and all of a sudden I heard
the distinctive click of no more film in the camera, and Billy
said, 'That's it, we're out of film,' but Hickman finished back
to the starting point with the same energy and speed that we
had going there. The car just never rolled to a stop.

"We stole that shot," Jurgensen says. "Just Billy and Bill
Hickman and myself. And whenever we'd get stopped by a cop
I'd take out my badge."

But Jurgensen is positive that no siren was used to warn innocent bystanders, "Because then they would look at the car!
What we did was the dead opposite, if you go back and look,
of what they did in *Bullitt. Bullitt* in San Francisco is devoid of
people on the streets when that car chase is going on. And Billy
Friedkin determined that was not going to happen."

Even though the high-speed driving was saved for last, the
equally complicated stunt work was carried out in a more traditional way.

Five specific stunts were planned: Doyle, looking up at the
El, narrowly misses an oncoming car and spins into a gas station; Doyle tailgates a truck with a "Drive Carefully" sign on
it, tries to pass on the right, and has a collision; Doyle, his view
obscured by a truck, sideswipes a fence; Doyle drives wrong

way up a one-way street paralleling the El in the distance; Doyle almost hits a baby buggy.

"What we hoped would not happen, happened," Friedkin recalls of the first stunt. "The stunt driver who was in the other car mistimed his approach to Doyle's car [with Hickman driving] and instead of screeching to a halt several feet before it, rammed it broadside. Both cars were accordions, and so on the first shot of the first day of shooting the chase, we rammed our chase car and virtually destroyed it on the driver's side.

"Naturally, right after the spectacular crash occurred, all four cameramen chimed out, 'Ready when you are, B.F.'"

Hackman's near-miss of a woman pushing her baby carriage continues to draw gasps. Although it looks like a near hit, in actuality the car swerves wide of the (empty) carriage and stunt woman. Then a quick zoom in on the woman's face was made from a stationary camera and, when edited together, the moment appears harrowing when, in fact, it is not even happening.

Jerry Greenberg won an Oscar for his editing of *The French Connection*, the most visible section of which is the chase. But as a whole it possesses a level of uneasiness the director craved.

"You approach a scene by saying, 'How would I photograph this scene and extract the most meaning,'" Friedkin reflects. "And I'm not always successful at doing that, but that's how I approach each scene. It's not with a style in mind. I try and cut where it's least expected: either too early or too late, and that's conscious, because one of the things I feel is that most audiences are ahead of filmmakers today. I think they know exactly where the cut's going to come before it's made and I think all the cutting that's done on television and in most American films today is predictable. If there was any innovation in *The French Connection* it was the editing style. It was elliptical and nerve-racking because it was unexpected. There was nothing to fall back on."

It also reflected Friedkin's fascination with the streets.

"A lot of *The French Connection* really comes out of Billy's own street smartness and the fact that he is a street guy, a downtown guy," Walon Green feels. (Green also won an Oscar that year for writing and directing the documentary *The Hellstrom Chronicle*.) "*The French Connection* was the first cop movie I ever saw where cops really acted like cops and didn't act like Hollywood people playing cops."

Friedkin and D'Antoni delivered *The French Connection* to a studio in corporate turmoil. Twentieth Century-Fox was then going through a number of executive shake-ups and *The French Connection* became the film on which everybody wanted to demonstrate his decision-making abilities, rightly or wrongly. At one point someone even thought of changing the picture's title to *Doyle* and using the sales slogan, "In the great tradition of American violence."

Despite Fox's doubts, audiences and critics responded vigorously. Theater managers even reported getting calls asking when the chase sequence began so that patrons could arrive early and stay through the next show.

The French Connection opened in a handful of theaters in October of 1971 (today most films bow at between 750 and 1,500 screens to maximize first-weekend income) and steadily built into a blockbuster, returning $26,315,000 in rentals from America alone. Compared with current bonanzas such as *E.T.* and *Star Wars* this may seem low, but in the pre-video, pre-mass-marketed era of the seventies it was a phenomenon.

It also divided the critics. Coming out the same year as Don Siegel's *Dirty Harry, The French Connection* fueled the debate begun in the late 1960s (especially at the 1968 Democratic Convention in Chicago) about the police as the problem, not the solution. Jimmy "Popeye" Doyle and "Dirty" Harry Callahan came to represent the rogue cop whose illegal actions, born of decent motives, were increasingly sanctioned by the conservative Establishment. While the courts were becoming more liberally attuned to the rights of criminals and the nation's police were being forced to stay within the law (at the same time fighting those who worked outside it), two movie cops seemed to hold the answers.

"I remember going to Italy when it opened and being told by a group of journalists that it was the most profascist film they'd ever seen," Friedkin remembers. "That certainly wasn't my intention. Then I'd come back to America and hear from people like the American Civil Liberties Union that it was really showing the cops for what they were: a bunch of thugs who shouldn't be let loose with guns, breaking heads. And I thought the film was even-handed."

Nothing in *The French Connection* served to generate more debate than Popeye Doyle's final gunshot—off screen—unseen—before the film's final blackout.

"If they're talking about what something means in a movie, usually you've got a movie that people will want to see," Friedkin told the Fellows of the AFI in 1974. "Example: the obelisk in *2001*. People went around for years sitting around

McDonald's, cocktail parties in Bel Air, saying, 'What the hell is the obelisk?' And that's why I put the gunshot at the end of *The French Connection*.

"It simply means that the movie ends with a bang. That's all. It wasn't in any script and I did it in the dubbing room on the day before I left as a kind of a joke. I said, 'Let's put a gunshot in offstage.' And the mixer said, 'Why?' So I said, 'So we can end this thing with a bang.' So we stuck it in there and just let it go. A number of studio executives said, 'What the hell is that gunshot?' I gave them all kinds of stuff—I said, 'It's possible that Doyle has become so crazed that he's firing at shadows. Another possibility is that his partner in the room offstage put a bullet in the dead cop to take the onus off Doyle for having shot the guy.' I ad-libbed about three or four possible explanations, none of which was in my mind when I put the gunshot in."

As the man who is portrayed as having killed the federal agent, Eddie Egan is irritated that history now regards him as a trigger-happy renegade, even though he did not shoot the real-life FBI man, Frank Waters.

"I used to beat up on him once a week just for exercise, but I never shot him," Egan now jokes. "I've only drawn my gun three times in my whole career."

Nevertheless, it was Egan's reputation as a spoiler that gave Roy Scheider the clue as to how to play Egan's partner, Russo.

"You said something to me one day about your partner," Scheider reminisced with Sonny Grosso on Grosso's TV show, *Cop Talk*, "who I found to be a rather blustery, boastful, loud-mouth Irishman. I knew his reputation as a cop was enormous; he was a good cop. He *told* me he was a good cop. But sometimes he'd be a little hard to take. I said to you one day, 'How do you put up with this?' and you said to me, 'If *I* didn't like Eddie, who would like him?' I thought, 'Oh, my God, that's the whole basis for the character. That's the whole basis for the relationship.' So I rode in on that one."

There is a fine line between someone who is obsessed and someone who is merely committed, and that line is one that Friedkin daringly addresses—and Hackman brilliantly acts—in *The French Connection*. Unlike most crime films which become consumed with the facts of the case, this one breathes with the lives of the people involved in the work. Like Moore's book, which ultimately reduces the crime to a patchwork of police procedures, lucky breaks and regulations, the film—which draws upon only a few incidents and invents its screen action completely—is probably the best presentation of law enforcement mindset in movie history.

That authenticity became apparent to many of the 3,078 members of the Academy of Motion Picture Arts and Sciences, who nominated it in eight categories for the Oscar.*

The competition was stiff: *A Clockwork Orange, The Last Picture Show, Fiddler on the Roof, The Hospital, The Conformist, Summer of '42, The Garden of the Finzi-Continis, The Emigrants, Carnal Knowledge, The Hellstrom Chronicle, The Sorrow and the Pity, Shaft, The Andromeda Strain, Sunday Bloody Sunday, Straw Dogs, Nicholas and Alexandra, Klute, The Go-Between* and *McCabe and Mrs. Miller* were all nominated in various categories.

Friedkin had had an inkling of the Oscars-to-come when the Hollywood Foreign Press Association had given him their Golden Globe award as the year's best director. He had also enjoyed snapping his bow tie at Alfred Hitchcock at the Directors Guild ceremonies when they handed him their "Best Director" award. But he was still modestly praising his competitors—Stanley Kubrick, Peter Bogdanovich, Norman Jewison and John Schlesinger—in pre-Oscar interviews.

But when April 10, 1972—Oscar night—arrived, Friedkin almost didn't make it to the show. He and his date, Jill Krementz,† were picked up on schedule by Ed Gross and his wife in Gross's 1965 humpback white Rolls-Royce. Tony Fantozzi and his wife were with them.

"I had had the car serviced to make sure that when we drove up to the Dorothy Chandler Pavilion nothing would go wrong, that it looked good, and we'd get there on time," Gross recounts.

At that time Friedkin was living in a $1,000-a-month house above Sunset Boulevard.

"We started to drive down Sunset Boulevard and smoke started to come from under the hood," Gross continues. "I said, 'Oh, my God, something's gone wrong. So we pull into a gas station and there was no water. I put water in, we went three blocks, smoke started to come out. By the time we had gone from Fairfax to La Brea (less than a mile) we had to pull over three or four times. So we pulled into a gas station at La Brea

---

*Nominations for *The French Connection* included: Best Picture (Phil D'Antoni); Best Director (William Friedkin); Best Actor (Gene Hackman); Best Supporting Actor (Roy Scheider); Best Cinematography (Owen Roizman); Best Film Editing (Jerry Greenberg); Best Sound (Theodore Soderberg and Chris Newman); Best Adapted Screenplay (Ernest Tidyman).
†Photographer Jill Krementz later married writer Kurt Vonnegut, Jr.

and Sunset, the fellow looked at the car and said, 'The water pump is blown—you can't drive this car. Stay here.' "

Panic. Mindful that taxicabs in Los Angeles are as easy to find as agents who return phone calls, Friedkin, according to Gross, "was going through all of his nervous breakdown warmups.

"Just then a guy drives in in a Chevy Chevette—one of those tiny little two-door cars. He's wearing a metal hat—he was a construction worker. Billy, in his flip manner, says, 'Hey, you wanna go to the Academy Awards?' to this guy. The guy says, 'No, I don't wanna go to the Academy Awards.' Billy says, 'Well, will you take us to the Academy Awards?' The guys says, 'Oh, sure, come on, pile in.' "

Friedkin wound up inviting the man and his wife to the post-Oscar Governors' Ball; they diplomatically declined. In short order the celebrants, crammed into the microscopic car, arrived at the Los Angeles Music Center's Dorothy Chandler Pavilion.

"You know how they have all these limousines lined up for blocks?" Gross laughs. "And they announce them all? Well, we pulled up and it's, 'Now here comes Academy Award nominee William Friedkin,' and here we come out of this car! People were hysterical, laughing, it looked like we would never finish coming out.

"Anyway, it was a big night because everybody won. Hackman won, Billy won, D'Antoni won. Fantozzi was a winner, too, because he represented Billy. That was a big night—one of the best nights I've ever had."

It did not take Friedkin long to flex his Oscar-enriched muscles. As a now-confirmed *wunderkind*, he was proudly touted by the American film industry as proof that they were making room within their respectable ranks for "The New Hollywood." At the age of thirty-two, he had become the youngest director ever to win an Oscar. In truth, of course, at his real age of thirty-six, he was not. But the appellation of boy wonder stuck.

It even stuck when, the morning after the Oscars, Rochelle Reed of *The Hollywood Reporter* ran an item quoting Friedkin's assessment of the movies' rating system (which had given *The French Connection* an R, restricted) as "a stupid, destructive system based on a firm lack of understanding of film."

The next morning a contrite Friedkin again spoke to Reed.

"The fellow who's sitting here talking to you today doesn't feel that way," he said. "I don't stand behind any of those remarks. In fact, I categorically deny those remarks. I'm not denying I said them, but I honestly don't feel that way now."

It may have been politic of him to quell the fires, but there was no doubt that he had also meant what he had said the first time. Honesty has never been Friedkin's problem, only discretion in dispensing it.

Following his Oscar win (and the upping of his directorial asking price), he announced a flurry of projects including two for Universal, another with D'Antoni and one for Warner Bros. But the most startling announcement had to do with Paramount: the August 1972 formation of The Directors Company. Comprised of Peter Bogdanovich, Francis Ford Coppola, and Friedkin—the three hottest filmmakers in the industry—the company would deliver twelve films over the next six years, four per director. Paramount would bankroll the enterprise to the tune of $31,500,000 (three per director at $3 million and one at $1.5 million) with all three directors, plus Paramount chief Frank Yablans and two others, sitting on the board of directors. It was to be an unusual example of artists running their own firm; all parties had to approve the first three films from each filmmaker while the fourth could be at the filmmaker's own discretion with or without his colleagues' consent.

The announcement luncheon, held at New York's "21" on August 20, said that Bogdanovich would direct *Paper Moon*, Coppola would make *The Conversation* and Friedkin would complete *The Bunker Hill Boys*, which would be a follow-up to the themes of *The French Connection* but not a sequel.

The attraction of The Directors Company was its autonomy. Although the trio of young heavyweights would take less salary up front, all would share in the returns once their films were released. They might even go public or produce films for others, it was hinted at the luncheon. But more than anything else it offered control.

Said Friedkin at the time, "We hope to profit from our experience—mostly negative—of observing how studios operate. Most of the problems Francis and I have had in the business* have been with the so-called middlemen of the studios, the guy who is supposed to 'help' you but, because he knows nothing about how to make movies, winds up being the bane of your existence. Now we have our own company and all that's going to change."

---

*While shooting *The Godfather* in 1971 Coppola had held out against massive studio opposition, threats of firing and interference to create a work from which, afterward, the studio profited immensely.

But before he could deliver a film to his own company, he became attracted to one that was being produced by the writer he had met five years earlier in Blake Edwards's office. This time the man was far more secure about his work and wanted an equally secure director to guide it to the screen. William Peter Blatty knew that the public would accept no compromises in the film of *The Exorcist*.

CHAPTER 7

POSSESSED

Father Merrin is about to enter the MacNeil home in the single most famous image from *The Exorcist*.

THE REASON WHY *The Exorcist* exists is contained in a single exchange of dialogue that did not make it into the movie.

It is in the very last scene in which Chris MacNeil, the mother whose daughter has just gone through hell, turns to Father Dyer to ask why there is so much pain in the world.

"If you're asking me if I believe in the devil, the answer is yes," she tells him. "Yeah, I do. Because the devil keeps doing commercials."

For a moment Father Dyer looks at her, and then asks quietly, "But if all the evil in the world makes you think that there might be a devil, then how do you account for all the *good* in the world?"

The struggle by author/screenwriter William Peter Blatty to get his line in the motion picture, and the equally passionate efforts by director William Friedkin to keep it out, symbolize the dynamics that have surrounded this popular and controversial film. Until the creation of *Star Wars* in 1977 no movie so captured the hearts and headlines of the public as did *The Exorcist;* but unlike *Star Wars, The Exorcist* has not blended into popular culture or inspired a commerical empire. There are no *Exorcist* action figures. No store stocks *Exorcist* bed linen. *The Exorcist* will never show up on school lunch boxes.

To this day there are adults who resolutely refuse to see it and an equal number of others who cannot dismiss it from their minds. The reasoning behind both decisions is the same: the ability of *The Exorcist* to unsettle lies not only in its skillful storytelling but in its spiritual roots in the very foundations of Christianity.

On August 20, 1949, William Peter Blatty was a junior at Georgetown University in Washington, D.C., when he read a *Washington Post* article about a fourteen-year-old boy living in nearby Mount Rainier, Maryland, who had apparently been exorcised of a "demon."* Blatty, who had been raised with a deep faith in Catholicism, was fascinated with this modern manifestation of tangible evidence of transcendence.

"If there were demons," he later wrote in *The Exorcist: From Novel to Film,* "there were angels and probably a God and a life everlasting."

The idea stuck with Blatty, who eventually became a Hollywood screenwriter of light comedies (*A Shot in the Dark, John Goldfarb, Please Come Home*) but always longed to express his spiritual views in dramatic form.

---

*Blatty maintains that the 1949 case suggested the topic but not the story.

In 1969, tired of being thought of only as a gagman and perhaps, as he had admitted, partly as an apologia for all the froth, Blatty took a year off from screenwriting to commit *The Exorcist* to paper. On its publication in 1971 it entered and remained on the nation's best-seller lists for some sixty weeks.

The public response to the book was swift, massive and varied, precisely the reaction that would greet the film version two years later. Some people accused Blatty of knocking Catholicism back into the Dark Ages while others embraced its affirmation of faith. Some called it vulgar; others understood the need for vulgarity in portraying the forces of evil. Some merely said it was sensationalism. But nobody could put it down.

One was producer Paul Monash who, fresh from the success of having made *Butch Cassidy and the Sundance Kid*, was able to offer Blatty $400,000 for the screen rights to his novel.

"I saw it as being extremely visual if we could find out how to get a young girl to do it," Monash said. "I also [felt] that the book was going to be enormously successful . . . it was such outrageously evident film material. I thought it would have the substance of a very successful horror movie. I though there was substance in it which had kind of gotten buried and could be uncovered in the screenplay."

Monash's interest apparently put him in the minority. According to Blatty, "The manuscript had already made the rounds of every studio, mini-major, major-major, fly-by-night independent from here to Panama and nobody wanted it. I never got anything more than a mimeographed form rejection slip."

Monash's reaction was different, although later to Blatty's chagrin. It seems that Monash was working on a project at Warner Bros., brought them *The Exorcist*, and got an immediate deal. And then he wanted changes in the property without, as it happened, letting Blatty know.

"He uncovered a memo I had written to someone—I don't know how he got it—in which I criticized certain [things], told him certain changes we would have to make," Monash recalled.

Among them were combining Fathers Merrin and Karras into one priest, moving the location away from Georgetown, putting Chris MacNeil into some profession other than acting, and making Lieutenant Kinderman less colorful. Or, as Monash put it, less *"Bridget and Birney*—this over-Jewish guy . . . just seemed terribly artificial."

Blatty sharply referred to the memo as "screwing the author," admits to copying the document from Monash's Warner

Bros. office, and used it to separate Monash from any control
in the film. He then went to bat for Friedkin as director despite
learning that the studio was already negotiating with Mark Ry-
dell (*On Golden Pond, The Rose*) for the job. When Warners refused to consider Friedkin, Blatty threatened to sue; Warners
backed down.

Finally able to work with the director he admired, Blatty was
shocked when Friedkin handed him his own screenplay back as
unfilmable.

"It isn't faithful enough to the novel," Friedkin told him. Of
particular concern to him was Blatty's use of cinematic tricks
in telling his story: flashbacks, quick visual intercuts, change
in narrative tone, etc.

Discussions between Blatty and Friedkin resulted in the
streamlining of the novel in ways that acknowledged how the
film would be consciously designed to play to a theater audience. A number of subplots were removed, much to Blatty's
disappointment, but all in service of Friedkin's pragmatic reasoning that everybody knew the little girl was possessed and
that any red herrings would just frustrate them.

But Friedkin was also concerned with making the film as authentic and believable as possible despite its grounding in the
fantastic. He decreed, therefore, that there would be no optical
effects—that everything happening in the story would actually
take place in front of the camera. This decree meant instant
surpassing of the $5 million budget Warner Bros. had provided
and the simultaneous invention of a roomful of mechanical and
makeup devices, the combination of which—solely from the
camera's point of view—would give the *appearance* of the litany of phenomena *The Exorcist* required.

But all the effects in Hollywood would mean nothing if the
audience didn't care about the people enduring them, and to
that extent *The Exorcist* had to work as a credible story:

Somewhere in Northern Iraq Father Lancaster Merrin (Max
von Sydow), a Jesuit priest and archeologist, is supervising an
historic excavation at Nineveh. A strange object is brought to
him from a newly uncovered ruin; it is a St. Joseph medal that
dates from the 1500s. Merrin examines the area where the
Christian amulet was found and discovers something not to his
liking: a small model of the demon Pazuzu.

By the time he tells the curator that he has to leave, he is
even more dismayed. What are these pagan and Christian symbols doing together in a pre-Christian dig? A clock in the room
stops when he says, "There is something I must do," as he pre-

pares to leave Iraq. Standing one last time at the site of the excavation, Merrin is confronted with a huge statue of Pazuzu. Nearby two dogs growl and fight.

Dawn in Georgetown, a tony district of Washington, D.C. Actress Chris MacNeil (Ellen Burstyn) is studying her script for a "campus unrest" movie she is filming on this location. Her concentration is broken by irregular rappings coming from the bedroom of her eleven-year-old daughter Regan (Linda Blair). Later that morning she tells her butler, Karl, to check the attic for rats, and is then off to work.

On the movie location that morning Chris lets the director, Burke Dennings (Jack MacGowran), know in no uncertain terms that she feels the scene is awful while the movie's producer (William Peter Blatty in a cameo role) stands by. Walking home that night she sees a brooding priest (Father Damien Karras, played by Jason Miller) rapt in conversation with another, troubled priest. She also sees groups of costumed hobgoblins— because it is Halloween.

In New York City Father Karras arrives at his aged mother's clean but cluttered apartment in Hell's Kitchen. Mrs. Karras (Vasiliki Maliaros) has injured her leg and as her son changes the dressing he pleads with her to move from her solitary surroundings. She refuses. She also recognizes that something is troubling her son, even though he has not spoken about it.

Back in Washington Chris discovers a Ouija board and asks Regan why she's been using it. Regan tells her that she and Captain Howdy play with it. When Chris tries to touch it the planchette jumps from her hand. It will be Regan's twelfth birthday on Sunday and she misses her father, who is in Rome.

At night Father Karras and his supervisor, Reverend Thomas Bermingham (himself), have beers at a campus pub. Father Karras, who is a psychiatrist counseling troubled priests, is himself troubled. He tells Bermingham, "Tom, I think I've lost my faith."

On Monday morning Chris awakens to find Regan sharing the bed with her.

"My bed was shaking," the girl complains. "I can't get to sleep."

That same morning at the Dahlgren Chapel on the Georgetown University campus a priest is preparing the altar for services. He gasps in horror when he sees that a statue of the Virgin has been desecrated with clay and paint forming breasts, phallus and a whore's bright makeup.

One afternoon in the charity ward of New York's Bellevue

Hospital Karras and his uncle (Titos Vandis) visit his mother, whose leg has necessitated her hospitalization. When he sees his mother she asks him accusingly, "Dimmy . . . why you did this to me, Dimmy? Why?" Karras, ashamed that with all his medical training he cannot afford to give his mother the care she deserves, later tries to work off his anger in a gym.

In Chris MacNeil's Georgetown house a cocktail party is in progress. Burke Dennings, typically drunk, insults Karl's German heritage. Father Dyer (William O'Malley, S.J.) enjoys playing the piano and identifies Father Karras to an inquiring Chris. Suddenly Regan appears in the room. She looks coolly at one of the guests* and tells him, "You're going to die up there," and urinates on the rug.

Later that night, after the party, Chris bathes Regan who asks, "Mother, what's wrong with me?" Chris tells her it's nerves and to keep taking the pills the doctor prescribed.

After Regan has been tucked in, Chris tries to rest when a sudden stream of screams comes out of her daughter's bedroom. Rushing in, Chris sees that the entire bed is jumping wildly. She throws herself on the mattress but it continues to shake.

At night in the Jesuit residence Father Dyer helps Father Karras get drunk with an "appropriated" bottle of good scotch. Karras still feels that he should have been with his mother.

Chris's doctors are unable to diagnose Regan's malady. Even an arteriogram proves inconclusive. One afternoon Chris's secretary, Sharon (Kitty Winn), summons the doctors to the MacNeil home: Regan is suffering convulsions. When they arrive, Regan is violently bouncing on the motionless bed. Her throat swells to the size of a basketball, her voice changes into something ripped raw and bloody from the base of her spine, and she fights off the doctors hissing, "Keep away! The sow is mine!"

More doctors and more tests, all worthless to an increasingly distraught Chris MacNeil. Entering Regan's room at night she closes the wide-open windows and confronts Sharon, who is just returning with a prescription, admonishing her for leaving Regan alone. Sharon tells her that she had left Burke Dennings to babysit. Moments later an assistant director appears to tell Chris that Dennings has died—fallen down the long flight of steps just outside the MacNeil house.

Under hypnosis, Regan reveals this "Captain Howdy" who

*The character, unidentified in the film, is an astronaut.

she says is "inside her." Rather than speak, "Captain Howdy" grabs the hynotist's groin and forces him to the floor in agony.

The next morning Lt. Kinderman (Lee J. Cobb) visits Chris on his investigation of Dennings's death. He also speaks with Damien Karras, an expert—thanks to a school thesis—on witchcraft. Kinderman feels that the desecration in the chapel and the manner of Dennings's death (his head twisted completely around) are the work of a devil-worshipper and wonders if Karras, as counselor, knows of a troubled priest who might fit the description. Despite Karras's stonewall, he and Kinderman begin to develop a friendship.

Chris finds a crucifix under Regan's pillow and does not know how it got there. Soon afterward, Chris is blocked from escaping Regan's room by furniture which slides across the floor. Regan then takes the crucifix, mutilates her own genitals, and turns her head completely around. Dennings's voice comes out of Regan's mouth.

The next day Chris finds Father Karras and asks him if he can arrange for an exorcism for her daughter.

Karras interviews the now-possessed little girl and brings the evidence to his church elders. Eventually approval is secured with the participation of Father Lancaster Merrin, who has had previous experience along these lines. Merrin is summoned to the MacNeil home and immediately begins the Roman Ritual.

The exorcisms are an ordeal that assault Karras's and Merrin's spirit and stamina. Merrin dies alone of a heart attack and, when Karras discovers his body, a gloating Regan/Demon is guarding it. Taking her by the throat Karras challenges the demon, "Come into me, come into me!" In a flash of light it does. But before a now-possessed Karras can harm Regan, he throws himself out the window to his death at the bottom of the same stairs on which Dennings was killed. At that exact moment, Lt. Kinderman arrives.

Crowds form around Karras's body at the foot of the stairs. Father Dyer pushes through the people and administers last rites to his friend.

Not many days later Chris and Regan leave Georgetown. Seeing Dyer, Chris stops their car and hands him the St. Joseph medal that had belonged to Karras. Father Dyer pauses atop the stairs where Karras died, then walks off.

Shooting began on August 14, 1972, at Goldwater Memorial Hospital on Welfare Island in New York—it was the scene in which Karras visits his mother on the charity ward and his guilt becomes insurmountable. The Reverend William O'Malley, S.J., who was portraying Father Dyer in the picture, recited a blessing prior to the first shot. Depending upon one's view of the power of prayer it either had no effect at all or greatly reduced the calamities that were to follow during the film's unusual nine-month shooting schedule:

- The MacNeil household, a set constructed at the Ceco 54th Street studios, burned to the ground early one Sunday morning;
- Jason Miller's five-year-old son, Jordan, was seriously hurt by a motorcycle during a beach visit; he has recuperated;
- Jack MacGowran died two weeks after his scenes had been shot;
- Max von Sydow's brother died in Sweden;
- Linda Blair's grandfather died during production;
- Ellen Burstyn wrenched her back and was out a week;
- A gaffer (lighting technician) lost a toe in an on-set accident;
- The film's budget rose from five million dollars to—by some reports—more than twice that.

"Such negative energy in that film!" remarks Shirley MacLaine, William Blatty's California neighbor and the person on whom the character of Chris MacNeil was admittedly based. "Of course, I was Chris MacNeil," the Oscar-winning actress confirms. "Bill used the French couple who ran my house in his book, he used J. Lee Thompson as the basis for the director, and the first séance I ever went to, he arranged in my house.

"He also," she adds with an edge, "still claims that the picture on the front of [the book] *The Exorcist* is not my daughter, Sachi [Stephanie Sachiko], but it is; he took it himself and distorted it photographically. Her friends used to ask her about it."

The MacLaine-MacNeil comparisons were extended, MacLaine says, "Billy [Friedkin] came over to visit me. I made him pancakes. He was getting down my movements so he could coach Ellen Burstyn in how to play me."

If MacLaine's notation of "negative energy" is to be questioned, there seems ample proof of it in the numerous production delays. Some could have been anticipated, even if not avoided: the groundbreaking nature of the effects (which had to be invented for the film but have since become industry routine) required a high level of research and on-the-job experimentation. In terms of set construction, the entire interior of the MacNeil house had to be built with movable walls inside the Ceco Studios in New York. To create the intense cold of the "possession" bedroom it was enclosed in a cocoon and drained of warmth by a massive air conditioning unit which had the annoying habit of setting off the building's sprinkler system at odd times, flooding the set. The air conditioning, however, allowed the spectacular effect of seeing the breaths of the actors suddenly appear when they moved from the warm hallway to Regan's cold room. After several hours' uncomfortable filming (Linda Blair was covered with electric blankets while she lay in bed), the temperature would invariably rise above breath vapor level and required a complete shutdown until the air conditioner could once more do its job.

The MacNeil home that appears in the film is the third one that was actually built. The first, designed by John Robert Lloyd (who had worked with Friedkin on *The Night They Raided Minsky's* and *The Boys in the Band*) was determined by Blatty and Friedkin to be unusable and a new designer, Bill Malley, was engaged. Then, at 2:30 A.M. one Sunday morning, with only a security guard in the building, Malley's set caught fire—possibly the result of an electrical short circuit—and burned. The third set replacing it was the one that finished the film.

It was Friedkin's desire to shoot the film in New York and Washington, D.C., to remove his cast and crew from California in the same way he insisted on making *Minsky's* away from the distractions of Hollywood.

"I didn't want to get up in the morning and see mountains as I was driving to work to do a scene that was supposed to take place in a Georgetown townhouse," he repeated. "I didn't want Ellen Burstyn and the others in the film to have to do it either. I wanted them to be more connected with a city kind of life."

But there was a more pragmatic reason than environment for the move to Manhattan. The child labor laws of California under which Linda Blair would have to work were unbendable in limiting a minor's availability to four hours a day. Given that it took two hours to put on Dick Smith's demon makeup and another hour to remove it, this would have left barely an hour for Blair to do any acting. New York's more liberal restrictions made it possible to use her within a reasonable framework.

To accommodate the various effects demanded in the script, Regan's bedroom had been constructed with a number of hidden devices. Small air vents were placed on windowsills so that curtains could blow about even though the windows were shut.

The bed was capable of being raised by a fork-lift device on the other side of the wall; the bed's high backboard covered the holes. The mattress on which the terrified youngster would unaccountably bounce was fitted with false bottoms to hide a cantilever which would violently jerk Blair back and forth and, at times, appear to throw her into the air.

Another effect proved just as uncomfortable. For the shot in which Regan hurls green vomit into Father Karras's face, thin tubes were run behind her thick makeup and bent down into her mouth where they would be hidden in the natural shadows at the back of her throat. On a signal from Friedkin she would lurch forward, open her lips and a technician would squirt a stream of liquid. The same device was used for the copious amounts of vomit required when Father Merrin blesses the girl during the Roman ritual and bile flows onto his vestments.

"We could only do sixteen or seventeen takes before she started choking," Friedkin once joked about Blair's ordeal; in fact, the two developed a deep trust and to this day the actress regards Friedkin as her mentor. But at the time others—without any basis in fact—felt differently. Rumors circulated widely that the twelve-year-old had, herself, become somehow "possessed" during the shooting and that she bore psychological scars afterward. Anyone who knew the tedious process of filmmaking would recognize such assertions as ignorance, but such talk fueled the public's curiosity about the film. It would also eventually work against it at Oscar time.

Three of the more noteworthy effects in *The Exorcist* were Regan's levitation, her 360-degree head turn, and her enormously controversial self-mutilation with a crucifix.

The first was done with wires, although Friedkin at the time staunchly refused to admit it, hinting that it might have involved magnets, force fields and even magic. In fact, an inspection of the frames (something allowed on a good video copy or any print) reveals that Blair was in a harness with piano wires attached at the center of gravity and running into a small slit in the ceiling of the set.

Of greater artifice is the complete head turn, something that would instantly kill the girl and, as reported by Lt. Kinderman, did kill Burke Dennings.* Blatty objected to the effect: "I fought that from the beginning," he says. "If the head turns 'round—I

---

*Incidentally, Burke Dennings was to have been played by—and was clearly modeled after—British director J. Lee Thompson, who shot Blatty's *John Goldfarb, Please Come Home*. Thompson changed his mind just prior to production.

remember the conversation—you have the *effect* now of turning around, but originally the shot was so that you saw it three-sixty. I said, 'Billy, the head falls off and there's a lot of blood, that's what happens! *Supernatural* does not mean *impossible!*' And he fixed it [by inserting a cutaway at mid-turn] but the fix still gives you the impression that the head is going completely around."

The third effect is the notorious crucifix scene. Although some viewers mistakenly believe that the girl is masturbating with the icon, in fact she is mutilating herself. A stand-in, Eileen Dietz, was used for the close shots in which Regan's hand drives the cross beneath her bloodstained nightgown. For more distant shots Regan is represented by a life-size doll whose head rotates.

The assortment of effects that would so dominate the attention of critics and viewers of the finished film proved a constant frustration to Friedkin—just like the repeated queries about the gunshot that ended *The French Connection*—who wanted to maintain the illusion of the supernatural. Those who dared ask for details received what became known as his "Felt Forum speech":

"I went to New York's Felt Forum and saw the Great Renaldi who does a festival of magic and the occult and he calls this trick the 'ultimate illusion' and what he does is he gets this set, which is an operating room, and he wheels out a woman and he says, 'I'm going to saw this woman in half.' And he brings out a huge, thick log and he tests it under a buzz saw. Zip! Boom! The saw goes right through these logs, breaks them up. Then he brings the woman out. He brings the saw down and runs it through the woman and blood spurts all over the place, all over the stage, the attendants, the whole damn thing and it smells of death.

"And the audience goes, 'Oh, my God, Jesus Christ!' And I dig this and they're sitting there in the Felt Forum in New York and you see the guts of the woman pour out, all the lights on the stage are up. I'm staggered. Everyone's staggered. People are saying, 'Oh, shit!'

"Now he steps out and he says, 'Ladies and gentlemen, there may be doubters among you. I invite you to file up on both sides of the stage and review the remains.' So everybody in the joint forms two lines and they're going up and I'm going up and when you walk by this thing, you're looking, and the woman's color has changed. She's got this deathly pallor. The guts are there. It stinks of death and formaldehyde.

"But the closer you get, something looks wrong, you can't put your finger on it. And people are buzzing and guys are saying, 'Aw, she's not really dead.' Then they all sit down again and the Great Renaldi walks back out on stage and he says, 'You're right. The woman isn't really dead. I am unable to kill a different assistant each night, for each performance. All I ask you is, did the illusion work? Were you convinced?' To which he got a standing ovation. Now, that is a long way of saying to you, did it work? Don't ask me how or why, but did it work? That's the only question, as a filmmaker, that I ask the audience."

Friedkin may have asked the same question of Bill O'Malley. According to Howard Newman, the film's unit publicist, O'Malley had to play a tough scene where, as Father Dyer, he had to offer last rites to Father Karras at the end of the film. The company had gone well into the night in Georgetown. According to Newman in *The Exorcist: The Strange Story Behind the Film*, "It was almost midnight by this time but the exhausted O'Malley played it like a trooper as the absolution and death scene was shot over and over again from different angles. Each time the angle changed the lights and cameras would have to change also and O'Malley would trudge back to the camper with Jason to try to warm up just a bit.

"After going through the scene about fifteen different times, Billy Friedkin called O'Malley aside and told the priest he wasn't getting the expression of fear in his face that he had hoped to capture in the scene. Even priests can lose their patience and the weary O'Malley pleaded with the director, 'Billy, it's two in the morning! When you've seen your best friend die fifteen times in one night, you've really got to pull the emotions out of your guts.'

" 'Do you trust me?' asked Friedkin. The priest nodded. Friedkin stepped out of hearing range to talk with the soundman and cameraman. He then came back to O'Malley and spoke to him quietly for a few seconds, again asking the priest if he trusted him. The priest assured him again without really understanding what the director was up to.

"Friedkin then nodded to the soundman, who yelled, 'Speed,' just as the cameraman boomed, 'Rolling,' With that Friedkin hauled off and belted O'Malley right across the face. Stunned, the priest turned around and went through the scene a final time. With a trembling voice O'Malley absolved Karras for the last time, his hands shaking and tears welling up in his eyes. As Karras died, O'Malley threw himself down on the bloody corpse sobbing uncontrollably. 'Cut!' yelled the delighted Friedkin, who ran over to the shaken priest, grabbing him up in his arms and planting a big kiss right where he had struck him."*

Other incidents were less stressful. One was designed to play a practical joke on the Warner Bros. executives three thousand miles away. "On a Friday before the Monday that we were to shoot events at the MacNeil house beginning with the arrival of Father Merrin," Blatty recalls with a smile, "Billy and I were having dinner. Over the wine I said, 'Wouldn't it be funny if instead of Max von Sydow showing up at the door, removing his hat and saying, "Mrs. MacNeil, I'm Father Merrin," it was Joe Fretwell, the film's costume designer, who speaks with a southern accent?' And Billy said, 'What if it were Groucho Marx?'

"I said, 'Groucho's in town and he's a friend of mine.† Would you actually do this?' "

Friedkin was game and Groucho agreed to impersonate the Exorcist provided that it would be filmed on Monday; on Tuesday he was due to leave New York.

"The plan was," Blatty explains, "that not only would he appear at the door—he'd take off his hat and it's Groucho Marx—but that Jason Miller would precede Groucho into the room and we'd have Eileen Dietz, as the demon, tied to the bed. And when she screamed a certain ten-letter obscenity the duck would come down!"

The gag was never shot—Blatty claims that Friedkin "got psychosomatically ill that Monday"—but it shows the closeness that developed between the men.

"We have a common background in that we are deeply connected to a mother," Blatty offers. "He is the only child and I, effectively, am the only child because I was the youngest. I would say in my case my grief [over a mother's death] could be described by an outside observer as neurotic, overdrawn, and one might describe Billy's reaction as the same as mine. And who knows what deep psychic effect it had on both of us."

*Another instance of this shock technique that had earlier worked on Paul Crump came out in *To Live and Die in L.A.* in 1985. For a scene in which actor John Pankow was to discover his wife in bed with another man, Friedkin asked, "John, do you trust me?" Told yes by Pankow, Friedkin rolled the camera and slugged him to get a dazed reaction on the first take rather than spend time on a reasoned, gradual buildup. Later, Pankow understood. The scene did not make the film's final cut.
† Blatty had appeared on Groucho's TV show, *You Bet Your Life*, and traveled in Hollywood's comedy circles.

Understandably, the mother imagery in *The Exorcist* is the most affecting in the entire film. In the casting of sad-eyed Vasiliki Maliaros both men found counterparts to their Old Country maternal memories.

"Coming to the set of Karras's mother's apartment, Billy wasn't there yet, but the set decorator was," Blatty reports, "and I said, 'What is this? This is all wrong.' Everything was as neat as a pin, unlike my mother who, in her later years, [said] Eh! [so let it be messy]. I went to Billy about it [and he said], 'Oh, she would be neat.' What he was really saying was, '*My* mother would be neat.'"

This realization also lends extraordinary resonance to Karras's relationship with his mother. Karras feels suffocating guilt at not having been able to provide for his mother and, later, the demon taunts him with it. Blatty, too, is unhappy that his success did not come early enough to ease his mother's later years. Friedkin, whose mother shared the beginnings of his fame, well knew these emotions and infused them into Karras's anguish at betraying his mother's welfare. The line of dialogue, "Dimmy, why you did this to me?"—used first by Mrs. Karras and later repeated by the demon—is easily the most emotionally devastating in the entire film.

It also points out that Friedkin and Blatty never intended *The Exorcist* to be purely a horror film, a fact that its legions of imitators were unwilling or unable to realize. Its power comes not merely from shocks (it is easily half an hour before anything truly scary occurs) but from the overbearing sense of dread that suffuses the entire work.

It begins in the prologue, set in Iraq, in which Father Merrin (who is modeled after priest/scholar Teilhard de Chardin) confronts a statue of the demon Pazuzu.

"The prologue shows that there is nothing more terrifying than evil when it is unavoidable," Blatty explains, adding that his publisher had originally wanted to cut the pages. So did Warner Bros.—for budget reasons—but Friedkin's and Blatty's insistence caused them to allow a trip to Iraq after U.S. scenes had wrapped. Production manager William Kaplan was dispatched to the politically unstable but historically valuable locale and began to get it ready for Hollywood.

"Bill Kaplan was a legend in most of Iraq as the man who was making sacrifices to a demon statue," Friedkin recounts. "They thought we were a bunch of devil worshipers and were spooked by us!" This was the result of Kaplan's pursuit of the giant prop Pazuzu which had somehow been sidetracked during air shipment from Los Angeles and wound up in Hong Kong. "It was packed in a ten-foot crate," Friedkin wonders. "How do you lose something like that?"

Nevertheless, the "devil worshipers" were invited to a meeting with the Yezede, a sect that—according to Friedkin—were the real thing.

"They're really very pleasant people," he reports, even if "they have some unusual customs. For example, they don't use any words beginning with the *sh* sound because the Arabic word for devil begins with that sound. Therefore, they never take the devil's name in vain! If words beginning with that sound are deliberately used in front of them, they are required to kill the person."

Friedkin took a meeting with, as he describes, "some old guy who looked like Khomeini and had a thousand flies in his beard and you had to sit there and they told me going in 'don't wipe the flies.' The flies are all over. 'Don't brush 'em away 'cause you'll embarrass him.' So if you want to meet this guy, use self-control."

The Iraqi sightseeing was balanced by the hardships of work. In the desert where they shot the scenes of Merrin confronting Pazuzu the temperature rose to 120 degrees. For the moment when Merrin encounters his old enemy at the same time two dogs begin to fight, the desert seemed even more unforgiving.

"We were trying to get shots of vultures circling over Pazuzu's head—every morning that we would shoot we'd take raw meat and set it by the statue of Pazuzu. And no vultures came. Then we wanted to get these dogs fighting, so we said, let's throw the fucking raw meat to the dogs. They starved the dogs for three days, then threw them out. The dogs ran out—we're shooting—and the dogs sniffed the meat and walked away. It turned out these dogs had never eaten meat; they ate bread. They're *vegetarian*."

But the dogfight that truly threatened the *Exorcist* company occurred within the warring factions of the Iraqi government.

"The country was in a state of flux," Friedkin reports. "President [Said] Ahmed Hasan al-Bakr was out of the country holding meetings in Poland. The chief of the secret police, Nazim Kassar, tried to take over the country. He had a forty-man hit squad waiting at Baghdad airport to assassinate the president. It turned out that the president's plane was four hours late coming into the airport. The hit team was in groups around the airport and they panicked—thought it was a trap—and started to give themselves up. It wasn't a trap; President Al-

Bakr just decided to stay later. But when they gave themselves up, it turned out that Kassar was camped out around where I was shooting and the guys who were our hosts came in and said, 'We don't go out today.'

"I didn't know for a couple of days what the problem was. We were sort of confined in a house arrest while they tried to figure out what was going on.

"They rounded up the forty guys and they had a one-day trial. They were all tried in one day and hung the next. Took 'em two days."

Returning to cutting rooms in New York, Friedkin was as energized as everyone else was depleted. Looking forward to the intricate editing process, he also began investigating solutions to his most difficult post-production problem: the personality of the demon.

"You can't make demonic forces behave like Shirley Temple," William Peter Blatty had stated. "This is true or you're kidding yourself." During production, Father John J. Nicola, who was on the set to ensure authenticity (and who opposed the crucifix and church desecration scenes), offered the comment that the demon's obscenity during the exorcism itself was too tame.

"Billy said to me one day out of the blue," Blatty recalls, " 'Tomorrow we're doing the scene. I want the most steaming, horrendous obscenities that you can give me.' And I handed him the page like this—by one corner."

Even with the new dialogue it was apparent that a voice other than Linda Blair's would have to be heard speaking it; if not, Blatty reasoned, it would sound like a schoolgirl talking dirty— not the forces of evil. Some new approach had to be found.

The Exorcist soundtrack was to be mixed at Todd-AO under the skilled supervision of Robert "Buzz" Knudson (who would win an Oscar for his work). In 1973, when the various dialogue, music, and effects tracks were to be blended, sound techniques had not yet entered the computer age. In casting a wider net than Hollywood possessed, Friedkin, as he had in the past, sought help from Chicago.

"We would listen to what was there and try to substitute sounds for it that would aid and abet the horror of the possession at that particular time," explains Ken Nordine, Friedkin's friend from the WGN days. Nordine, by now a highly successful commercial producer, "bought special equipment to play with and distort Linda Blair's voice."

"A lot of what I know about sound came from listening to

Ken," Friedkin acknowledges. "So he was the first one I reached out for, and we paid Ken a lot of money to go out and experiment. He was going to go out and use computers to mix the voice with animal sounds and come up with that distortion. At a certain point Ken played some tapes for me . . . and it basically sounded like Ken Nordine doing a demon voice. It was wrong. But what it told me—while I'm listening to this voice that is trying to sound demonic which basically sounds comic— is that I had to go for a kind of unnatural sound, neither male nor female. Otherworldly. But what *is* otherworldly?"

Nordine reports learning that his work was rejected when he sent Warner Bros. a bill and the studio refused to pay it, "figuring they weren't going to be using anything." Nordine sued. Five years later it was settled with one important casualty: the Nordine-Friedkin friendship.

"Bill was placed in the position, because of his relationship with Warners, that he had to take a deposition that was against me," Nordine says. "We had experts—voiceprints and all that— but when you really get down to it it was an episode in my life where I felt I should've gone to an exorcist myself to get rid of this evil that had been placed on me."

To perform the voice of the demon Friedkin next turned to Mercedes McCambridge, the Oscar-winning actress whom he remembered for her mastery of the technique of dramatic radio. Associate producer David Salven located McCambridge— whose voice and career had both tasted hell—in a Texas production of *Who's Afraid of Virginia Woolf?*

"The minute she walked into my office I knew that was it," Friedkin says.

McCambridge insisted on suffering abuse while lip-synching the demon's voice. She smoked to excess, ate raw eggs and a pulpy apple, and even asked that her hands be bound with bedsheets, all in the service of conveying such anguish that it would express a kinship with the possessed Regan MacNeil.

"It was her idea to drink," adds Friedkin, noting that the actress was a recovering alcoholic. "She asked me to let her drink, which was a traumatic thing for her. She asked me to tie her to the chair and I did. She was really up for shit and we tried everything, she did everything, and she was really incredible."

In addition to McCambridge's mouthing of Blair's on-set lines, Friedkin, Knudson and their sound crew added the squeals of pigs being led to the slaughter, voices played backward, different microphones and various levels of distortion on the combined tracks. Friedkin's own voice is used as a sweetener in some instances.

As the firm December 26 premiere approached, Friedkin had to go outside the Todd-AO facilities to complete the reel containing exorcism itself.

"Reel eleven of *The Exorcist* was *the* motherfucker reel," he says. "We were so behind schedule that I took that reel over to Fox, to the guys that I did *The French Connection* with—Ted Soderberg. It took me one month just to mix reel eleven at Fox, but I was going to Fox in the morning for two hours, then I'd shoot over to Todd-AO in the afternoon, and back and forth for a twenty-hour day."

Then there was the problem of the film's music. Friedkin's first choice was Bernard Herrmann, the feisty composer who had scored the classics of Orson Welles and Alfred Hitchcock. Living in England, Herrmann flew to Los Angeles to view a rough cut of *The Exorcist* and to meet Friedkin.

"I want you to write me a better score than the one you wrote for *Citizen Kane*," Friedkin said, according to one story.

"Then you should have made a better movie than *Citizen Kane*," Herrmann replied, and returned to London.

Executive producer Noel Marshall then suggested Lalo Schifrin, the Argentinian pianist-composer who had become highly successful in Hollywood through such soundtracks as *Cool Hand Luke, Bullitt* and television's *Mission: Impossible.* Friedkin had met Schifrin some fifteen years earlier when the musician had played with Dizzy Gillespie. The two discussed the score and, according to Friedkin, agreed on a sparse, atmospheric style, "like a cold hand on the back of your neck." Schifrin then went off to compose.

"Lalo came in and we went into a little projection room," says Bud Smith, who was again editing for Friedkin for the first time since their Wolper days. "He wanted to play Billy what he thought was a theme and Billy said, 'I can't tell what this is; go record it and then I'll know,' " which was arranged.

According to Smith, Friedkin halted the recording in midsession.

"What he was recording was this 110-piece orchestra playing Brazilian music for the score," Smith says. "Billy stopped him recording it right in the studio. I was trying to convince Billy to go ahead and record the stuff and if we didn't want it we can let Warner Brothers use it for some other movie; he's gonna be paid anyway."

Smith later tried to place some of Schifrin's score in the

MacNeil party scene but Friedkin objected.

"He hated it," Smith reports, quoting, " 'Get that shit out of my movie!' He took the roll of [sound] film, took it out in front of Todd-AO, right in the street and just threw it into the parking lot and he said, 'That's where that fucking music belongs. In the parking lot.' And that's the honest-to-God's truth."

Friedkin's evaluation of the music reflects distaste and betrayal.

"It was big, loud, scary, wall-to-wall, accent, accent, a guy picked up, accent, accent," he says. "I don't like any musical accents. It pained me to do it, but I would rather have Lalo Schifrin denounce me on the front page of the *Los Angeles Times* every day for the rest of my life than use one note of his score in my picture."

Eventually he licensed other music from records and the Mike Oldfield cut, "Tubular Bells," became as closely identified with *The Exorcist* as Strauss's *Also Sprach Zarathustra* was with *2001: A Space Odyssey*.

As the Christmas deadline neared, word then began seeping out of the editing room that there were disagreements between director Friedkin and producer Blatty.

"There came a certain point where I was barred from the post-production by Warner Brothers," Blatty reports. "First me, then Lalo!"

Although at the time there were wild rumors in the trades about lawsuits, firings and egos at play, both Blatty and Friedkin denied any real conflict.

"I was sick in bed with hepatitis, anyway," Blatty says. "There was no point in barring me. But they didn't want me around. Billy showed me the first cut; it was a masterwork. Really, a classic film. Which I don't think the version we've all seen is."

The first fine cut of *The Exorcist* ran two hours and twenty minutes. Anxious about hitting a commercial two-hour running time, Friedkin reduced its length further. Blatty was not pleased.

"They [Warners] knew I would explode over the cutting of the twenty minutes," Blatty says, still steaming. "I'd seen only one version and approved one version, and I guess someone wanted to prevent trouble."

The "trouble" was Blatty's predictable reaction to Friedkin's removal of several scenes he considered essential to the preservation of the religious content of the picture.

"If it were merely the artistic considerations," a skeptical

Blatty asks, "why would he choose to create great gaps in the carpentry of the story?"

Friedkin was more direct: "I'm not making a commercial for the Catholic Church."

Blatty maintains that his purpose in writing both the novel and the film was to demonstrate how faith can help mankind conquer despair. He used the illustration of the possession not as an example of the torment one demon could cause one little girl, but as a warning of the doubt it could instill in those around her.

"The point was to make us despair at our own humanity and to feel so bestial and vile that, if there were a God, He could not possibly love us," Blatty says of the demon. By extension, he believes that the moral center of the film—contained in long dialogue stretches that Friedkin removed—would have allowed the audience to wallow in the shock and obscenity so that they would afterward consider the question, "Why?"

"And that, I think, is what removes it from possibly the level of a truly masterful film to what is only a superb thriller," he says.

Why, then, did Friedkin cut the film from what Blatty feels was a remarkable longer version into a more commercial two-hour length?

"Billy didn't know he had a hit," Blatty says. "But apparently audiences are either so wrapped up in the story or so heedless of story in films of these kinds that they never notice."

Both men continue to ride each other about the final exchange between Chris MacNeil and Father Dyer involving Father Karras's St. Joseph medal. Blatty wanted Chris to keep the medal as a symbol that she was open to accepting faith. Friedkin refused.

"I think Bill's wrong," Friedkin insists. "You get a sense of the rhythm of a picture and those scenes were out of rhythm. They were the author's message. I shot them, had trouble getting them to work on the set, finally thought they were badly done. I didn't know what to say to the actors. I took them out."

If *The Exorcist* had squabbles between its own people, it was nothing compared to what was happening elsewhere. In June of 1973 the U.S. Supreme Court had defined *obscenity* as, among other things, material that violates community standards. Horrified that they would have to prepare a myriad of different versions of their film, Warner girded for some tough legal challenges. Few came; some communities (notably Boston and

Washington, D.C.) circumvented possible censorship battles by self-applying an X rating and restricting attendance, when monitored, to people over the age of seventeen.

By December 26, 1973, it hardly mattered. People wanted to see *The Exorcist* and they lined up around blocks to do so.

And there was something else they started to do: throw up.

Psyched into near hysteria by the long wait in lines and further keyed into reaction by the film's power, audiences savored the cinematic roller coaster ride. And as on a roller coaster, some got sick. Surprisingly, it wasn't at the scenes of possession.

"At the first public press preview in New York City I stood throughout the film in the back of the theater, behind the audience," says Blatty, wryly claiming to be "the only person who *knows*" why people got sick at his film.

"At a certain point a young woman came up the aisle and, walking by me, was a little unsteady and I heard her saying, 'Jesus. Jeeeeesus,' and I thought, 'Oh, boy, we're dead. She hates the picture.' But I marked the point at which she left. And that's the point at which *everybody* got ill and at which I always have to lower my head: it's when they're giving Regan the arteriogram and the needle goes into her neck and the blood comes out. *That's* the moment it's always been."

If audiences were getting sick at *The Exorcist*, the filmmakers were getting rich. And that's when two hitherto unheralded people stepped forward to claim their share.

The first was Mercedes McCambridge who, in an impassioned interview with Charles Higham in *The New York Times*, accused Friedkin of denying her an agreed-upon screen credit. Friedkin fired back that McCambridge's contract did not call for a credit, that he wanted to give her one, but Warner Bros. prevented it. The settlement was to add the words *and Mercedes McCambridge* to subsequent prints.

Then Eileen Dietz, the woman hired to serve as Linda Blair's stand-in, petitioned the Screen Actors Guild that she, and not Blair, had acted the possession scenes. Warner Bros. disputed her claim and called in Bud Smith to measure those few shots ("It came out to 133 frames," he reported, or about six seconds) in which Dietz doubled Blair.

"Eileen Dietz did some acrobatics that we experimented with but are not in the picture," Friedkin advises.

"I know what I did; I did every possession scene in the film," Dietz maintained. Eventually, lacking credibility, she faded from view.

Nevertheless, Dietz's public statements, in Friedkin's opinion, "cost Linda Blair her Oscar."*

But beyond the McCambridge-Dietz controversies there appears to have been an organized movement against *The Exorcist* within the Hollywood establishment. George Cukor, one of Hollywood's most traditional directors, was dead set against *The Exorcist* receiving any recognition from the filmmaking establishment. According to those who heard the elder Cukor waxing against the picture, he called the film "an abomination" and "if this thing wins an Academy Award it's the end of Hollywood."

Cukor had also released *Travels With My Aunt* the same year that *The Exorcist* was in competition. It had not fared well at the box office. Word was getting around town that Academy members were splitting into two camps.

One indication of rough seas came when the Academy of Motion Picture Arts and Sciences decided that no film was worthy of their nomination for "Best Special Effects" for the 1974 ceremonies. Director Tom Gries defended Friedkin's film in a meeting at which George Cukor assailed it. Sources say that when *The Exorcist* won its vote, the whole category was nixed.

There was further opposition from the Directors Guild of America, again credited to Cukor who, by this time, by all accounts was taking it personally.

At a luncheon hosted by the DGA for directors of the year's foreign language film Oscar nominees, Friedkin recalls being greeted by Cukor who suddenly began spontaneously denying the rumors that he had been bad-mouthing *The Exorcist*. Friedkin was amazed that Cukor would even acknowledge their existence.

"He came up to me and absolutely copped out on it," Friedkin says. "The only other thing I remember was the Directors Guild awards, which I was favored to win. I remember seeing that, when they announced that George Roy Hill had won for *The Sting*, Robert Aldrich, who was president of the Guild, was standing on the stage, smugly nodding his head and clapping, and there was a wave you could see. I saw it in Aldrich and there were other guys around the stage who were sort of nod-

---

*Friedkin does acknowledge that Dietz appeared in the shots of Regan driving the crucifix under her nightgown as well as in a rear view in which the girl backhands a doctor who enters her room. Friedkin also shot a sequence in which Regan, her long furry tongue licking at Kitty Winn's heels, follows her spider-like around the house. The scene was removed when its inclusion upset story construction.

ding in assent and, in a sense, breathing a sigh of relief. It was that moment that made me feel that a bunch of people did get together and influence votes away from my film."

William Peter Blatty adds an equally bizarre note to Friedkin's story.

"It may not even be connected," he reveals, "but only one director other than Billy Friedkin ever contacted me and/or met with me about his desire to direct *The Exorcist* and that was Bob Aldrich. The only one."

If some remembered, others forgot. *The Exorcist* was nominated for seven Golden Globes and won four.* It then was announced for competition for a staggering ten Academy Awards.†

On April 2, 1974, the difference between the Hollywood Foreign Press who had voted the Golden Globes and the three thousand Academy members who chose the Oscars became apparent. Buzz Knudson and Chris Newman won the Academy Award for sound and William Peter Blatty accepted his for screenplay. Everything else went to *The Sting*.

Critic (and later music producer) Jon Landau, on the NBC *Tomorrow* show after the Oscar telecast, opined that Friedkin's behavior had hurt the film.

"I also have an intuitive feeling—-again, that's all it can be— that Mr. Friedkin himself worked against the acceptance of the picture. I think that he added a certain unpleasantness, apart from the movie itself, in his interviews and in his way of handling himself."

For his part, Friedkin did not appreciably alter his conduct following the Oscar snub. According to Hollywood etiquette, he didn't need to. *The Exorcist* was becoming one of the top-grossing films of all time (and it is still one of the very few R-rated motion pictures among that impressive group with rentals of $89 million in an era when the average ticket was $1.77). It has also, understandably, not played widely on television†† and loses most of its impact on home video.

---

* Golden Globes: Best Motion Picture Drama (winner); Best Actress: Ellen Burstyn; Best Supporting Actress: Linda Blair (winner); Best Supporting Actor: Max von Sydow; Best Director: William Friedkin (winner); Best Screenplay: William Peter Blatty (winner); Most Promising Newcomer: Linda Blair.
† Academy Awards: Best Picture; Best Actress: Ellen Burstyn; Best Actor: Jason Miller; Best Director: William Friedkin; Best Screenplay, Adapted: William Peter Blatty; Best Cinematography: Owen Roizman; Best Film Editing: Jordan Leondopoulos and Bud Smith; Best Sound: Robert Knudson and Chris Newman; Best Art Direction: Bill Malley/Set Decoration: Jerry Wunderlich.
†† It was Chris's casually profane mouth that needed cleansing more than the demon's for the television version, a change that Blatty—who always felt un-

By all standards, then, *The Exorcist* was due a sequel. Not if William Friedkin had anything to say about it.

"Not for any price would I do a sequel to *The Exorcist*," a resolute Friedkin told Joyce Haber in February of 1974. "Not for one hundred percent of the profits. Nor was I asked." He disputed a report in *New York* magazine's "The Intelligencer" column suggesting the contrary with, "I don't like *New York* magazine or its brand of journalism, and that's for publication. I think they distort the facts. They didn't check with me on this report, but they have called me in the past."

After turning thumbs down at Warners over any sequel, Friedkin held up a different finger when it came time to tote the ledger. In the spring of 1975 he sued the studio for $5.8 million alledging breach of contract, fraud and usury. According to the suit, Friedkin said that the film had grossed $90 million and returned rentals of $40 million; his original fee of $325,000 plus 10 percent of the net profits should have resulted in the figure for which he sued.

Filmmakers rarely sue their studios—litigious people are not popular in the industry—although *threats* to sue are as common as false compliments. Friedkin's action was applauded by A. D. Murphy of *Variety* who called it "a direct challenge to 'boilerplate' provisions of production-financing-distribution contracts written over the decades by all major companies."

The complicated action was settled privately and did not form legal precedent, but it typifies Friedkin's regard for money— not that he craves it, but he wants what is his. Despite a lean childhood, he shows little hesitation to spend what he needs and invest the rest. When he travels, he travels first class; he drives a top-of-the-line BMW; he keeps an apartment in New York City, property in the Hamptons, a cabin in California's Big Bear region, and will impulsively buy such trendy items as Swatch designer wristwatches—not just one or two but the whole line. At the same time he is notoriously stingy with money for business and constantly watches his office expenses (unless a studio is paying for them).

These things do not come from buying savings bonds; they come as rewards when a film hits the box office lottery. And that's exactly what *The Exorcist* was doing in the winter of 1973– 1974. Instead of a vacation, however, the energetic Friedkin

---

comfortable with her language—wholeheartedly supports. When such safer lines as "Your mother still rots in hell" were required to replace a far less acceptable one spoken by the demon in the theatrical cut, Friedkin—who perhaps symbolically discovered he could do a pretty fair impersonation—lip-synched the new phrases himself.

embarked on a series of college speaking engagements that had been booked before his film had begun dominating his time and spirit. Near exhaustion from the ordeal of completing the film, he was joined in some cities by Father William O'Malley and together they explained to eager young audiences the intricacies of the filmmaking process and also the mysteries of faith raised by the motion picture.

Friedkin was accompanied on this journey by Jennifer Nairn-Smith, a young Tasmanian woman who had been his companion since April of 1973. Born into a business family on the island just south of Australia, Nairn-Smith started dancing at the age of six and won a scholarship to the Royal Ballet in London. She later studied in New York under George Ballanchine and would eventually teach dance privately with the Balanchine method between appearances in *All That Jazz* and *The Best Little Whorehouse in Texas* on screen.

She and Friedkin lived together for three years until April 1976, according to the suit she filed against him on March 29, 1978, demanding $2 million in support plus $100,000 a year when they separated. The newspapers did not report one aspect of the relationship, however: on November 9, 1976, Jennifer Nairn-Smith had given birth to a son, Cedric, whose father is William Friedkin. It is a subject Friedkin refuses to discuss, although it later played an important part in his 1985 child custody battle opposite Lesley-Anne Down.

The turmoil surrounding *The Exorcist* disrupted the lives of all who contributed to the film. Although spurned by the Academy, it nevertheless generated a string of imitators and forever altered the style of screen horror.

For Friedkin his status as an "A List" director was confirmed with his two back-to-back smash hits. His activities during this period reflect this royal status. In 1974 he resigned from the board of the American Film Institute in a flamboyant manner, calling it "The Chuck and George Show" after Charlton Heston and George Stevens, Jr., two of the AFI's prime movers.

"I was there at Friedkin's last meeting at the AFI," recalls director John Hancock *(Bang the Drum Slowly, Weeds)*. "It was, indeed, the Chuck and George show. It was like a course in comparative religions—all points of view. I was a fellow and there weren't many actors on the board; they didn't last more than one meeting. Heston got through whatever he wanted and Friedkin would slap the table and fight him—only a guy who'd just made *The Exorcist* could do that."

In late March of 1975 Friedkin returned to the AFI as a film-

maker-in-residence, although he stayed off its board of directors citing "irreconcilable differences over programs and
policies."

Friedkin was more generous with his money than he could
be with his time. He made a large donation to Cedars-Sinai
Medical Center for its Rae Friedkin Nursing Center. He also
gave to Research to Prevent Blindness both in memory of the
operating room accident that had cost his mother the sight in
one eye and to honor the charity's co-founder, Jules Stein of
MCA, Inc.

At the same time he vehemently withdrew his support of a
new filmmakers' prize at the Chicago Film Festival over a dis-
agreement about how that competition was being run.

Despite these activities, he was haunted by a gnawing doubt
about the ending of his most recent film. Wherever he spoke
about *The Exorcist*, he was finding audiences misinterpreting
the ending. Rather than viewing Karras's death as a sacrifice
by which the priest gives his own life in order to save Regan's
(carrying the demon "with" him through the window), some
fans of the movie thought the demon had somehow caused him
to jump. Some even had not realized that Karras had become
possessed in his final moments on earth. For these people *The
Exorcist* ends on the depressing note that Blatty had feared.

Friedkin asked Warner Bros. if he might do the unheard-of
thing and add a new ending to those prints of the film currently in circulation. He then contacted a jubilant Blatty and
discussed filming a new sequence in which Father Dyer would
be walking down the seventy-five-step staircase next to the
MacNeil house and momentarily think that he sees Karras "as-
cending" them toward him. It would be a symbol of Karras's
rebirth following the restoring of his faith.

Blatty had an even more elaborate and chilling idea for a
new ending. In it, Dyer would have gone into retreat following
his friend's death. One day, while walking, he would be confronted by a jogger who ignores his desire for solitude. Instead,
they talk.

"As he talks," Blatty explains, "what they're really talking
about is the problem of evil. Very gradually we notice a subtle
change in his voice and then finally you realize that it's the
voice of Damien Karras! And then you play off Dyer looking at
someone whom you don't see, but you *know* it's Damien Karras. He says, 'Don't you know me, Joe?' And suddenly Joe Dyer's
gaze begins to go this way and then up—he starts looking up—
up—and then you continue to hear a voice saying, 'We are the

light, Joe.' And up there are millions of white lights in the day-light sky. Everywhere."

The new ending was not to happen. Warners estimated the cost would be $400,000 and Friedkin also felt the weight of tampering with success. If Blatty had his way, *The Exorcist's* deleted twenty minutes would be restored for a special home video version, but even as producer he has not been able to bring it about.

Yet *The Exorcist* continues. The sequel, *The Heretic*, was released in 1977 and generally debased everyone involved; Blatty himself called it "the worst 'A' movie ever, ever made."

In 1988 Blatty was continuing his efforts to write and produce *Legion*, his 1983 novel that again brooded on the mystery of transcendence by developing the lives of the survivors of his original *The Exorcist*. He was interested in attracting Friedkin to direct it, exactly the thing that Friedkin had so firmly stated that he would never do, and negotiations often were as turbulent as anything that had gone on in Regan MacNeil's bedroom. In 1989 Blatty directed it himself as *The Exorcist: 1990* for Morgan Creek Productions and Twentieth Century-Fox.

The triumph of *The Exorcist* was also a burden. While it opened doors for Friedkin they were in the direction of feeding the insatiable hit-making machinery whose crassness he so despised. But the other road was far riskier; it, of course, was the one he took.

Recently he pondered where it has led him: "You know what it's going to say on my tombstone?" he asked with a mixture of sarcasm and bitterness. "It's going to say 'The man who directed *The Exorcist*.'"

CHAPTER 8

THE WAGES OF SUCCESS

Friedkin and Jeanne Moreau attend a premiere in 1977, just before their February wedding in Paris.
COURTESY OF AP/WIDE WORLD PHOTOS

LIKE A WEREWOLF, Hollywood destroys the thing it loves most: success. At the beginning of 1974 nothing in Hollywood was more successful than *The Exorcist* and no one connected with it was more successful than William Friedkin.

According to ritual, therefore, William Friedkin was to be given *carte blanche* in making his next motion picture. Such power has its logic: since nobody really knows what makes a hit, anyway, it makes as much sense as anything else to give the nod to the most recent person who appears to have a clue.

In the early 1970s that nod went most frequently to a group of filmmakers collectively referred to as "the New Hollywood." These were the current Young Turks who, it was believed, would take movies into the next generation. They included among their ranks the first directors to have graduated from America's burgeoning film school population. They had not tasted war, had not had their childhood formed by television (but had encountered it in their teens), and were inspired by Hollywood tradition without being mired in it.

Such filmmakers as Martin Scorsese, Brian DePalma, Hal Ashby, Roger Corman, Peter Bogdanovich, Francis Ford Coppola, and Bob Rafelson were asserting their countercultural sensibilities on movies and their increasingly youthful audiences. Bogdanovich and Coppola, especially, had delivered smash hits *(What's Up, Doc?, The Godfather)* that were both traditional and visionary. The New Hollywood, it seemed, was in tune with the new audience.

The benefits accorded such prophets accrue in Faustian proportions: budgets, once tight, suddenly become loose; agents, once silent, suddenly return phone calls; studios, once fastidious, suddenly become profligate; and the press, once blasé, suddenly becomes curious.

Yet if the rewards are like those offered Faust, so are the penalties. Hollywood is strewn with the souls of filmmakers who, when handed unlimited freedom, responded with unchecked ambition. The pressure to become a hit-making machine is enormous, often insurmountable. Some directors entrench by rehashing the same slasher or sitcom products that initially propelled them into profits; others use this newfound power to get financing for old projects deemed suddenly bankable; still others regard it as a chance to expand the boundaries of the art form.

The third is by far the riskiest, for it means abandoning both the comfort of formula and the security of studio support. An artist with vision confounds those who must foot the bill for his impertinence; in less lofty terms, Hollywood loves to watch hot shots fall on their ass. Friedkin was working without a net and, in true Pyrrhic fashion, didn't disappoint the throngs.

More precisely, *Sorcerer*—his next fully completed project—both fulfilled the curse and confounded it. In concrete terms it took four years, two studios, and $22 million to become the first unqualified commercial disaster of what journalists had come to call the New Hollywood. In aesthetic terms it remains one of the great films of the sound era, an uncompromising personal achievement and a work of tenacity and gumption that has only grown in stature despite an abortive 1977 release.

Friedkin came to *Sorcerer* the long way around. He had set up offices at Universal with a two-picture deal, one of which was supposed to be an informal, guerilla-type project shot quickly with the kind of off-the-back-of-the-truck, boyish spirit he hadn't enjoyed since *Good Times*. He had planned to make an informal horror film about a documentary filmmaker who gets wrapped up in his work: making a documentary film about horror films. The self-reflexive project was to be filmed throughout Universal's richly historic back lot. Some thirty to forty minutes of test footage may actually have been shot (studio records conflict) before the idea was abandoned in favor of what, at the time, was meant to be merely a modestly budgeted ($2.5 million) action remake of *The Wages of Fear*. In a short time it exploded into *Sorcerer*.

In hindsight, it would have been unusual for a filmmaker coming off of two smash hits to make the kind of small movie that *Sorcerer* was originally meant to be. Most directors relish the freedom that runaway success gives them; they recognize how ephemeral it is and eagerly use it whenever—if ever—it comes.

Moreover, there is a noblesse oblige involved. In the protocol of the studio system, anyone who achieves success must share it. Bigger budgets, longer periods of crew employment, more leisurely shooting schedules, and more distant locations (because studio reps love to travel on the picture's expense account) are the spoils that arrive with clout. Ironically, the effect of success is therefore to reduce a director's choices because of the burdens it carries.

Then, too, filmmakers sometimes develop an appetite. William Friedkin wanted to taste *The Wages of Fear*.

Although he was being offered virtually everything then circulating around the industry, Friedkin decided to return to the well of those films that had inspired him to become a filmmaker. One day in 1974 screenwriter Walon Green *(The Wild Bunch)* happened to run into Bud Smith who told him that

Friedkin had been wanting to speak with him about writing a picture to be set in South America. Green instantly felt it would be *The Wages of Fear.*

"I don't know why he picked me," Green says. "I'd never worked with him before. I guess he liked *The Wild Bunch,* but we'd never talked about it. I came in and I wasn't even interviewed. He said, 'You know the story?' and I said, 'Yes,' and he said, 'Let's do it.'

"I sort of got freaked out," Green confesses. "He had become so big, I had to reacquaint myself with him because it had been my experience with other people that if you knew them when they started out and if they had made a movie like *The Exorcist* you didn't come back to them on the same level. With Billy that was not true; if you know Billy you will always know him."

Green and Friedkin went in several script directions, some of which looked interesting, most of which did not work out. Their inspiration was John Huston's *The Treasure of the Sierra Madre,* a favorite of both men.

"We wanted a cynical movie where fate turns the corner for the people before they turn it themselves," Green explains. "We set out also to write a real movie about what we thought was the reality about Latin America and the presence of foreigners there today. Because of the kind of guy he is, that had to be tested."

In fashioning their remake, Green and Friedkin faced an unusual provision in French copyright law regarding the Georges Arnaud novel on which Henri-George Clouzot's *The Wages of Fear* had been based. Under the principle of *droit moral* the artist's work remains under his control. In the case of *Sorcerer,* Friedkin could shoot another motion picture based on Arnaud's book but it could not include anything Clouzot had devised for his original film.

"Actually, we had no problem with that," Green admits. "I didn't want to sit there and copy this guy's film. It's a story and we see it a different way."

In his film, Clouzot (to whom *Sorcerer* is dedicated) uses Yves Montand, Charles Vanel, Peter Van Eyck and Folco Lulli as the quartet of fallen men who volunteer to drive a pair of trucks laden with unstable explosives on what becomes an absurd (in the existential meaning of the word) mission. Clouzot introduces the men at a point when their odyssey is already in the cards, and once they have been portrayed as tough but sympathetic figures it is only then shown how they have all transgressed and been condemned to this living hell for their antisocial actions.

Arnaud's theme of the relentless nature of fate beyond the existence of original sin is presented emotionally in the 1952 film (which was released in America in 1953). For Clouzot, the men's crimes are seen in flashback and they are revealed in counterpoint to their present ordeal. Friedkin and Green used a chronological structure.

The screenplay was originally written for Steve McQueen, who was then starring in *The Towering Inferno* and enjoying a well-publicized marriage to actress Ali MacGraw. The brooding, rugged McQueen, however, wanted the movie shot in America. Friedkin and Green balked; they wanted McQueen but they were adamant that *Sorcerer* had to be made on location. McQueen dropped out.

Eager to commence, Friedkin started the film in Paris in April of 1976 without an American star. By the time the company reached New Jersey two weeks ahead of schedule, Roy Scheider, now a major star following *Jaws*, had been signed, and they were off for the tropics.

The film draws its mysticism from those jungles. Its title comes from the name of one of the two trucks in the story, although the word is never spoken; it is only glimpsed briefly on the rusted door of the vehicle Scheider drives. As the odyssey begins, a Pazuzu-like demon's head carved in stone fills the screen, a gatekeeper of what is to come. It cuts to a man staring at a Mexican fiesta from a hotel room in Veracruz. Without knocking, another man (Francisco "Paco" Rabal) enters and coldly kills him with a silenced pistol.

Jerusalem. Three students wait for a bus in front of a public building. It comes, they board, but leave a knapsack behind. As the bus rounds a corner an explosion levels the structure and all standing near it. By the time the young terrorists make it back to their hideout, Israeli forces are in pursuit. The trio flees; one is shot, one is arrested, and the third, Kassem (Amidou), escapes.

France. Victor Manzon (Bruno Cremer) and his wife prepare to celebrate their tenth wedding anniversary. All is not well. She favors him with an inscribed watch but he is currently in disfavor with the law: he has used fifteen million francs from the family bank (in which he is an officer) to cover losses in the stock market. He begs twenty-four hours from the bank's directors to raise the funds* and pleads with his brother-in-law to

---

*The first three sequences of *Sorcerer*—in Mexico, Jerusalem, and France—were filmed in their original languages, then subtitled. It is a full twenty minutes before English is heard in this English-language picture. Says editor and as-

intercede with his father on his behalf. When mercy is refused and his partner takes his own life, Manzon looks at his watch and sets off on foot.

New Jersey. It's bingo night at Our Lady of the Snow Roman Catholic Church, and in the back the priests and their accountants are tallying the take from the entire diocese. They have made quite a haul, and this has attracted a quartet of thugs (Gerard Murphy, Desmond Crofton, Roy Dittrich and Roy Scheider) who stage a bold robbery of the church's counting room.

"Do you know whose parish this is?" one of the priests asks, incredulous at the brazenness.

"Up you and the horse you rode in on," one of the men says, and shoots him.

In the chapel there is a wedding in progress between a man and his recently beaten bride.

Outside of the church, escaping with the cash, the gang celebrates in their getaway car, driven by Scanlon (Roy Scheider), but their joy is soon tempered by the sin of having shot the priest. They start to bicker among themselves and, when Scanlon tries to quiet them, they collide with a tractor trailer. The car flips and skids, throwing bodies onto the pavement, shears off a hydrant and finally slides to a stop. Scanlon alone manages to crawl away as the police arrive.*

The police, though, are the least of Scanlon's worries. That night he meets a friend, Vinnie (Randy Jurgensen), who tells him, "You're on the hit list." Apparently the priest who was shot is the brother of the local don, Carlo Ricci (Gus Allegretti), who has vowed revenge at any cost.

Paying Scanlon back a favor, Vinnie tells him to scrape together two thousand dollars and, "Get a train down to Baltimore. Go to Pier forty-seven and at customs ask for Nat Glick and don't mention my name, 'cause at this moment I don't know you and I don't want to know you. I owed you a favor and this is it."†

---

sociate producer Bud Smith, "The Paris sequence, in the examiner's office, was shot from every angle you could possibly think of in that room. You're dealing with French dialogue and holding it in a wider angle would have been boring. He even had a guy in the background picking his nose. There's 360-degree coverage."

* The company totaled twelve cars before building a small hidden ramp so that the thirteenth would shoot into the air as Friedkin wanted.

† This dialogue set off an affectionate running gag between Friedkin and Randy Jurgensen, who has worked with him on numerous films. "A couple of years later," Jurgensen recalls, "I was involved in an investigation where the jury

One morning, Scanlon awakens in the Latin American country of Porvenir. This is the safe haven he was promised: a godforsaken armpit of the world where he and other sinners can live out their remaining days. Coincidentally, Manzon and Kassem (now called "Serrano" and "Martinez") are here too. All work for an American oil company clearing swamps and laying pipeline. In exchange for their subsistence wages, no questions are asked. Here no one is to be trusted, no identity is to be believed.

Porvenir is a fascist country whose people live at the whim of the local martinet. Scanlon is a marked man; he is singled out for his forged identity papers and is shaken down for what little money he earns. He is desperate; at a bar he gazes longingly at a painting of a woman who is reaching for a Coke. It is a toss-up as to which he would rather savor.

It is then that Nilo (Rabal) makes an auspicious arrival.

Nilo bribes the customs official and says he is traveling to Managua, but instead takes a room in the village. He does not seek work and soon draws attention from others who, like him, long to leave on one of the planes that come and go on the nearby airstrip.

One morning a series of explosions destroys the main drilling rig and incinerates dozens of workers. The oil company, fearing instability in the local regime, insists on calling it an accident even though they have proof that it was sabotage. They summon consultants who (like Red Adair in *The Bold Men*, the Wolper documentary) advise them that the only way to cap the geyser of fire is with dynamite. The cache of TNT, however, has been allowed to decompose and become unstable in its humid jungle storage shelter.

The solution is to offer four men the chance to redeem themselves, obtain a new identity and receive a reward for fetching it—if any of them manages to survive.

Four men qualify following an audition sequence both tense and funny: Scanlon, the former professional getaway driver; Manzon, a car enthusiast; Kassem, a cold-hearted killer who won't even stop for children playing in the road; and Marquez (Karl John), an old German of equally murky background.

The four form two teams (Scanlon and Marquez, Manzon and Kassem) and are assigned their pair of trucks for the 218-mile

---

was investigating me. Billy was involved in something else and I called [him]. I got a note from Billy because I was unable to reach him. It said, 'Dear Randy, I hope things turn out all right. If they don't, catch a train down to Baltimore and see a guy by the name of Nat Glick.'"

trek. They cushion three crates of dynamite on beds of sand in each truck and wait nervously for the predawn departure.

That night Marquez's throat is cut. Nilo is suspected, but instead of being accused, he is hired to join Scanlon in the cab of "Sorcerer."

At each moment of crisis in their journey, the man facing it acts in a way defined by, and defining, his character. The one who fabricates an explosive device to clear the road is Kassem, the terrorist who blew apart a building in Jerusalem. It is Manzon, the banker, who demands higher pay from the oil company boss. Scanlon, the driver, is the first to qualify for the job ("Teamster?" the boss asks him. "Greyhound," Scanlon replies wryly.) And the mysterious Nilo proves adept at outshooting a band of marauding guerrillas, although he is mortally wounded in the process.

The two trucks with their four desperate drivers encounter a series of obstacles as they work their way out of hell:

- Roads that dissolve into mud as the rains arrive;
- Rickety, rotted wood bridges that heave under the weight of the monstrous vehicles;
- A jungle that flagellates machine and man alike;
- A huge, fallen tree that blocks the road and must be cleared by pilfering some of the volatile cargo;
- A flimsy rope-and-log bridge swinging hazardously low over a swollen, debris-strewn river.

Once they clear all these obstacles, the men allow themselves to feel euphoric. In their cab, Kassem and Manzon talk of Paris, and Manzon shows Kassem the watch his wife gave him on their last day together.

"It's five minutes before nine in Paris," he smiles just as the truck blows a tire and begins to plunge over the embankment. The three cases of explosive in the rear lurch violently forward and the truck is torn into a thousand fiery bits.

Behind them, Nilo and Scanlon notice a puff of smoke on the road ahead to mark their comrades' grave. By the time they reach the spot, only a rock slide and rubble are left of the two men.

Guerrillas have been drawn like sharks to the disaster. When they threaten to steal the load and murder both drivers, Nilo pulls out a gun and kills three of them; Scanlon grabs a shovel and finishes the fourth. Nilo, however, has been fatally shot. That night as Scanlon weaves through more and more surrealistic landscape—all the while reliving his life from the church robbery to the last day's horrors—Nilo dies, and with him the truck. Barely 1.3 miles from his destination, Scanlon carries one crate of explosives by hand and in the dead of night arrives, exhausted, at the camp where he is greeted as the redeemed hero he is.

Shortly afterward he is proudly handed a passport that confirms his assumed identity and is bought a drink by Corlette (Ramon Bieri), the oil company foreman. Rejecting (but probably accepting) a suggestion that he head toward Managua as an even more obscure place in which a man could lose himself, he decides—before leaving for his plane—to ask a woman with a weatherbeaten face for one dance.

While the two move awkwardly across the barroom floor a taxi pulls up outside the cantina and a pair of men step out: one is Scanlon's friend, Vinnie, and the other is the second hit man hired by don Carlo Ricci to settle the old vendetta. The credits appear and then fade out leaving only the haunting rumble of a truck engine lost in the darkness.

As an essay on themes of fate and betrayal, *Sorcerer* represents all of Friedkin's fascinations: men in secret societies (terrorists, killers, thieves, robbers) within societies (outcasts, expatriates) who have their own codes of honor more stringent than society's. They are compelled to complete the job even at the expense of their own lives and, above all, to reconcile themselves to increasing isolation from those around them. It could be a metaphor for the filmmaking process as well; in the course of its production, Friedkin almost became like one of his characters.

"It was a *very* tough film to shoot, probably *the* toughest," says Mark Johnson, then a second assistant director on the picture (and, since, the Oscar-winning producer of *Rain Man*). "It was so physically hard, and Billy was an absolute perfectionist. I was just starting in the business and I had no idea that directors were quite as driven as he. He knew exactly what he wanted and if he didn't get it, he wouldn't shoot, so everyone was on their toes."

Johnson recalls the complexities of the perilous bridge-crossing sequence. It lasts a full ten minutes on screen and is a marvel of cinematic tension.

Whipped by winds, stung by needlelike rain, continually threatened by unraveling support vines, and beset by the danger of rotted timbers exposing the flooded stream only inches below, the four men face an unrelenting, physically demanding ordeal. Both trucks cross it—barely, in a display of virtuosity in film editing—and their near destruction is all the more believable because it is done entirely without miniatures or special photographic effects.

"It took forever to set up," Johnson says. "We had a team of about fifty Mexicans upriver who would start throwing kindling and different debris into the stream, and to time it so we were making a shot when the debris started coming under the bridge."

To fan the calm Mexican weather into the storm called for in the script, two helicopters were hired to fly close to the action. Their rotors served as huge wind machines.

"They would come up and go over the set, immediately over what we were shooting," Johnson recalls, "to give us the wind and pick up the water and everything else. And we would have to coordinate the swinging of the bridge, which was actually swung by some underground cables and could be lowered.

"We also had three water towers, very large towers, and the special effects people were spraying water onto the bridge. It would literally take forty-five minutes to do a single shot, and then the shot itself would take forever, so we're talking several hours to do one shot. At one point everything was perfect but somebody forgot to turn on the windshield wipers."

The finished sequence contains some 137 shots, only a few of which (such as those of drivers through the windshield) are cut from the same take; the rest, nearly 80 percent, are from painstakingly varied separate angles.

The unrelenting pressure took its toll, especially as the budget began to increase. In no hurry despite the entreaties of two separate studios (Paramount and Universal), Friedkin kept to his vision.

"I don't think that anybody could push Billy then," Johnson remembers. "He had won an Oscar for best director and the movie preceeding this one was one of the top-grossing movies of all time, so he was the Christ. I was totally enraptured by him. I thought he was so bright and so magnetic, he knew how to use power better than anybody I knew, and could turn in a second to just devastate you and tear people to shreds. So we were all intimidated, scared, and extremely respectful of him."

It was on *Sorcerer* that Friedkin earned his reputation for firing people from his pictures. Most survivors place the body count at seventy, including several production managers. On many occasions crew morale was minimal and on one instance it turned cruel.

"I remember when Billy, who had probably just fired a rash of people and really devastated them in unsympathetic fashion, was driving with one of the stuntmen in a Jeep through one of the villages and ran over a pig," Johnson cites. "The pig was dying on the side of the road, screaming in pain. Billy went over to it and started to cry. And I think every single person on the cast and crew had very snide comments about the fact that he shed a tear for this pig and yet the location manager, who was a very sweet woman, had been fired and sent running from the set in tears. And yet this is how Billy chose to show his sympathy."

Friedkin extracted rare control from the two studios who were financing his film.

"I'm sure that both of them regarded his actions on that picture as a form of arrogance," reasons business manager Ed Gross. "Let's face it: you had a fellow who was making a picture in the Dominican Republic, far removed from studios, except when they chose to fly down there and see what was going on. You had a filmmaker who had absolutely total control, which he has on all his pictures and which he insists on now; you've got to swallow that if you want him to do a picture for you.

"On the other hand, if you have a multimillion-dollar negative in the hands of somebody down there in Central America you are not about to tie his hands or throw him off the picture. So they were really at Billy's mercy."

Friedkin knew it, too. When one day he heard that Universal Pictures executives were screening his rushes ahead of him, he decided to use humor instead of clout to get even.

Before the first shot of the next day, while the camera was shooting the identifying slates, he ordered one of the Spanish-speaking laborers (who had been taught phonetic English) to look into the lens and say, "More per diem, more per diem." The next day the same grip would be taught to say, "Mr. Wasserman, you a jerk-off."*

Friedkin's playfulness knew no favorites; he also took a swipe at Charles Bludhorn, chairman of Gulf and Western Industries, the parent company of Paramount, which has extensive holdings in Central America.

"He put Bludhorn's picture on the wall in the office in the scene where [the oil company foreman] finds out that the well

---

*Lew Wasserman, chairman of Universal Pictures and MCA, one of the most powerful men in the history of film. It was Friedkin's way of letting them know he was onto them without forcing anybody to admit it.

is blown by terrorists and they can't do anything about it,"
Walon Green reports. "When Bludhorn saw his picture on the
wall as the chairman of the oil company he had a shit hemor-
rhage!"

At times the behind-the-scenes dangers outdid those in the
movie. Bud Smith—who was editing the film as it was being
shot—had set up his cutting room in a shack behind the company's Dominican Republic hotel.

"Then this guy comes into my cutting room," Smith says with
bemused hindsight. "He shut the door and when I went to open
it he said, 'Sit down. I'm serious. I have a gun and I have a
bomb under this building and I'm gonna blow you up in ten
minutes.'"

Smith told the would-be bomber that he would stay behind
but that he wanted to warn his staff to evacuate.

"So I opened the door and told everyone, 'Run, run, you've
got to get out of here!' and the man didn't shoot me, so I took
off, too! I went outside and told the guard, but the guard didn't
understand English. So we're all out there and the guy comes
out and says, 'I'm just kidding! I just want a job on your picture and wanted to show you I could act!' They arrested him
and we never heard what happened to him."

Smith's task of wading through the footage became a sub-
stantial one as *Sorcerer* took on a look more textured than anything Friedkin had ever before attempted. Poetic images are
intercut with action sequences to form cinematic epigrams.

The gnarled faces of the peasants who depend on the United
States-based oil company for their livelihoods—their land having been wrested from them in the first place—make assorted
commentary on the desperadoes in their midst. The old barroom charwoman, a pipe-smoking man, the horrified families
of the fire victims (now suddenly recognized as individuals in
their anguish) and children of the mud all pass silent judgment
of the interlopers around them.

Portents embroider the mood of fate that Green and Friedkin
have decreed. A hawk continually glides overhead, a ready
scavenger hovering over the players in the drive of death. As
the four men set out on their mission, a young Indian dances
around their truck; is it a felicitous blessing or an omen of
madness to follow? Or both.

Fittingly, as they begin their descent into hell, the first few
miles are downhill.

An intricate soundtrack (Buzz Knudson was dubbing mixer)
is even more complex than the Oscar-winning aural tapestry of

The Exorcist, although few theaters at the time of its release were equipped to reproduce it fully. Given all its production elements (helicopters, water, languages, road surfaces, machinery) the majority of *Sorcerer* was built in postproduction and contained an unheralded symphony of audio components. The drone of truck engines, the shifting and stripping of gears, the awful sound of explosions, the crinkling of plastic body bags, the buzzing of insects in stifling hot jungles, the groaning of bridges, and the omnipresence of strangling vegetation combine into a mood of suffocating oppression that is heard and felt as well as seen.

Specific effects are also shocking. When Scanlon clubs a highwayman to death with a shovel, the noise includes the growl of an animal being slaughtered. A crowd of bystanders watching the bodies of their dead arrive in plastic bags hushes into a nervous silence of the sort that movies seldom get right. Even the subtle sound of a switchblade flicking open or a rock striking another rock carries a twinge of danger.

With its constant sense of dread, it is easy to regard *Sorcerer* as a negative, defeatist film. Certainly it is not an uplifting road movie in the sense of traditional Hollywood product, but a philosophical examination reveals that it is far more affirmative. Here are four men (among others in Porvenir) who, despite the havoc they have created in the lives of others for which they are currently paying the price, are nevertheless compelled to survive. They may even care to atone. That they do so without their original victims' knowledge or consent makes their purging even more pure.

The intellectual weight of their fates is worth measuring, for their payment of the wages of their sins with the currency of fear is significant. That they are working for the all-controlling multinational oil conglomerate—itself the greatest sinner in the film—is an exercise in absurdity.

Sorcerer is additionally unsettling because, as with *The French Connection* (and increasingly with his subsequent work), Friedkin refuses to grant the viewer a consistent point of view. For example, although Kassem kills innocent people with his terrorist explosion, he is portrayed not as a devil but as a fanatic; in essence it is his faith that is the villain, not him. Victor Manzon remains a gentleman and his exile is a romantic *beau geste* despite the harm that his fifteen-million-franc debt caused others. Scanlon's crime may have bruised the hypocrisy of the church (which in the film harbors gambling and sanctions wife-beating) but he is still a sinner. And Nilo is the most elusive, although there is a delicious irony that he is killed by one of the very guerrillas his high-level assassination probably helped to inspire.

The final blow is the exchange between Scanlon and Corlette, who hands him his paycheck in the cantina just before the two killers arrive.

"If you find anything that's good, send me a postcard and maybe I'll join you," Corlette tells him.

"You mean you'd give all this up?" Scanlon asks, sarcastically.

"In three months' time, who knows? I may have no choice."

In other words, either politics or the oil supply will force him out too. Not only might Scanlon's ordeal have been for nought, but so will Corlette's. The difference is that the oil company will not die, it will only relocate to another part of hell.

During the postproduction of *Sorcerer* Friedkin, as was his custom, took time to regroup his own life. He traveled back to Paris, where he had begun the film, and on February 8, 1977, married actress Jeanne Moreau. The two had met on the set of *Monte Walsh*, a western in which Moreau had starred with Lee Marvin, in 1970.

Moreau, fabled romantic star of the French New Wave *(Jules and Jim,)* had by the time of her marriage to Friedkin emerged as a director in her own right with *Lumière* in 1976. The marriage of the fifty-year-old Moreau and the forty-three-year-old Friedkin in a Parisian municipal ceremony symbolically linked the French film renaissance with the New American Cinema.

The Friedkin-Moreau marriage in 1977 extended a professional collaboration that had begun earlier that year. They had planned to film a ninety-minute television special featuring composer-singer Neil Diamond at various stops on his European tour. While Friedkin would handle the performance sequences, Moreau would direct dramatic material. She would also appear under her husband's direction with Brigitte Bardot, Jacques Tati, Catherine Deneuve and Jean-Paul Belmondo (making it a quintet of Europe's greatest stars). By the end of January, however, Moreau announced in Paris the cancellation of the project due to "friendly disagreements." No more was said.

The newlyweds did finally work together on a television show, although its success remains a matter of intense debate. Persuaded that they needed a new approach to kick off Oscar's fiftieth year, the Academy of Motion Picture Arts and Sciences in Los Angeles asked Friedkin to return to TV to produce their forty-ninth annual awards ceremony to be aired Tuesday, March 29, 1977, on the ABC network.

"They wanted a change—to do almost anything but what they were doing," Friedkin explains. "Obviously there were limitations; we had to give the award, you know? But I tried to cut away whatever they didn't have to do."

The results were described by Variety's reviewer, "Mack": "On a level of quality, maybe half the differences belong on the plus column. The rest was just—well, different." Friedkin is less diplomatic in his evaluation: "It was awful," he admits.

"Once I got into it I realized how impossible and thankless a job that was," he reports with hindsight. "The people you really want to get on the show, for various reasons, would just never do it, because they're too shy or they have an axe to grind. I tried to get Woody Allen to come on, clearly film's most important comic presence. He couldn't even think about it. Mel Brooks wouldn't come on the show because he said the Academy didn't give a fuck about comedy, that Charlie Chaplin never won an Academy Award. Then I got into all kinds of beefs because I had told Jack Nicholson that he could present the Best Picture award and then I got a call from John Wayne. John Wayne said he'd like to go on the show. I said I'd love to have him come on the show. He said he had to present Best Picture. I said, Jesus, I'd already promised that. He says, 'Well, take it away.' I said I can't do that. I can give you almost anything else. He said, 'Well, no, I think I'll pass.' I feel bad about it because I should've let him present Best Picture; he was the right guy to do that and at the right time in his life. The whole fucking world calls you and you can't do it."

Feeling his producing oats, Friedkin assembled a succession of presenters whose participation announced the arrival of the New Hollywood. The live telecast (which clocked in at just under three hours) included Richard Pryor, Tatum O'Neal, Tamara Dobson, Marty Feldman, Roy Scheider, Marthe Keller, Ellen Burstyn, Sylvester Stallone, William Holden, Red Skelton, Donald Sutherland, Jane Fonda, Ann-Margret, Lillian Hellman, Warren Beatty, Liv Ullmann, Louise Fletcher, Jack Nicholson and, of course, Jeanne Moreau. Chevy Chase hosted.

The changes were evident from the instant the show opened inside the Pavilion—not outside to watch the costumed arrival of the celebrity guests.

"I got thousands of letters of hate mail for that, as did the Academy," Friedkin remembers, realizing that the fashion show is what many viewers tune in to watch. "I now understand that," he avers.

The short subject category was the first hint of real trouble. Presented by wall-eyed British comedian Marty Feldman (who had scored a popular success as "Igor" in Mel Brooks's *Young Frankenstein*), the award for animated short went to Suzanne Baker, producer of *Leisure,* who was unable to attend the ceremony. Feldman—who had already endeared himself to the audience by deadpanning, "I would just like to point out that God made me in His own image"—was clearly rattled by this change in the live scheduling. He then added of the Oscar, "It's not Jewish. You can tell."

Feldman's nervousness caused him to move directly to the opening of the next envelope without first announcing the names of the slate of nominees for live action short subject. Proceeding to the podium, winning producers Andre Guttfreund and Peter Werner *(In the Region of Ice)* earned grateful applause from the audience when Guttfreund said, "Since the nominations themselves were not announced, I would like, out of respect for those people who were nominated with us, to announce them as well," and then did so.

But Feldman's (and Friedkin's) most memorable gaffe was a stunt that the two of them had arranged but which was not included in the script for the event: while examining an Oscar, Feldman purposely dropped it. It shattered into dust on the stage floor.

Oscars are heavy items cast of metal and plated with gold. They haven't been made of plaster since World War Two when, as a gesture to the metal shortage, the Academy allowed ersatz statuettes to be produced. Feldman's Oscar was obviously a prop, but the joke fell as flat as a priest handing out rubber communion wafers.

Richard Pryor, although equally nervous, fared better. His monologue—a brilliantly acted tirade explaining why no black people would ever win an Oscar—was something of a rebirth for the nightclub comic who had fallen to taking writing jobs *(Blazing Saddles)* when his performing career meandered through small parts.

Fourteen-year-old presenter Tatum O'Neal managed a good swipe (scripted) at the proceedings: "In all my years in Hollywood, I have never seen a more outstanding list of candidates."

Other presenters represented Friedkin's company of actors known more for their performances than their celebrity. Roy Scheider—probably wondering how his *Sorcerer* work was being edited across town—handed out the Special Visual Effects award in deadly earnest, scoring two uncharacteristic laughs. Ellen Burstyn introduced Sylvester Stallone, whose *Rocky* was winning hearts, only to have the screen champ interrupted by the real thing in Muhammad Ali who chided him, "You stole my script!"

Veteran comedian and clown Red Skelton then stopped the show with an extended sketch about the Hollywood soundman, a performance that is both moving in itself and as a tribute to the movies' unsung technicians.

"It's nice to be asked here," Skelton said. "Everyone backstage says, 'Gee, you look good.' That's one of the Three Ages of Man: Youth, Middle Age, and Gee-You-Look-Good.'"

Barbra Streisand sang her nominated song, "Evergreen," marking a rare television appearance for the reclusive artist.

Political and social activity were the key for the remainder of the evening: Jane Fonda introduced Pearl Bailey to hand out the Foreign Language Film award. Fonda, whose every Oscar appearance causes speculation on whether she will discuss politics, had just portrayed blacklisted writer Lillian Hellman in the film *Julia*. Friedkin had flown Hellman to the ceremony to present the documentary award and her presence was being noted throughout the crowd.

"Look around the room," a still-bitter Hellman told a friend before the ceremony. "I see three people here who named me to the House Un-American Activities Committee."

Other appearances were equally controversial. Norman Mailer presented the writing Oscars and spoke of Voltaire visiting a brothel for homosexuals: "The next day a friend asked if he liked it and would go again. 'No. Once a philosopher, twice a pervert.'" He then unaccountably likened this to a writer who allows someone else to direct his script.

The Oscar show was outspoken, to say the least, and political beyond what the Academy had expected.

"I had the power and I thought I would try to make a liberal statement," Friedkin concedes. "For example, I cut the word *best* out of the show. At the end of the show I had Warren Beatty explain this because, 'Filmmaking is a totally collaborative medium and between filmmakers no one work is better than any other.' It was 'Academy Award for Actor in a Supporting Role,' or whatever."

In 1989 producer Alan Carr tried the same egalitarian policy and achieved the same precious—and criticized—results. As screenwriter Paddy Chayefsky has remarked, "What do you think

the Academy Awards are all about? Ladies and gentlemen, this
is Mrs. Norman Maine!"

Friedkin now knows this.

"I made a lot of mistakes doing the show," he says, "and I
think, ultimately, it was not a good show. It was a debacle. No
political statement belongs on that show."

Although he had taken the Academy's mandate seriously and
shook the stuffiness out of old Oscar at its half-century mark,
he also succeeded in shaking his own prestige. Since that 1977
Oscar show no William Friedkin film has won an Academy
Award in any category. With the sole exception of *Sorcerer*'s
sound recording, none has even been nominated.

Following the show, Friedkin returned full-time to readying
Sorcerer for its May 1977 release. The summer was to be crowded
with films.

The competition was stiff but not unbeatable: *The Deep, The
Spy Who Loved Me, A Bridge Too Far, The Pink Panther Strikes
Again* and *Smokey and the Bandit*—all with stars, all various
forms of escapism. The only unknown quantity was a modest-
budget science fiction film with nobody in it, and science fiction films hadn't been popular in years.

The film, of course, was *Star Wars*. In one historic week it
ushered in a new era of commercial filmmaking while it destroyed the public's interest in thoughtful, often downbeat
movies that filmmakers like William Friedkin sought to make.
Star Wars (even more than *Jaws,* the previous runaway blockbuster, released in 1975) identified the youth audience as the
most powerful in America; it was an audience ill prepared and
certainly not interested in the philosophical complexities of
Sorcerer.

That summer a shattered Friedkin went into self-imposed exile in the south of France where he took stock of his position.
As the first unparalleled flop of the celebrated New Hollywood,
the film's rejection attracted more than its share of attention.
How could the director of *The French Connection* and *The Exorcist*, who had known the public's taste so keenly, suddenly be
wrong? The critics had no answer—most compared *Sorcerer*
unfavorably with *The Wages of Fear* and noted Friedkin's gall
in remaking it.

In Hollywood, as elsewhere, success has a thousand fathers
while failure is a bastard child. *Sorcerer*, according to that
measure, claimed parentage of William Friedkin alone. Nevertheless, few valid reasons—and none that survives hindsight—
explain its rejection by the public.

Some have suggested that Roy Scheider's committed but noncharismatic performance failed to provide the audience with the clear-cut hero that Steve McQueen would have offered in the same role. Writer Walon Green admits that he may have done Scheider "a certain amount of injustice" in not rewriting the part to better suit his talents, but recalls that Scheider wanted to be made more sympathetic (including a subplot with a youngster in the town), a tangent both Green and Friedkin rejected. Scheider still harbors resentment over the final product and refused to discuss it.

Moreover, *Sorcerer* became a football in a partnership game between Paramount and Universal, whose Film Partners International had been created to handle it. Distributed by one company in America and another abroad, yet with the revenues shared, *Sorcerer* remains caught in the corporate cracks and, at this writing, has never been licensed for network, syndication or videocassette presentation despite its cult status.

Among Friedkin's associates it is generally considered to be his best film. The few others who saw it remain baffled; some say it was mistitled (*Sorcerer* alluding too much to *The Exorcist* without delivering on the promise), others feel that it does not compare with Clouzot's *The Wages of Fear*.

It may be that *Sorcerer* is a film that is out of its own time. Begun during that brief period of self-examination that followed American involvement in Vietnam, it was finally released at a point in history when audiences, having examined themselves and not liked what they found, were opting for pure escapism.

To Friedkin, self-deception is a capital crime, and one that he is incapable of aiding and abetting in one of his films. The grueling, uncompromising nihilism of *Sorcerer*—and its ultimate truth—applies to Friedkin's life and may explain why the filmmaking community respects, yet fears, the zeal of his pursuits.

"As you know, the film is a disaster, critically and with the public," he communicated privately in August from La Garde, in the south of France, "and this hurts and disappoints me beyond measure. I feel it's the best thing I've ever done, and to be so far off the mark is a real blow.

"I'm working on four or five projects now—don't know which will come off, but I have to come up to bat more often. This business of taking two years to make a film, then if it's not a home run I'm as asshole—can't live like that anymore.

"Though it's easy to criticize *Sorcerer* and find many flaws in it—all of my films have been flawed, and those that worked did so, if not *because* of their flaws, then at least in *spite* of them. Anyway, next case."

As *Sorcerer* faded into the red, Friedkin took to pursuing other things. In September of 1977 he announced that he would direct a production of David Rabe's *Streamers* at the Westwood Playhouse, marking his first venture into theater. He also expressed interest in mounting a production of *Macbeth* at the Ahmanson Theatre. Neither happened.

Citing schedule conflicts with two possible film projects—*The Brink's Job* and *Blood and Money*—he bowed out of stage work for the present.

In early 1978 Moreau and Friedkin were back in Europe and he was turning his interests toward *Act of Vengeance*, Trevor Armbruster's nonfiction account of the 1970 murder of United Mine Workers leader Joseph A. "Jock" Yablonski (it was eventually made for HBO by director John Mackenzie).

The European sojourn ended abruptly. On March 28, 1978, Jennifer Nairn-Smith filed suit against Friedkin in Los Angeles for over two million dollars demanding half his income earned between April of 1973 and April of 1976, the three years they had lived together in Bel Air. She asserted that she had put her career on hold in order to "devote her full time and attentions to caring for [his] personal needs as his companion, housemaker and confidante" and said that he had earlier agreed to share with her the fruits of his success, a bounty that included sums still coming in from *The French Connection* and *The Exorcist*. She also requested an additional $100,000 per year to maintain the style of life to which her three years living with Friedkin had accustomed her. Their son, Cedric, was not made part of the public issue.

Two days later—on March 30, 1978, according to papers he filed in June of 1979—Friedkin separated from Jeanne Moreau. Moreau's response to his petition disputes this date and sets it at March 3, 1979. In either event, the marriage was finished.

It was formally dissolved on December 11, 1979. It was also time to do something about The Directors Company. In actuality, it had already been done; in September of 1974 Friedkin had, in the words of the trade paper, *Variety*, "ankled" the company.

In its brief life The Directors Company had produced three pictures: Peter Bogdanovich's *Paper Moon*, Francis Coppola's *The Conversation* and Bogdanovich's stylish *Daisy Miller*. Friedkin never delivered a production to the company under which arrangements all the partners were to have received a share of the proceeds. Like Liberty Films and First Artists—two other past entities invented to put artists in control of their own product—The Directors Company could not survive the realities of the industry at large. After *Sorcerer*, William Friedkin faced the same problem.

CHAPTER 9

BOSTON BAKED BRINK'S

Mt. Rushmore-on-the-Charles: (left to right) Sonny Grosso, Noel Behn, Friedkin, Lou DiGiaimo, and Randy Jurgensen hold a press conference in Boston on December 15, 1978, to deny allegations of financial payoffs during the making of *The Brink's Job*.

PHOTO BY JOHN THOMPSON, COURTESY OF *THE BOSTON HERALD*

"I'M TRYING TO mix farce, fantasy and reality," William Friedkin said midway through filming *The Brink's Job* in Boston in the summer of 1978. "I think that's the best blend in a motion picture. If I were to take a perspective on life, itself, I think it's equal parts of farce, fantasy and reality. My own is, anyway."

Accordingly, even the making of *The Brink's Job* became as much circus as the story of the original robbery in 1950.

As reported by Noel Behn in his book, *Big Stick-Up At Brink's* (which was the basis of Walon Green's screenplay), the January 17, 1950 robbery of $2.7 million from the supposedly impenetrable Brink's vault in Boston's North End had already been brought to the screen before—in *Six Bridges to Cross* in 1955. It was called "the crime of the century" by headline writers at the time and the FBI spent over $29 million solving it, despite the fact that everybody who lived in Boston's North End supposedly knew who had pulled it off. Less than fifty thousand dollars of the actual cash was ever recovered, and the caper endures in local folklore not just because of the notoriety of the escapade but because it was carried out by the most unprofessional menagerie of misfit amateurs that ever could have come together.

In Friedkin's version, the man in charge of it was Tony Pino (Peter Falk), a small-time hood. As the film begins in 1938, Tony, his bumbling brother-in-law Vinnie Costa (Allen Goorwitz, né Allen Garfield), Gus Gusciora (Kevin O'Connor), and Sandy Richardson (Gerard Murphy) are just four scalawags earning a penny ante living at the fringe of Boston's disorganized crime. A prison sentence for a bungled slaughterhouse break-in does little to temper their interest in pulling jobs and, when Tony is released from jail in 1944, he returns to his indestructible wife Mary (Gena Rowlands) ready to go. He has, however, no immediate prospects for work. Times are tough, and minor league boosters like Tony and his gang—those who haven't been taken by war service—must do whatever they can, even if it means an honest job.

The family diner isn't exactly raking in the cash for Tony, but he turns down an offer by Joe McGinnis (Peter Boyle), a tough mobster and an instantly dislikable thug, to plan heists together.

Sandy Richardson's discharge from the navy inspires Tony to reunite the old gang ("Are ya ready to do some honest thievin'?" the unrepentent hood asks) and, with local bookie Jazz Maffie (Paul Sorvino), the Pino gang manages to break into a gumball factory and liberate its safe. It contains thirteen dollars, of which a disgusted Maffie says, "You can keep my share."

One day, still scouting for possibilities, Vinnie and Tony happen to notice a string of Brink's armored trucks entering and leaving a Prince Street garage with relatively little security. In fact, the place might as well be wide open. Tony devotes his next few weeks to charting the Brink's activities from nearby rooftops, finally posing as an auto parts salesman to flim-flam his way inside (during which he lifts a key from an open cabinet). He later uses it to swipe a couple of loose bags of cash off the back of a Brink's truck making a routine stop— just like that. He has also seen the vast cash flow in the counting rooms.

One night Tony actually enters the Brink's garage alone. Astonishingly, he finds no guards, trip wires, or signals of any kind—the Brink's reputation, it seems, is just an image. Standing in the vault room, Tony safely removes his mask and looks around him.

"This joint is mine," he says to himself. "I own this joint."

Soon he tells his wife, "That building is asleep and all that money is there and is being held prisoner. It's screamin' at me through the walls. It's yelling, 'Hey, Tony, come in and grab me. Get me outta here.' Well, I'm goin' in and I'm gonna get it out."

A routine police roundup for ex-felons throws Tony together with Specs O'Keefe (Warren Oates), who seems to possess the know-how to break into a safe. Tony recruits him for the job and —with Gus, Sandy, Vinnie and, reluctantly, Joe—they decide to pull off the Brink's job.

Tony instantly finds himself out of his league; the problem with money, he knows, is how to unload it, and the only fence who can handle any amount of cash, Mutt Murphy (Malachy McCourt), demands seventy-seven cents on the dollar. They have no choice but to accept Murphy's law.

Deciding that an armed robbery is preferable to Specs' D-Day level assault on the vault, Tony and the gang—with Vinnie as lookout—daringly enter the Brink's garage and take the cash from under its understaffed guards' noses. They are astonished to find a ledger sheet which details that the safe contains not a few thousand dollars as they had thought but, instead, $2.7 million.

In less than five minutes, the robbery has been carried out.

The aftermath is everybody's undoing on both sides of the law. FBI director J. Edgar Hoover (Sheldon Leonard) is convinced that the heist was a communist plot and commits the

Bureau's entire facility to bringing the perpetrators to justice.

The perpetrators, however, are starting to have their own problems. There is spreading belief that Joe McGinnis, who was supposed to go through all the bills and weed out those that were consecutively numbered and destroy them, may have, instead kept them and shortchanged the members of the gang of their shares.

Specks and Gus are busted in Pennsylvania for other crimes; Specs is given three years in jail, Gus twenty. When Gus mouths off to the police and refuses to answer questions about the Brink's robbery, he is beaten to death.

As years pass, the feds are relentless. Knowing that Specs' war experiences have weakened his hold on sanity, and aware that his sister is dying in a hospital's charity ward, they threaten him with an even longer sentence than his twenty years. With days to go before the statute of limitations runs out on the robbery, Specs cracks.

The Brink's boys are rounded up and brought into jail. They are paraded up the courthouse steps where they are treated more as folk heroes than the criminals they are.

As the film's end credits roll—over a fantasy shot of the gang members joyously rolling in a mountain of real cash—one final assurance appears:

"Since 1859 nobody has ever lost a penny entrusting their valuables to Brink's."

Unlike the intense realism of *The French Connection*, *The Brink's Job* is almost a romp, an agreeably lightweight picture that articulated the romantic side of Friedkin's fascination with crime. These are characters straight out of *Guys and Dolls*, mismatched ne'er-do-wells who somehow managed to pull off a crime that shook the financial community into a state of panic.

Brink's is a prime example of the screwy side of Friedkin, the side that playfully introduces actor and friend Gerard Murphy (a former longshoreman who jokes about having done prison time) as "the inventor of the bazoom (!) lens" while obliging reporters dutifully write down the fiction. The director who gently torments his property master, Barry Bedig, by suggesting that there be milk and cookies on a tabletop for one scene, then sends him scurrying for sugar wafers when he shows up with Oreos. The artist who admires a painting hanging on the wall of a warden's office in a prison location, then enjoys hearing that a crew member has thoughtfully swiped it as a gift.

The mixed tones of *The Brink's Job* are established from its very first shot, as a forlorn saxophonist serenades the air in a side alley near a bustling market district in Boston. A throwaway, this device immediately calls attention to the film's conscious mixture of objective and subjective treatment of reality, keying the audience both to become involved and prepare to observe. The film, therefore, is firmly rooted in reality while it also asks audiences to accept just how unbelievable that reality was.

Its first demonstration of this on comic, rather than intellectual, levels is during Tony Pino's visit to Brink's in the guise of an automotive parts salesman. Not only is Peter Falk a winning con man purposely offering the office manager a deal he knows he cannot accept (and therefore one which won't have to be kept), but his body language when he sees the lax security rivals that of Oliver Hardy who can't believe Stan Laurel has been so stupid. As Falk sees carts full of money pouches casually thrown around, key cabinets left boldly open and guards acting at the level of civil servants, he constantly shifts his stance, cocks his head and rolls his eyes at the display. Friedkin does not choose to shoot this in close-up to punch home the mugging; he lets the viewer take it all in, too, better to share Tony's wonderment at what he sees.

He lays the foundation for the mixture of comedy and tension in the actual robbery during a nighttime surveillance visit by the gang. Apparently Tony and the boys made numerous prerobbery visits to Brink's using his stolen key. There they partied, hung out, and flaunted the contrast between the company's image and its reality.

On one particular night they happen to glance at the office paperwork and notice that Brink's handles huge payrolls for the area's biggest employers. For the first time they sense that their take may be in the millions. Friedkin shows the impact of this realization by moving the camera toward each of the gang members as he reads a roster of the accounts. The technique is a sharp change from the laid-back style of the comedy and adds a touch of anticipation to the enterprise. It is the moment when the robbers sense the enormity of their task and a hint of its implications. Friedkin had to carefully consider the tone he wanted to set in directing it.

He explains, "One of the actors says, 'We come in on a Friday and it's a million each,' and the other guy says, 'Who would've dreamed that they kept this much money in the safe?' Now, you can do that with a light touch or you could do it in a series of close-ups so that it is a very dramatic moment. It's a kind of

ultimate moment; it's not a moment when the guy says, 'Please
pass the butter.' " In the final film, Friedkin plays the discovery
for tension and then lightens up as the gang becomes giddy
with their prospects. It is that mixture of farce, fantasy and
reality all in one pivotal scene.

It continues in a following sequence. Walking that fine line
between farce and fact, Specs O'Keefe—engaged to peel the vault
by Tony after hearing of his World War Two demolition experiences—suggests a plan of action. His idea is to fire a bazooka
at the safe from a rooftop across the street. Of course, they'll
have to seize a bazooka by staging a machine gun raid on a
local army base, and a couple of guys might get shot, but, hey,
that's the price.

The reactions of Pino, Costa, Richardson, Maffie and Gusciora as they grasp O'Keefe's insanity knock the film back into
the kind of reality it needs to make the actual robbery so tense.
It also sets up O'Keefe's breakdown later in the story.

The robbery, which took barely five minutes in real life, is a
cinematic combination of time pressure, drawn guns, ludicrous
disguise masks, innocent passersby, alarms and luck. In style
it matches in many ways the robbery of the Libby, McNeil &
Libby plant in *The People Versus Paul Crump*.

Since, by definition, *The Brink's Job* is a story whose ending
is already known, its joys must come in explaining the hitherto
unknown details. But this makes the film meticulous, not cap-
tivating, and in the end reflects Friedkin's own indifference to
the project.

"I had no particularly strong feelings about *The Brink's Job*
in terms of passion," he admits. "And very likely it may be on
the screen. The best films I've seen are those in which there
seems to be a large quantity of passion on the part of the filmmaker. I made *The Brink's Job* for a number of reasons, not the
least of which was to come to Boston during the basketball
season, and that is the honest-to-God's truth. I didn't feel that
'here is a story that must be told' or something like that, that
'the world is not as rich if we don't have this.' "

Nevertheless, Friedkin had agreed to do *Brink's* after its producer, Dino DeLaurentiis, parted company with the original
director, John Frankenheimer, over the film's proposed tone.

"He didn't understand the humor in the picture," says
DeLaurentiis of Frankenheimer. "He wanted to do the Brink's
robbery as very serious; he wanted to be more realistic, more
straight, and more realistic is wrong, because Tony Pino was a
joke. He was like the guys in *Big Deal on Madonna Street* (a

classic Italian comedy about inept crooks). When Tony goes in
to rob the chewing gum factory and gets thirteen dollars, it's
impossible to be dramatic in this situation."

Friedkin, who had initially turned the project down, accepted
it when DeLaurentiis again offered it to him just before Celtics
basketball season was to start. The fact that it was fully fi-
nanced, mainstream property dealing with the romance of street
crime may not have been far from his mind, either. Although
Sorcerer had not shaken Friedkin from Hollywood's A List it
did allow studio heads to question him with more confidence.
The fiercely independent DeLaurentiis would be a good buffer.

Rejecting previously written screenplays, Friedkin again
contacted Walon Green. In some ways, he was asking Green to
cover the same territory as he had traveled in 1969 for *The Wild
Bunch*. Green shared Friedkin's sensibilities of honor among
thieves.

"In Boston you have an 'old school' kind of person you don't
find in places like L.A. where the crime is very hard and very
mean," Green notes. "And totally impersonal. I know burglars
in L.A. but they don't know other burglars; in L.A. nobody knows
anybody because they don't grow up in the same neighbor-
hoods together. These guys, here, they've known each other all
their lives."

Like DeLaurentiis, Green agreed with Friedkin that their
model should be *Big Deal on Madonna Street* "because the guys
were a goofy band of jerk-offs so it could really be a fun, enter-
taining film."

Noel Behn shared this interpretation and reports he found
the same spirit when he was researching his book.

"I had fifteen guys come and say that they were supposed to
be in on the robbery but nobody came by that night to wake
'em up," he laughs. "It was almost whimsical. And the police
were aware of this the whole time. I talked to a cop who'd been
on the force forever and he said they all knew these guys were
going in and out of that place and *talking* about taking it, but
they didn't believe that they ever *would*. They thought them
incapable of doing it."

Rewriting and preproduction took the early part of 1978 and
threatened to move the actual shooting into Boston's uncomfortable summer season. DeLaurentiis's line producer, Ralph
Serpe, was trying to arrange location clearances and brought
in a new production manager, Jonathan Sanger, when friction
between Friedkin and the first one developed. In the transition,
details of contracts with Boston Teamsters may have been

overlooked that would catapult the whole production into the national spotlight, not as a movie but as a front-page crime story.

The Brink's Job was the first big-budget production to be filmed entirely in Boston since *The Friends of Eddie Coyle* in 1972. It promised huge opportunities for extras, property owners and, above all, the powerful Teamsters union. Moreover, the enormous construction demands required to turn 1978 Boston into 1938, 1944 and 1950 Boston dictated a nearly twenty-four-hour-a-day regimen of shooting, commuting, and set building. Production designer Dean Tavoularis alone would be marshaling a large carpentry crew, each of whom would have to be driven by a Teamster when on the clock.*

"Teamsters were on the payroll twenty-four hours a day," Jonathan Sanger, who inherited the previous contracts, reports. "As it turned out, you had a driver captain who, according to his contract—and of course it was ludicrous, he had to be sleeping some of those hours—was on call twenty-four hours a day because he always had drivers working, so he put in a time card for twenty-four hours a day."

The narrow streets of the North End created situations that looked strange to the auditors. The normal tractor trailer equipment trucks could not negotiate the sharp turns of the neighborhood streets surrounding the Brink's garage, so many smaller trucks—each with its own Teamster driver—had to replace them at a resultant increase in costs.

The Brink's Job ballooned into a $12 million picture, and word got around that a guy could get rich by putting the touch on Dino.

The production did little to discourage them. Stipends were paid for homeowners to remove their television aerials and air conditioners, fees were paid those whose property was invaded, hundreds of local residents became extras for a day, and restaurants attracted the expense money of the actors and crew.

---

*Tavoularis's most elaborate set, by the way, goes completely unnoticed. In order to use the actual Brink's garage on Prince Street in Boston, the production had to enclose the entire window side of the building in a huge lightproof cocoon. This allowed night scenes to be shot during the day so that the cast and crew could live with some semblance of order to their lives. Because the 1978 skyline was different from the 1950 skyline, Tavoularis and his staff built an optically correct diorama of buildings, houses, street lamps, windows, and streets that looked like a complete view but was only about three feet high and stood on scaffolding in a ten-foot arc right outside the garage windows. Better than a theatrical background painting, it afforded varying perspectives no matter where Friedkin and cinematographer Norman Leigh decided to place their camera.

Friedkin, too, enjoyed himself in Boston, although while on the set—isolated from press and public—he showed another face. The failure of *Sorcerer* seemed to make him more self-critical and, although it did not shake his confidence, it increased his impatience with others.

"He really kept me on my toes," remembers assistant director Mark Johnson, who had come to *Brink's* for what he hoped would be an easier job of staging crowd scenes. "We had several hundred people and I thought I did a masterful job, because these were not movie extras, they'd never been in movies before. You couldn't just go up to a sixty-year-old woman and say, 'Action.' I'd have to say, 'You go over to the butcher and pretend you're buying this,' and so forth.

"I had to do that with some two or three hundred people. I thought I'd done some great work. Billy would find the fifteen people I hadn't been able to get to or who were confused. If it had been anyone else's eye he would've said, 'Gee, that's believable.' But he would find the ones and yell, 'What the hell is this? What is that, one of your relatives? You owed somebody a favor here?' The last thing you wanted was to be dressed down by Billy in front of everyone else."

The firings began again.

"You see," Johnson continues, "the amazing thing about the people who were let go on the movie is, from Billy's point of view, all of them deserved to be let go. There wasn't anything arbitrary. There wasn't anybody who was doing a great job and he just didn't like the color of their socks. If you have an off day you probably shouldn't even show up, because he'll come after you."

"I was up for the challenge," Jonathan Sanger feels. "I also knew that it was a situation where if, for some reason, I had gotten fired, it wouldn't seriously impact my career because enough good people have been fired by Billy over the years that it wouldn't really have hurt me that badly. But the important thing was that I stuck up for what I believed in."

Friedkin sometimes tested that, and nowhere more sharply than a sequence that didn't survive the final cut of *The Brink's Job* but still pushed the director's power to its limits.

"We were looking at a building that we could hit with a wrecking ball," Sanger recalls. "Well, we went to Urban Renewal in Boston and we found a number of buildings that were up for demolition and we showed them to Billy. He showed us the building that he liked.

"We went back to the office and I get a call from the Urban

Renewal guy in Boston who says, 'It's very embarassing, but the building you selected, we *thought* it was on the Urban Renewal list but it turns out we sold it to some guy for five thousand dollars who's gonna refurbish the whole building.' I go to Billy and I have to say, 'Billy, we can't do this—this building we can't do.'

" 'We *have* to do that,' " Sanger says, quoting Friedkin. " '*That's* the building. That's the *only* building.' "

"So I go to the producer, Ralph Serpe, and say, 'Ralph, Billy wants to hit this building with a wrecking ball. I don't think it's a very good idea. He's convinced that it has to be that building. He likes the view, there are a lot of other buildings we could use, but that's the one.'

"Ralph said, 'I'll take care of it.' It was the first time I was glad not to be in the loop; I wrote a letter saying I don't want to be responsible for this one, whatever happens. Ralph and Billy were not getting along at that point; generally Ralph would talk to Billy through me or Billy would talk to Ralph through me and I wound up being in the middle."

Eventually Friedkin, according to Sanger, promised just to hit the building with the wrecking ball once on the advice of the construction crew that a single tap wouldn't be that hard to repair in a structure already designated for rehabilitation. In the end a single hit was not enough and the company wound up paying more for the sequence than the entire building was worth.

"I could've been wrong, but I was right, and I wasn't happy to be right because it cost the company more than they expected," sighs Sanger, who concludes, "If you don't like Billy Friedkin, then you don't hire him to do your picture. But if you want to make the picture that he wants to make, you have to make the picture. Billy is not financially irresponsible. He is not someone who shoots an inordinate amount of film. He designs his shots very carefully and when he's got it, he's got it. But the route to getting there is where the mishaps happen."

The Brink's Job was the first major film in years for Peter Falk who, despite a solid background in theater, had garnered his greatest fame as television's rumpled *Columbo*. Tony Pino was a big responsibility for him, and Friedkin knew this.

"What Peter has, as a result of many years' experience, is a consistency from moment to moment," he had noticed. "Sometimes only an actor and director notice that, it's so subtle; I had to discover it. You see a film done this way, shot by shot, and you think that every shot should have something tremendous in it. Not necessarily. The actor is protecting the cycle of his performance from shot to shot, from moment to moment."

The ensemble cast was aided by the real Vinnie Costa, Jazz Maffie and Sandy Richardson, three surviving members of Pino's gang who advised their screen counterparts on details of their lives. Sometimes Friedkin had to resort to less intellectual methods. Randy Jurgensen, who played an interrogating FBI agent, remembers one in particular.

"I was doing a scene with my back to the camera and I don't think he was getting the response and the look that he was supposed to get from Paul Sorvino," Jurgensen says. "My dialogue was something along the line of, 'Come clean, you're not telling me everything.' Paul's character says, 'Yes I am.'

"Whatever [Friedkin] saw that he didn't like, he whispered in my ear—he's done this several times—and the camera rolled. I said, 'Look, you Guinea sonofabitch, you're gonna tell me exactly what it is I want to know or I'll beat the shit out of you!' And Sorvino says, 'Uh, I told you everything there was.' Billy says, 'We got it.' He does that. He does it to get what he's originally going after, which he feels he hasn't had."

Sorvino, an actor not lacking in self-confidence, accepted Friedkin's manipulative technique.*

"I'd rather succeed or fail on my own merits," he evaluated, "and not because my piece of the mosaic shined brighter or less so; that's my own nature. Of course, when you're working with someone like Billy Friedkin you can leave it in his hands, because his judgment is impeccable—probably much better than mine."

Allen Goorwitz shared Sorvino's trust in Friedkin.

"I took the film without reading the screenplay," he said in an interview prior to seeing himself in the finished film. "I loved the project, loved Noel's book enough and came up blindly because of the association with the ensemble and the director."

Peter Boyle was in an even more unique position. His Joe McGinnis was an unwhitewashed version of Dillon, the turncoat bartender he had played in *The Friends of Eddie Coyle* six years earlier.

"It was a similar character, but that's what happens around the movie business," he offered pragmatically. "One of the main things is working with Billy Friedkin because he's the best and I thought it would be a very interesting meeting of the director, the material and the rest of the cast. We didn't have any problems with it at all."

Although he did not let his cast know of his self-doubts dur-

---

*The sequence did not survive the final cut of the film.

ing the filming, Friedkin confided them to friends as shooting dragged through a brutally humid New England summer.

"I think my trend-setting days may be behind me," he revealed at the midpoint. "I think I got very lucky with *The French Connection* and *The Exorcist;* I never thought that they would be as successful as they were. I thought that my last film, *Sorcerer,* which was a failure critically and at the box office, was the best film I've ever done. So you never really know. You just do stories which interest you and let the chips fall where they may."

For Friedkin, who uses self-denigration as an interview ploy, this was not an unusual revelation. What was unusual, however, was his maintaining the same attitude when the press was not around.

"He was very different than he had been when we were filming the beginning of *Sorcerer,*" remarked Jonathan Sanger, who had also worked on that film's set. "Then he was on top of the world and couldn't do anything wrong. He had total control. [On *Brink's*] he questioned himself a lot more. He was very concerned about the cast chemistry and his own fallibility; he seemed to question his own thoughts. He was more introspective; it was clear at the beginning. Once he went ahead with the film I didn't see any of those moments of vulnerability. He asked question of people that he probably wouldn't have asked questions of before. He wasn't sure about things. Once he got involved and he had a cast that he was happy with, he rallied around it and that was it and he didn't show that face anymore. But in preproduction there was a change in him."

The first change was in his health.

"On *Sorcerer* I lost fifty pounds during the course of filming and on *The Exorcist* I lost fifty pounds," Friedkin recapped midway through *The Brink's Job.* "Bearing that in mind, I've tried to eat a lot of junk food on this picture so that I don't become dehydrated. I'm six feet tall and I was down to 137 pounds at one point."

While watching his weight (and developing a penchant for frankfurters that would continue for ten years), Friedkin also pursued a work schedule that burned up the calories faster than he could put them on.

"You get a natural high that comes out of the work itself," he elucidated. "Most filmmakers who work on a film that takes twelve weeks or more, as this one will, are in the same position. You have very little personal life; I have none. I work on this film a hundred to a hundred and ten hours a week, between rehearsals, production, and preproduction planning, and then I work in the cutting room evenings and on weekends. I never really bothered to add it up, but that's what it amounts to, and there's very little time or energy left for anything else. Your whole life becomes this movie. I'm not asking for any sympathy; it's a terrific job."

It also proved to be a dangerous one. In a move that rivaled the brazenness of the Brink's heist itself, at noon on Friday, July 28, three gunmen entered the company's location offices at 441 Stuart Street in Boston's Back Bay and stole thirteen cans of footage intending to hold it for ransom when they called a week later with their demands.

Bud Smith, who seems to attract strangers to his editing room, happened to be late to work that day.

"My editorial crew was there working when someone came and knocked on the door," Smith says. "My son, Scott, was apprentice editor then. He opened the door and they hit him upside the head with a gun so as to say, 'Pay attention, we're serious about this' and took him into the first room and hand-cuffed everyone. They put cotton in their mouths and tape around their faces. They left one guy unhandcuffed and made him run film for them to decide what scene to take."

The trio seemed to know what they were doing. They made off with crowd scenes, period material that would be expensive to reshoot. There was only one flaw in their plan: they didn't realize that professional films, unlike home movies, are shot on negative which is archived at the main studio. Quickly made positive prints from the camera negative, called workprint, one then used for the editing process. What the thieves took was a cheap copy of safely stored original material worth a few hundred dollars in lab fees. And they didn't really get even that.

"What they stole, which was ironic, was the trims and out-takes," Smith chuckles. "All the cut reels were lined up in *my* room; everything else was in the room with the outtakes, and that's where they went."

Before the extortion call came in on August 7 it was thought that one of the extras had had second thoughts about appearing in the film and sent a goon squad to retrieve it. The FBI placed taps on the production office phones, scripted a response that Friedkin was to give to whoever called with ransom demands, and in that way hoped to snare the culprits. The FBI was right about the thieves but wrong about Friedkin.

The first figure named by the thieves was $300,000, a fairly accurate estimate, it turned out, of what it would cost

DeLaurentiis to reshoot the purloined sequences around Scollay Square and Haymarket. According to Boston Police Superintendent John Dyle, Friedkin's people were told to make a counter offer of $20,000 and not to leak that the footage had already been replaced.

Instead, Friedkin reportedly told the callers, "Go rent a projector and enjoy yourselves" and hung up.

Boston Police Detective Edward Walsh had warned the company to expect trouble.

"I already told them, way back about a month ago, that this might happen," Walsh said to *The Boston Globe* after the robbery. "We had information that an attempt might be made to get money being used in some scenes.* I told them it could happen to the film, but they said they had special security to take care of it, that this could never happen.

"They had to have inside information," Walsh felt. "They had to know what to do."

It was only after the film premiered that the full meaning of Walsh's assertion came to light. That was when NBC News ran a three-part report on mob influence in Hollywood. Produced and hosted by Brian Ross, the network's specialist on organized crime, the series revealed that Gerald McDowell, head of the Federal Organized Crime Strike Force in New England, was probing allegations that several film productions had had associations with underworld figures. The first title that was mentioned was *The Brink's Job*.

At issue were two alleged violations of the Hobbs Act, a federal statute involving extortion from a commercial enterprise, by the Teamsters union.

Ross's report included an interview with DeLaurentiis in which the producer said, "It is true, absolutely, absolutely true. We are obligated to take more people (hire more people) than we . . . really need. Oh, for sure, we spent at least an increase of a million [dollars] or more."

Named as people who had ties not only with the film but with organized crime were Ralph LaMattina and Joseph "Joe Shoes" Cammaratta. Quoting unidentified Boston police sources, the NBC report named LaMattina as an "underworld chieftain" in the North End and Cammaratta as an aide to him. Both were supposed to have convinced North End residents to accede

---

*After the robbery the Pino gang wallows in a room full of real cash. The company rented a garage and filled it with a million dollars in small bills. Police and understandably nervous Brink's guards stood by. After it was collected and counted (which took two days) only sixteen dollars had vanished.

to the film company's requests in exchange for cash payments.

The next day, December 15, William Friedkin flew to Boston. With him at a hastily scheduled press conference were Noel Behn, Sonny Grosso, Randy Jurgensen and casting director Lou DiGiaimo.

"I personally have no knowledge of any attempts of extortion made against us," Friedkin assured the press. "I have no knowledge of anyone on this picture having paid extortion or bribes or anything else."

Given that Friedkin's activities restricted him to the set or editing rooms, there is little question that he was telling the truth. There was also no reason for him to have made a disclaimer in the first place. Nevertheless, he was enjoying jousting with reporters, even when they queried him about his penchant for hiring roughnecks.

"I was not aware that it was against the law in this country to hire a worker with a criminal record," he responded facetiously.

Four men were ultimately indicted for racketeering, mail fraud and extortion on five productions between 1977 and 1979, one of them *The Brink's Job*. The June 13, 1981 charges were against Teamster organizer and trustee Joseph "Gus" Manning and drivers William C. Bratton, Hartley E. Greenleaf and Ernest C. Sheehan. All were accused of collecting money from the producers of such films as *Oliver's Story*, *International Velvet*, *James at 15* and *See How She Runs* as well as *Brink's*. Producer Ralph Serpe testified on their behalf at the trial.

On February 5, 1982, Bratton and Greenleaf were found guilty and on March 8 were sentenced: Bratton was handed two years for racketeering and three years (suspended) for mail fraud; Greenleaf got two years for racketeering and two (suspended) for mail fraud. Manning and Sheehan did not withstand trial; Manning suffered a heart attack during the proceedings and Sheehan had cancer.

For Friedkin the fallout was less serious but more profound. The interest of the FBI, grand juries and other investigators ran in sharp counterpoint to the Damon Runyonesque images of tough guys that had been the colorful edge to his films from *Crump* to the Wolper shows to *Minsky's* Trim Houlihan to the genuine scum who informed the authenticity of *The French Connection*. The "Phantom of the School" had ventured onto the turf of some real bullies and they brought the feds in with them, and not as story consultants, either.

Rather than back off, Friedkin reaffirmed his fascination with the crime milieu. The challenges and vague threats repeated by the press only inspired him to delve into the secret society whose arcane ethics provided him with material and, perhaps, more.

"I'm a police buff and a crime buff," he said during a calm moment before the film opened. "I'll tell you something: I've been fortunate enough to meet guys who have been at the other end of a gun and try to communicate with them, and they with me, without having to look down the barrel of that gun. And I've found that, I have to say this, some of the people I admire most are the guys who have done violent crimes. There are qualities that I've found admirable, I'm sorry to say, but it's true. Oh, I'm not talking about cold-blooded murderers. I'm talking about guys who—I don't know the reasons, nor do you— why they led a life of crime. But there is certain code among these guys that I have observed or experienced. Most people that I meet are covering their true emotions, but guys who have had experience in a life of crime—if you meet them on a level where they trust you in some way—it's a terrifically cleansing experience."

With *The Brink's Job* opening and his ability to bring in a complicated film on budget reaffirmed, Friedkin began talking about new projects. As usual, he had his choice.

There was Thomas Thompson's *Blood and Money*, the journalistic account of the death of Houston socialite Joan Robinson which CBS still wanted him to do as a miniseries. And he was toying with Ron Kovic's soul-wrenching Vietnam autobiography *Born on the Fourth of July* with Al Pacino as the paralyzed veteran (eventually made in 1989 by Oliver Stone with Tom Cruise).

It was on the airplane to Houston to research *Blood and Money* that Friedkin began talking with Randy Jurgensen about yet another movie, one that involved an incident in Jurgensen's own past. It was in the form of a book that attracted his attention just as it had the attention of producer Jerry Weintraub. The title was *Cruising*.

CHAPTER 10

CRUISING FOR A BRUISING

Al Pacino, as an undercover detective seeking a vicious killer of gay men, turns down one man who is cruising him by heading off with another in *Cruising*.

BETWEEN 1962 AND 1979 two apparently separate series of vicious murders rocked New York City's gay community. The first occurred between 1962 and 1969 and were the basis for Gerald Walker's 1970 novel *Cruising*. The second happened between 1973 and 1979 and were combined with the previous cases when William Friedkin personally adapted the Walker book into his 1980 film.

Cruising remains disturbing both for its tone and its content and represents the first time Friedkin's penchant for "resonances" worked against him in a debate that has become a continuing source of controversy.

Part of that is because of the crime itself: the *Cruising* murders remain shocking even today. The victims, all homosexual men familiar to Manhattan's leather bars, were frequently found in various forms of dismemberment, brutally knifed, their bodies wrapped in black plastic bags that washed up on the New Jersey shore of the Hudson River. Because complete bodies could not always be found, many of the victims could be identified only by tattoos, remnants of unusual clothing and arcane sex tools which had been found with them. Some of the murders—where not enough limbs or torsos could be matched—remain unsolved. The police department calls them CUPPIs (Circumstances Undetermined Pending Police Investigation) but the press nicknamed them "Bag Murders."

The seventeen years of killings became a nightmare of homophobia that was compounded by another incident that seemed to involve New York City's police department and bears even more closely on the film than Walker's novel.

In the early 1960s the district attorney's office of New York City began hearing that two men—one black and one white, thus earning the nickname "salt and pepper"—were blackmailing gay men by representing themselves as police officers. Their shakedown scheme was to patrol New York's West Village where gay men were known to cruise, find a pair in a compromising position, pretend to arrest them and then encourage a bribe to forget the whole thing.

"The gays were truly still in the closet by their own admission," recalls Randy Jurgensen, whose undercover work on the case earned him the gold badge of detective. "It was very easy to take advantage of these people."

The scam involved the salt and pepper "cops" driving the two gay men to the NYC police station on Fifth Street, a building that had a large front window so that the victims could see inside.

"One man would get out of the car and go inside and would begin talking to the desk sergeant," Jurgensen explains. In actuality, he would be doing nothing more than asking directions, but to the panicked men in the back seat of the car it looked like negotiations for their freedom.

"They'd keep them out all night and throw them into the back of an arraignment court," Jurgensen continues. Again, one of the fake "cops" would approach the bailiff and ask some unheard question that appeared like discussion. He would then report to the exhausted men, "Okay, the judge'd let it go for a thousand bucks."

"This doesn't sound like a lot of money," Jurgensen says, "but we were in the 1960s. They'd get it from their mothers or from their own account. This was going on and the word was that it was two cops who were doing it."

Jurgensen, who had managed to work undercover narcotics without ever being in the position where he had to shoot up, felt confident of working undercover on this case without having to become sexually compromised.

"I got an apartment [in the West Village] and I had to answer to only one inspector. I got paid every two weeks and I never went to the precinct. My wardrobe: a leather jacket with a star over my eye. And I got extraordinarily lucky. I would, within five months, come up with these guys. Nothing but good detective work. And I was extremely pleased to find out at the time that they were not cops. What they were—and the job exists today—was, literally, watchmen. The job had been created during the 1940s when the first German submarine had come up in Long Island Sound. Well, the job was to patrol the Hudson River and stop anybody with flashlights who might be signaling German submarines. When the war ended, the job was never done away with, and these guys were still patroling the Hudson River!"

And also, it turned out, those who cruised it.

What evolved the "salt and pepper" flim-flam into *Cruising* was that, while the investigation was going on, two of the gay men who had filed complaints with the district attorney's office lost their lives.

The police were never able to tie together the Hudson patrol with the murders, and they remain CUPPIs. The frustration arising from that situation is reflected in *Cruising*'s many ambiguities, which audiences, raised on neatly packaged mysteries, often find unnerving. The semiresolved plot, combined with Friedkin's growing interest in textures, details and resonances, makes it the most controversial of all his films.

Cruising opens without a main title; appearing on the screen in tightly lettered lines is the disclaimer:

> This film is not intended as an indictment of the homosexual world. It is set in one small segment of that world, which is not meant to be representative of the whole.

Morning. New York City. A tugboat chugs along the Hudson River when its skipper spots something floating in the water: a gangrenous, severed right male arm.*

In the police lab, Detective Lefransky (Randy Jurgensen) and Dr. Rifkin (Gene Davis) try to match the limb with a torso or one of the organs that litter their CUPPI morgue. Lefransky resists Rifkin's suggestion that a fingerprint from the hand of the limb could easily establish the victim's identity; Lefransky doesn't want a homicide on his hands that can't be solved.

Late one night along the West Village waterfront two patrolmen (Joe Spinell and Mike Starr) break from their casually sexist banter to harass two transvestites into orally servicing them in their police cruiser. While they are so engaged, the man who will later be identified as the killer wanders past—bedecked in crinkling leather and clinking keyring—and into a nearby leather bar.

Inside, the exclusively male clientele is displayed in its ritual regalia; jockstraps, leather face masks, studded collars and artfully torn clothing. The mysterious stranger picks up another man and they wander to the nearby St. James Hotel for sex.

After the coupling (not shown) the stranger binds his frightened prey hand and foot, pulls out a knife and, singing a children's song, suddenly stabs the man to death with repeated thrusts of his wide, serrated blade.

At the morgue Captain Edelson (Paul Sorvino) learns what he can from Dr. Rifkin: that the man did not struggle until after the first wound and that his anus was dilated at the time. Moreover, the semen in the anus was devoid of sperm. Edelson is nearly sick at the sight.

No sooner does Edelson return to his office than one of the transvestites from the squad car shakedown arrives to complain about the two officers who have been hitting on gays.

---

*In a glaring continuity jump, a panning camera shot of the tug is abruptly intercut with a static insert of the floating arm.

Edelson rejects the idea but, later, summons a young police officer, Steve Burns (Al Pacino), to see him. He tells Burns that a killer is stalking gay men and he wants the young cop to go undercover to try and catch him.

"Why me?" Burns asks.

"Because all the murder victims fit your description—dark hair, dark eyes," he is told.

That night Burns says goodbye to Nancy, his girlfriend (Karen Allen), and the next day moves into a recently vacated Greenwich Village apartment to assume his new identity as "John Forbes." Immediately he befriends neighbor Ted Bailey (Don Scardino), a gay playwright whose lover, Gregory (James Remar), doesn't share Bailey's faith in his writing talent. Bailey and Burns discuss the killings and Bailey is skeptical of the police's interest in capturing the murderer.

"If they did, they'd probably make him a member of the vice squad," Bailey feels.

Soon Burns begins scouring the leather bars. He cruises and is cruised by, among others, one of the shakedown cops and by Stuart Richards (Richard Cox), the man who will be revealed as the killer.*

Burns is still educating himself. Walking into a sex tool shop, he casually asks the clerk (Powers Boothe) what a display of colored handkerchiefs indicates.

"Light blue hankie in your left back pocket means you want a blow job, right pocket means you give one; the green one left side says you're a hustler, right side you're a buyer; yellow one, left side, means you give golden shower, right side you receive; red one means—see anything you want?"

Burns is just about out the door in embarrassment. "I think I'll have to go home and think about it."

"I'm sure you'll make the right choice," the clerk says nonchalantly.

Before long, Burns has become a regular on the cruising circuit—the Ramrod, the Cockpit, the Eagle's Nest, the rest. He learns the life but it is left unclear whether he actually takes part in it. *Cruising* becomes deliberately elliptical in an effort to place the viewer in Burns's disintegrating frame of mind.

One night a man whom Burns sighted (and possibly cruised)

---

*This first cruising sequence is unsettling. Shot from Burns's point of view, it involves a succession of men, all of whom look directly into the camera lens to "check out" the viewer. As in Hitchcock's *Rear Window*, this violation of the cinema's voyeuristic constraints is one of a number of Friedkin's primal techniques.

in the park is picked up by the killer and slain.

Momentarily back in the straight life, Burns makes forceful love to Nancy. He is troubled by something and, the next morning at breakfast, he tells her enigmatically, "Don't let me lose you."*

Burns is now finding himself more at ease in his undercover identity. He forms what is becoming a genuine friendship with Ted Bailey, learns the ritualistic dress codes in the various clubs (including "Precinct Night" where everybody dresses as cops) and freely enquires after the men he now sees. The outside world, however, is starting to slip away; when he and Nancy make love, his fantasies wander to the world of leather and sweat. When he turns down a possible encounter outside a club, he is told by the trick, "That bulge in your pants ain't a knife. Why don't we take a walk?" Burns's hesitation in saying, "Not tonight" is revealing.

Soon another gay man (Steve Inwood) is murdered in a peep show, his blood splattering the porn images on the screen. Capt. Edelson is now getting increased pressure from the city to clean up the cases before the Democratic National Convention arrives late that summer. Some clues help: apparently the killer left his fingerprint on a bloody quarter in the peep show booth.

Later the transvestite (who is also used by police as an informer) tells the police that two friends who happened to be at the peep show just before the murder heard someone singing a strange children's song, some kind of nursery rhyme.

Burns now feels that a man named Skip Lee (Jay Acovone), a troublemaker known to several bartenders, may be the killer. Checking on Lee, Detective Lefransky follows the suspect to work at a steak house and concludes that the murder wounds might have been made with a restaurant knife that Lee could easily have taken.

Burns lures Lee to a cheap hotel as police wait outside, ready to make a bust. When Burns's wire goes dead, the police raid the room and find him tied on the bed with Lee standing over him. No knife is found.

Both men are hauled into the station and separated but Lee is viciously questioned. When a large black policeman clad only in a hat and jockstrap enters the room and threatens to beat Lee, Burns loses all control; he is horrified at this mistreatment of a man whose only "crime" is that he is gay. After terrorizing

---

*Friedkin adds a playful sexual pun in this scene: At the moment that Pacino embraces Allen in her kitchen the automatic toaster pops up.

Lee for hours, the police release him. Burns, however, now feels
alienated from his police brethren and confesses obliquely,
"What I'm doing is affecting me," in a surprise visit to Nancy.
Confused, she says the wrong thing: "Maybe we should cut loose
for a while."

Burns is now at odds with himself and his sexuality. Meeting
Edelson in an elevated subway station, he angrily tells him, "I
didn't come on this job to shitcan some guy because he's gay."
Edelson is unmoved. He shows Burns a Columbia University
yearbook in the hope that Burns might recognize a student who
might have taken a class with one of the murder victims, a
professor there.

Burns does: a drama student named Stuart Richards, whom
he remembers seeing at the bars. He finds Richards's apartment, stakes it out and breaks inside one afternoon while the
young man is away. He discovers a closet full of leather clothing and a shoebox crammed with unsent letters to the youth's
father.

Eventually he allows Richards to notice him staring from the
park across the street from his window. He soon entices him
into a rendezvous. When Richards—taunted by Burns's repeating of the children's song—pulls a knife, Burns stabs him first.

In the hospital Edelson tries to make Richards confess not
just to the murder of the man in the peep show booth, where
they have his fingerprint, but to them all. Richards refuses and
will wait for his trial. Burns, meanwhile, has earned his detective's shield. While the police are cleaning Richards's apartment they learn from a neighbor that Richards's father had
died ten years ago. The unsent letters, therefore, are a psychological wish fulfillment.

Several nights later Edelson is summoned to the site of another gay murder. The victim is Ted Bailey. He notices that one
of the policemen on the case (actor Joe Spinell) is one that the
transvestite has claimed was shaking down gay men. But the
worst shock is that Ted Bailey's neighbor, John Forbes, has been
gone for two days and is the prime suspect in Bailey's killing.
Moreover, there was semen in Bailey's mouth.

Burns, meanwhile, has returned to Nancy with a promise to
tell her all that has happened to him. While he shaves in the
bathroom, she discovers his leather hat and jacket, which he
has taken to wearing even while off-duty. As she tries on the
clothes and watches herself in the living room mirror, Burns
looks into the bathroom mirror—into his own eyes—and into
the camera.

In synopsis form, *Cruising* appears as a far more unified narrative than on film, where it contains such a surfeit of nuance, digression and detail that, far from arriving at conclusions, viewers are encouraged to become stunned by the complexity of the issues. This, of course, is Friedkin's goal, just as it was in *The Exorcist* and *The French Connection*—literally saying, "The story is over but the world it's set in remains." The trick—and it worked less well in *Cruising*—is to satisfy the audience emotionally yet stimulate them intellectually.

It is the milieu of *Cruising* which, in hindsight, made this so difficult. Sexuality remains the most threatening aspect of American culture, and—regardless of the film's perfunctory disclaimer—viewers are apt to see their worst misconceptions visualized in the picture. The strain of homophobia runs deep within straight society, and *Cruising* mined it with explosive intensity.

At the time it went into active production in 1980 there had been few Hollywood films that dealt with homosexuality in any but the most exploitive ways; even Friedkin's *The Boys in the Band*, although sympathetic, still catered to the widely accepted theatrical notions of gay stereotypes. The far more closeted world of leather and sadomasochism was barely mentioned and never explored.

Yet here lurked a society (S&M) within a society (gays) within a still larger society (American life). Moreover, placing an undercover cop into it as a decoy added a fourth level to the strata. The emotional torment and dramatic potential were readily accessible to anyone who dared explore it, as Randy Jurgensen was assigned to do by his police superiors.

"I had the fear of being discovered in what I was doing," he recalls, almost clinically. "Not with my family and friends, but I'd find myself walking down the street and a police car was going the other way. After all, I was still a cop [searching, by design, for a possible police culprit] and I was scared to death."

Jurgensen formed bonds within the gay community and, from what he heard, learned that the various murder victims were known habitués of those clubs that cater to rough trade. It is a world that does not welcome outsiders.

"I would go to a bar and meet a gentleman and tell him I was 'coming out' and didn't know how to do it, and I would know a club that I wanted to get into. I would say to him, 'Would you meet me Thursday night at that club?' and I would wait there until he wanted to get in. Then I would approach the doorman who would say, 'I don't know you' and I'd say, 'I

know "John Jones." Go get him.' They'd go to get him and he'd
say, 'Oh, yeah, he's with me,' and I was in."

William Friedkin used the same technique when he asked
Jurgensen to bring him on a tour of the bars while the pair was
researching the film.

"I was in those bars almost every night for three months,"
Friedkin recalls. "I have friends who are regulars there and I
obeyed the dress code, which very often was nothing more than
a jockstrap. For me it was great, 'cause I'm not that good-look-
ing. I wasn't bothered that much, to be honest with you. If I
was John Travolta in a jockstrap, I mighta had some problems.
But I was just another fat Jew in a jockstrap." Was he slighted
by being ignored? "Well, you know, there's a certain ego. . . ."

In making the transition from book to script (for which for
the first time Friedkin received full screenwriting credit), he
had to confront the rabid homophobia of Gerald Walker's story.
For beneath its standard, if decorated, plot about a policeman
who stalks a killer of gay men, *Cruising* is also about a man
who comes face to face with his own emerging homosexuality
and how he chooses to deal with it. That Walker's solution is
to have the guilt-ridden cop assume the mindset of the killer
and continue his antigay mania is what both angered the gay
community and left Friedkin's film open to charges of exploi-
tation of and collaboration with the lie.

In July of 1979 *Cruising*—which was backed by Lorimar Pictures for United Artists release but for which Friedkin and producer Jerry Weintraub were largely financially responsible—
began filming in and around New York's leather bars. It caused
instant controversy.

"His film promises to be the most oppressive, ugly, bigoted
look at homosexuality ever presented on the screen, the worst
possible nightmare of the most uptight straight and a validation of Anita Bryant's hate campaign," wrote gay columnist
Arthur Bell in his widely read "Bell Tells" feature in the *Village
Voice* of July 10, 1979, just as production started. Bell's words—
which form a manifesto—were an impassioned alarm that
crystalized sentiment against the filmmakers. He continued:

> It will negate years of positive movement
> work and may well send gays running back
> into the closet and precipitate heavy vio-
> lence against homosexuals. I implore
> readers—gay, straight, liberal, radical,
> atheist, communist or whatever—to give
> Friedkin and his production crew a terri-

ble time if you spot them in your neighborhood (the film will be shooting for the
next seven weeks at Badlands, the Eagle's
Nest, the Underground, Police Plaza and
on Christopher and West Streets). And I
urge gay men whom Friedkin has signed
as extras and bit players in scenes to be
shot at backroom bars, piers, bathhouses
and Village streets to be aware of the consequences of his project. Owners of gay
establishments would do well to tell
Friedkin to fuck off when he comes around
to film and exploit.

Mark Johnson remembers, "To disrupt us became the fun thing. You know, find out where *Cruising* was filming and band together. No one threw bricks, but we had lots of whistle blowing which they thought, quite correctly, would disturb the sound takes. And then they had people climbing on top of rooftops shining mirrors onto our sets breaking up the whole lighting scheme.* There was almost a carnival atmosphere about it, the whistle-blowing and the chanting, 'Hey, hey, ho, ho, the movie *Cruising*'s got to go!' "

Johnson also recalls the readily available screenplay.

"At one point it was reprinted in some journal and everybody said they *had* seen it."

He also remembers that, rather than back off in the face of such opposition, Friedkin seemed to enjoy it.

"He's a madman," Johnson states. "He loved it. He loved the fact of that tension around him."

If Friedkin was getting any kick out of the demonstrators, his stoic silence during production seemed only to bait them further. Instead, Jerry Weintraub, in a *Variety* interview three weeks into production, said, "They're making a mountain out of a molehill and just looking for a cause to hang themselves on. I honestly don't think my film is anti-gay. They're basing all their complaints on the book. We're not doing the book, we're using the title and some of the characters to make a controversial murder mystery set within the gay community.

"I have no intention of letting them or anyone else see our script," Weintraub continued, responding to the charge that the filmmakers had refused to allow gay community representa-

---

* While the dialogue could be "looped" later in postproduction, errant reflections from mirrors and flashlights could very easily have ruined the photography and could not be corrected afterwards.

tives to read a copy of the constantly changing screenplay. "They have no right to try and stop our making this picture, and I explained our position to them very clearly. I just wish the picture were finished and ready for release."

Arthur Bell's importunings did not move New York City Mayor Ed Koch who, as a staunch civil libertarian (and a politician eager to bring money into his city), had refused to rescind the location permits that had been issued to the filmmakers. Koch's movie development liaison, Nancy Littlefield, gave a reason more pragmatic than the First Amendment: "Anything that brings in seven million dollars is good for New York," she said. Bell countered by calling *Cruising* "a snuff film."

Despite the pressure, Friedkin tried to keep the mood light on the set. Karen Allen recalls that while she and Al Pacino were shooting their scenes in a Manhattan loft, Friedkin was "really sweet and funny and kind of mischievous. *The Exorcist* was about to be rereleased in theaters and what he kept doing was that he would wait until moments before he said 'action' and he would sneak a big, bold red paperback copy of *The Exorcist* right into the middle of the shot—knowing, of course, that somebody was going to spot it and yank it off. But he'd do it like a little kid trying to get away with it. It was quite endearing."

"Why would I do that?" Friedkin counters emphatically. "I'm sure there is no copy of *The Exorcist* in the film *Cruising*. If she's serious, it's a fanciful story. If she's not serious, it's untrue. I mean, why would I do that? I didn't write *The Exorcist*. Some other guy did."

Mark Johnson also remembers some lightness on the set, albeit of a different manner, following a lengthy shoot in a gay bar.

"I asked one of the extras if he had had a good day after he had spent the entire day dancing in a bar scene, being given real beer and dancing and drinking and I think there were joints being passed around. And I asked, 'How did it go?' being polite at the end of the day. The guy said, 'It wasn't bad. I got blown twice.'

"I remember thinking, 'Give me back your voucher, pal, you expect me to pay for that?' "

It wasn't until after *Cruising* had wrapped that Friedkin broke his silence; it was to Janet Maslin of *The New York Times* in an interview objecting to being labeled a homophobe:

> "Anyone who knows me or knows anything about me knows that I am not anti-

gay," he said. "I don't make a film because I'm for something—I don't make
propaganda. If anything, all the films I've
made are enormously ambiguous.
    "Even *The Exorcist*, though it deals with
Catholic theology, isn't something you
could call a pro-Catholic picture. There are
many Catholics who resent it. But I
couldn't have made it if I was not sympathetic with that theology. I make a film
to explore something, and in the course of
that exploration, my attitudes get formed."

At times Friedkin would form his attitudes during the research process while at others he would encourage the actors
to collaborate; the "ambiguities" he noted to Maslin often remain undefined until they are set into a context within the film.
Among the most haunting images in *Cruising* is Karen Allen's
wearing of Al Pacino's leather accoutrements in the film's final
sequence. Its emotion comes entirely from Friedkin's manipu-
lation of cinema.

"As I remember, he talked me through it because there were
no lines and it wasn't scripted," she says, quoting his directions: " 'You walk into the shot, you pick up the jacket, you put
on the jacket, you look in the mirror . . .' He literally talked
me through it and maybe was making it up as we went along.
He actually had me do it many different ways. The impression
that stays with me is just an idea—whether he'd gotten it the
night before or dreamed it I don't know—because as I remember it was never scripted."

Friedkin's impatience in explaining to Allen his precise reasons for the mirror routine contrasts with the extended talks
he had with Al Pacino in his difficult role as Burns/Forbes. According to coworkers, Pacino eventually yielded to Friedkin's
point of view. Pacino continues to avoid discussion of the film.

This frustration with the collaborative process explains why
Friedkin chose to adapt the screenplay himself. Although directors always work with screenwriters to some degree, strict
guidelines from the Writers Guild of America limit the screen
credit a director may receive. With *Cruising*, Friedkin opted to
use the book's title and concept but work otherwise from scratch.

"I had no way of communicating my feelings about this to a
writer," he told Janet Maslin, once again mentioning the thin
line between the policeman and the criminal. As to which side
of that line he placed the gay community in general and its
S&M culture in particular, he didn't say. When his script hit

the streets, even in a version that wasn't the final draft, the protesters reacted to what they read, not what he may have had in mind but did not articulate in his pages.

"When I looked into that mob I saw a gang of unruly fanatics, blowing whistles, throwing bottles and cans at the trucks, at the actors and me," he said, reacting to their reaction. "So how could I believe that this group of people was representing the legitimate interests of a significant minority in this country? A legitimate group, with legitimate interests, does not threaten to kill you.

"Mass rallies and marches and sit-ins—that kind of civil disobedience is welcome, it's important. If that had been directed against *Cruising* I might very well have—no, I *would* have been persuaded—to stop filming." Improbable as that might have been, by the time of the September interview, it was a moot issue. It was Arthur Bell, Friedkin asserted, who inspired the violence. Reached by the *Times* for a comment, Bell expressed pride.

"What the Declaration of Independence was to Jefferson," he stated, "that column was to the gay community." Although Bell acknowledged that he had, indeed, urged violence during an ABC television interview, "it was last-minute advice, and I'd had only two or three hours' sleep the night before. If my head had been clearer, I would have said, 'Aim your violence against the cameras because their violence will be aimed at us.' "

The accusations flew back and forth—Friedkin claiming that Bell had no right to comment because he hadn't seen an up-to-date screenplay, Bell reminding Friedkin that he'd asked for one but had been refused—and by the end of it Friedkin admitted that the whole controversy would probably be counterproductive:

"My overall impression about every word that's been written on the subject, pro or con, is that I wouldn't have wanted any of it to happen. No amount of publicity can get an audience involved in a film. It might make people conscious of the name of a film, but that doesn't mean they're going to see it."

All that was left was for Friedkin, editor Bud Smith, and their staffs to piece *Cruising* together in a form that would reflect Friedkin's original vision while mollifying growing concern from the distributor that the graphic (and widely covered) scenes in the film would earn it a dreaded X rating. It threatened to venture into areas that major studio films had never dared—or wanted—to go.

In February of 1980 Friedkin, speaking to *Los Angeles Times*

writer Dale Pollack, attempted to head off that controversy by
suggesting that he was sensitive to the issue and was working
toward lessening the controversy.

"There's no experience or feeling on the screen in this film
that I myself have not felt or undergone," he told Pollack during postproduction from his Burbank Studios office. "It was
initially shocking to me. But the participants in this world show
enormous courage and freedom of choice. *Cruising* is as much
an antidote to gay stereotypes as you'll ever see," he concluded,
countering the homophobic view of gays as limp-wristed nel-
lies. "There's no such thing as one hundred percent male or
female person," he continued. "My film is an attempt to get
sexual ambiguity and violence and aggression as acts of sex out
into the open. The film will do more good than harm."

If it could ever be shown in public, that is. Despite Friedkin's
efforts, it appeared as though the Classification and Rating Ad-
ministration (CARA) of the Motion Picture Association of America was preparing to slap *Cruising* with an X rating, barring
audiences under seventeen from viewing it and effectively
shutting it out of most broadcast and newspaper advertising
outlets as well as America's more conservative theater chains.

On December 7, 1979, Friedkin and Weinbraub held a meeting with Richard Heffner, chairman of the MPAA rating board.
At that time he informed them that, unless they made certain
cuts in their film, it would be rated X. He also suggested—
according to Friedkin and Weintraub—that they secure the services of Dr. Aaron Stern, a New York psychiatrist who was
Heffner's ratings board predecessor, to lend his experience to
getting *Cruising* its preferred R rating.

Friedkin and Weintraub insist that Stern did not appear
before the full six-person board to plead *Cruising*'s case. He
did, however, receive a consulting fee of one thousand dollars
a day for thirty-two days from the producers to advise them
on what his former colleagues might find tolerable enough to
award an R.

Bud Smith, who was editing *Cruising*, took Stern's advice to
heart.

"We were trying to get it past the censor board at that time
because we had an X rating and we were trying to cut the murder scenes down. We employed Dr. Stern to come to Los Angeles and take a look at the movie and analyze it and tell [Jack]
Valenti what his evaluation of the movie was. First he saw it
and then we cut it down and cut it down and his evaluation
was that it was better than it was because you don't see the
violence and the blood spurting in the camera."

According to Steven Ginsberg in *Variety*, there were a series of contacts, meetings and changes in the film between December 17 and January 4, 1980, that resulted "in a removal of two shots as well as several frames from other shots," Friedkin is quoted as saying. Among them were the shortening of the first murder scene and the darkening, by Technicolor labs, of three shots; Friedkin produced a letter from Technicolor's senior vice president Jay Cipes as proof that this had been done.

Accordingly, *Cruising* received its R rating from CARA on January 4 and prints were shipped on February 15 for its national theatrical release. Then more hell broke loose.

On March 3, after the film had been playing for more than two weeks, Albert Van Shmus, administrative director of the ratings board, sent a memo to Friedkin and Weintraub insisting that two additional frame cuts must be made involving a scene of implied fellatio and a shot in a police bar.* Friedkin and Weintraub agreed to the Shmus mandate but argued that it might take as long as five weeks to do.

In the meantime, the nationwide General Cinema circuit had seen *Cruising* and felt, despite its official MPAA rating of R, that it deserved an X. Since it is General Cinema's policy not to exhibit X-rated films, they pulled *Cruising* off their screens. Immediately United Artists threatened to sue them for breach of contract. The matter was made even more complicated because *Cruising* had been offered to theaters under a process known as "blind bidding" in which exhibitors were compelled to compete for new films without having the chance to screen them first. Blind bidding is now outlawed in some twenty-three states, and *Cruising* is one of the reasons.

By June 2, in time for what he had hoped would be a lucrative summer release, Friedkin acceded to all the demands for cuts and darkenings and announced, "The film, *Cruising*, is the film I intended to make. The cuts I made were shot cuts, not scene cuts. Had they (the MPAA) requested cuts before, I would have made them."†

The decade between the release of *The Boys in the Band* and

---

*This was a potential shot of a practice known as "fist fucking" in which a lubricated hand is inserted into the anus. Sharp-eyed viewers can see two car license plates outside the club reading "FFA" (Fist-Fuckers of America, a cult allusion).

†One story bears noting to show the imprecision of the highly subjective movie rating system. At one point in their numerous versions Smith and Friedkin decided to splice in four frames of actual anal intercourse from a porno film. The various advisors screened the work, made no mention of the subliminal cuts, and pronounced the movie as being worthy of an R rating. The clip may still be seen by single-framing the murder of the man in the peep show booth.

Cruising saw major changes in the public's attitude toward gay people. On one side there was a clear awareness of the existence of homosexuals within the fabric of society (as many as 10 percent, according to Kinsey) and on the other there was the sense that this population had coalesced into a powerful social, political and economic lobby. The only place it hadn't had much of an effect was in the film industry which—possibly because so many executives and artists were insecure about their own sexual orientations—tended to avoid the subject where possible or misrepresent it where not.

Part of the problem is that any film dealing with a minority group is going to appear to be a statement about that group simply because of its existence in a vacuum. If it takes an extreme point of view without anything else to counter it, it will draw fire for its sins of omission as well as those of commission. *Cruising* had the added burden of dealing with a sexual minority group.

"It's speculative," Friedkin now feels with goodly hindsight. "I think it always would have upset and disturbed mostly straight people. You know, there are a lot of straight people who just don't want to deal with it and I understand that. Certainly I was very unhappy about the controversy because I believe that there are legitimate gay rights issues that are sort of swept out of the way by whether or not the film should be shown. The gay activists did not look good trying to get the film banned any more than I think the Saudis looked good trying to get *Death of a Princess* banned [from public television].

"I think the legitimate issues of gay rights like employment and housing opportunities and immigration are the very important things that the gay movement concerns itself with, but they don't make headlines. When a person looks homosexual to a guy in customs, he can be turned out of the country, and this is an important thing that people should be aware of.

"However," he adds, addressing the more provocative subtext of the whole controversy, "the film itself, very frankly, makes people think not about gay rights but gay sex. And I quite understand the position of gay activists not wanting people to think about that."*

---

*The issue of AIDS, of course, which was not defined when *Cruising* was made, is of unusual significance in a retrospective consideration of the film, which deals on one level with the dire consequences of sexual promiscuity. The killer is not, of course, a metaphor for AIDS, although the arguments the film raises are hauntingly like those which have been offered by such fringe groups as the fundamentalist community; i.e., to be gay is to court death.

If anything else, Friedkin's script tones down the hysterical homophobia of Gerald Walker's novel, from its two police joking about allowing the killer to "clean up this town for us" to the Ted Bailey character (named Dave Hooper in the book) griping about the risks of "ten minutes in the bushes" with a trick.

Other differences between the book and the film are crucial in relieving the characters of their compulsion to anguish so much that they knock the plot aside with their self-pity. On a less introspective level, the film also eliminates a scene in which Burns knifes a gay man who has come on to him only to learn later that the man was another undercover policeman who had been trying to entrap him. This presages his assumption of the killer's identity that exists in both versions.

Finally, the killer is caught only after he reads of the other murder, the one he didn't get to do, and goes berserk in the gay baths.

What Friedkin retained was Walker's disturbing premise that homosexuality can be "caught" and, one way or the other, leads to death. The ambiguities that he presents as *Cruising* concludes don't so much settle the mystery as open up four more, among them:

1. Did Gregory, Ted Bailey's jealous, belligerent roommate, kill him and then leave town?
2. Was Bailey killed by the shakedown cop who, after all, has been seen in his car, at the bars, in the park and now at the murder scene?
3. Is there a second killer?
4. Did Steve Burns, in fact, kill Bailey as the result of guilt for allowing the young man to bring him out of his closet?

Despite arguments to the contrary, the film leans toward the fourth contingency. It is, for example, only with Bailey that Burns can relax and even smile. Bailey is the only gay character in the film who is not portrayed as being into rough trade. And, both in his distance from Nancy and his edginess with Edelson, Burns is clearly undergoing some kind of change, more than likely his "coming out."

Burns's discovering his own homosexuality while working undercover is not what has enraged gay activists; his becoming another murderer is. This is the case despite the film's laying the groundwork for a more sympathetic resolution:

1. Burns is appalled at his fellow officers' harassment of Skip
    Lee who, had he not been holding the badge, could well
    have been him;
2. Burns's sexual activity with his girlfriend, Nancy (a rela-
    tionship not in the book), becomes increasingly mechanical
    and soon precludes kissing;
3. Burns has an erection outside one of the clubs;
4. Burns stoically allows a bar patron to massage his chest.

The film also goes to the unusual length of changing its own
point of view to provide killer Stuart Richards with a fantasy
in which he talks to his long-dead father about his "mission"
to kill gays, a scene that appears to explain the youth's insanity
and, with it, his actions.

"I had always meant to suggest the possibility, if not the
probability, that this cop, the Pacino character, flipped out and
killed this guy," Friedkin says. "I always wanted to suggest that.
And even people who were close to me or knew me were confused about it, and I love that. Because that is part of the sexual ambiguity that I was reaching for in the story. Now,
ambiguity is not everyone's cup of tea—when I say ambiguity
I mean I don't want to answer all the questions, wrap it all up
and this is what happens. I wanted to make a film where there
were many questions left, as there are with *The French Connection* and *The Exorcist,* and who's good and who's bad and what
really happened here." All of these resonances add texture to
the film—many were added while production was in progress—but do little to offer the viewer an emotional release.

That didn't keep viewers from becoming emotional.

"We are asking Hollywood to use the same system of self-
censorship they apply to other minorities," said Ronald Gold,
a former *Variety* reporter and media consultant for the National Gay and Lesbian Task Force quoted by Vito Russo in *The
Celluloid Closet.* "Nobody would dare to do a film about a group
of organized black men whose objective is to rape a white
woman. We always find ourselves in the position of having to
play civil libertarian to a bunch of bigots who want their constitutional right to express their hatred of us."

"The disclaimer is an admission of guilt," writes Russo in
the same book. "What director would make such a statement
if he truly believed that his film would not be taken to be representative of the whole?

"In essence Friedkin [is] saying of *Cruising,* 'I'm trying to
present a portrait of a group of people who get their sexual
kicks in ways that society doesn't approve, but I'm making no

personal judgement of these people.' Gay activists responded that the judgement was being made nonetheless by a misinformed and already prejudiced society and by a Hollywood that seldom portrayed any other aspect of gay life and thus created a climate for backlash and repression."

The flap over the content of *Cruising* is unfortunate because it happens to be an extraordinary achievement in narrative and sensory (but not necessarily sexual) richness.

Given that the torments it chronicles are internal, the film relies on that most ephemeral of attributes—the soundtrack—to establish a world of vague surrealism and often conflicting aural imagery.

Some of the devices are obvious: the sound of clinking chains (often forming a musical counterpoint) and footsteps on streets of differing surface. The sounds create a closeness to the characters that belies their physical distance from the camera. On most films this would be blamed on a bad sound mix; in *Cruising* it forces the viewer/listener into threatening, yet tantalizing, proximity.

"There's probably more leather sound than you'll ever hear in a film again," notes Paul Huntsman, Friedkin's postproduction supervisor who, along with the sound editors and mixers, devised the unusual and near-impressionistic audio effects. "We made the sounds by twisting a wallet full of credit cards near the microphone," Huntsman reveals, "and just played with it as we ran the film." The visceral sounds of the killer's knife cutting into muscle tissue and glancing off bone were also a ruse. "We took a kitchen carving knife and stabbed a piece of meat," he says. Was it a piece of steak or—pardon the expression—rump roast?

"Neither," Huntsman smiles. "We used a chicken. Beef costs too much."

Beginning with *The Exorcist* Friedkin had experimented with adventurous sound techniques given the freedom—and subtlety—of a burgeoning interest in theater audio technology. Ironically, the disruptive chanting of demonstrators during the filming of *Cruising* forced him to loop dialogue in postproduction, and in enjoying a "second chance" at making the film he moved farther toward the impressionistic style he would increasingly come to embrace. When Al Pacino shuffled along the rain-soaked streets of the West Village, his feet were making the normal sounds of shoes on pavement. But, more subjectively, he (and the audience) could hear the call of writhing leather blocking out the reality and seducing him.

Beyond that, the feeling one takes away most passionately

from *Cruising* is that of loneliness. Except for a confrontation with the team of cops that roughs up his first suspect, Steve Burns does not enjoy any relationships with more than one other person at a time. In contrast with Friedkin's other "cop" films, *Cruising* has none of the devotion between partners or the casual camaraderie among a group of friends. Burns works alone and his relationships can be counted on the fingers of one hand: Nancy, Edelson, Bailey, plus the occasional bartender, store clerk or suspicious trick.

Burns's isolation—the result of being sent into nighttown to spy on his peers, be they fellow cops, fellow gays or fellow homophobes—makes him the ultimate victim of the ultimate kind of betrayal. Not only does his girlfriend reject him, but his boss won't let him back out of undercover, he couldn't hang out with his friends even if he had any, he can't trust his own sexual desires anymore and, in any case, were he to act on them with a man he might get killed or exposed. Beyond that, his mission is to catch the killer by attracting him—in other words, by betrayal.

Of all Friedkin's films, *Cruising* is the one which remains most painful for audiences to watch.

"A woman told me that *Cruising* was the most deeply disturbing film she'd ever seen," Friedkin reports more in fascination than with glee. "She went home and had to take a bath. She felt unclean for days and weeks, and was profoundly disturbed and couldn't put her finger on why—she doesn't know whether it's because she was a woman or what."

Cruising affected most audiences in that manner. The noisy controversy over its depiction of gays only distracts from the core of what makes the film so viscerally upsetting: it is about secrets, about dark obsessions and about the individual's inability to confront the truth about himself. In choosing the subculture of S&M, Friedkin picked a secret that is both real and a metaphor, a modern Pandora's box into which he freely reached.

"I choose to make a film because I respond in some way to the subject matter and very often the subject becomes an exploration for me of what it is that's going on behind it," he says. "What was *The French Connection* all about? Was it about a lot of evil people bringing dope into this country or was it about loony, corrupt cops? I try to explore those topics within the confines of an entertainment film, not within the strict ground rules of a documentary. My films, though they seem to be on the edge of documentary, are basically my own fantasies on these subjects."

CHAPTER 11

DIVORCE OF THE CENTURY

Friedkin lines up a shot during the armaments-sale sequence in *Deal of the Century* with actors William Marquez and Chevy Chase.

COURTESY OF WARNER BROS.

"CRUISING TO ME is like a depression pill," Friedkin now feels. "It seems to me that the person who directed that film, who is remote from me, by the way—remote from how I perceive myself—was deeply depressed, clinically depressed. An extremely depressing movie. Not the subject—that's depressing enough— but it's like a flu virus, that movie. That's the only way I can describe it. It's flawed, very badly flawed, but it's also like a virus—you can't like it. When I saw it I recognized things about how I felt at the time, and what I recognized more than anything was that this is the work of a depressed person."

If Friedkin's self-diagnosis is correct, the time following *Cruising* can be seen as the nadir of his personal and professional life. The rest of 1980 had been filled with the customary search for projects and the activity of preparing *Cruising* for foreign release. He and writer Frances "Frankie" FitzGerald had become an item and spent time traveling and making appearances in the literary circles of New York and Los Angeles. He also spent time watching the Boston Celtics play, and even joining in himself.

"Billy went out to scrimmage with the team," reports A. Alan Friedberg, now a top executive with Columbia Pictures and then the president of Boston-based Sack Theatres, who housed the visiting director in the fifth-floor guest rooms in his Beacon Hill townhouse.

"My mind was boggled at the prospect of Billy Friedkin scrimmaging with the Celtics," Friedberg says, perhaps enviously.

"I remember his coming back from the scrimmage on a particular Saturday morning. I remember he was sort of winded, looking tired, and I remember a feeling of guilt that he had to go up to the fifth floor where he was staying. Well, it's funny in a way, but two weeks later he had a heart attack and I had this twang of guilt that maybe, somehow, I had contributed to that."

Friedkin denies that his heart attack altered his view of life, but a look at his subsequent films suggests otherwise. As the person involved, of course, Friedkin would be the last to see his own softening. Instead, he concentrates on the trappings of his condition: physical training, vitamins, medication to level his moods, and an omnipresent bottle of nitroglycerine pills.

But his films very clearly reflect an awareness, barely acknowledged consciously, of the frailty of human life. Prior to his hospitalization, Friedkin's films concerned themselves with the cheapness of life and how capriciously it could be spent. After, they would focus on the value of life and family. Al-

though he has never been a maker of "splatter" films that excite the baser sensibilities of the public, he has never been
reluctant to take a life on screen in order to make a point.

But after his heart attack he begins to dwell on the lives he
loses, whether it is in the gnawing sense of guilt that suffuses
the D.A. prosecuting a mass murderer in *Rampage* or the hu-
manizing of the undercover soldiers of *The C.A.T. Squad*, a genre
not known for vulnerable characters.

The first foray back into the business following his hospitalization and rehabilitation was in the unusual arena of live theater, a dream he had often discussed but never brought to
fruition.

As with his film projects, Friedkin announced several stage
productions that never happened. In 1974 he had wanted to
direct Vanessa Redgrave and Charlton Heston in *Macbeth* at
the Center Theatre Group/Ahmanson. Apparently the curse of
"the Scottish play" prevailed and the project was called off.

In September of 1977 he was set to direct David Rabe's controversial *Streamers* at the Westwood Playhouse. Friedkin, then
working with playwright Rabe to develop *Blood and Money*,
planned to start rehearsals in October and open in November.

"We're absolutely going to terrify the audience with a play
that is about the violence in everyone," producer Norman Twain
told John C. Mahoney of the *Los Angeles Times*. "I still can't
believe that I've got the best naturalistic director in the world
to direct it."*

Twain should not have banked on it; in November, instead
of starting rehearsals, Friedkin left to address preproduction
duties on *The Brink's Job* and was replaced by Milton Katselas.

By the summer of 1981, however, Friedkin was ready to make
another attempt to direct his first official theatrical work.†

Duet for One, written by Tom Kempinski, is the story of Stephanie Abrahams, a concert violinist who has been struck with
multiple sclerosis and can no longer play. Her composer-hus-
band suggests she undergo therapy with Dr. Alfred Feldmann,
a music lover as well as psychiatrist. In the course of their encounters Feldmann removes Abrahams's confident veneer to
reveal a childhood tormented by parental rejection and professional uncertainty. The violinist is said to have been modeled

---

*It is interesting, albeit senseless, to speculate on how Friedkin would have
handled the homosexual subplot in *Streamers*.
†Friedkin told *The New York Times* that he had worked in theater in the late
1950s in "Chicago's equivalent of off-Broadway." This would have been an allusion to his television gambit with Second City.

on cellist Jacqueline Du Pré, who succumbed to multiple sclerosis in 1987.

"It doesn't make much sense as a play. It's almost like taking a clinical relationship," Friedkin admits. "I'm surprised that anyone thought it was worth putting on Broadway."

It was Ellen Burstyn who brought the play, which had already opened in London, to Friedkin's attention.

"It's one of the best plays I've read," he told *The New York Times* on June 12, 1981. "I've done plays on film—*The Boys in the Band*, *The Birthday Party*—and I'm going to direct *That Championship Season* with George C. Scott.* I wish I'd been offered them as plays first. I feel as excited as though I was just starting out. The play is very simple—about the therapeutic alliance—and it's ideal for Ellen. In many ways it's director-proof. Keep it subtle and simple. If it turns out well, the direction will be unnoticed."

Friedkin committed to the play and then, he reports, Ellen Burstyn changed her mind about Max von Sydow, whom Friedkin had already contacted in Sweden and arranged to bring to New York.

Friedkin disagreed with Burstyn's sudden preference for her acting coach, Lee Strasberg, for the analyst's role. After much debate, Burstyn withdrew and was replaced by Anne Bancroft.

"At the point I got into rehearsals with Bancroft I wondered what I was doing there," Friedkin continues. "I realized I had a responsibility to these people, primarily to Max and secondarily to [producer Emanuel] Azenberg. I would have a responsibility to Ellen but I didn't agree with her and still don't. I thought that the teaming of Max and Ellen would have been terrific. And Ellen has as much or more steam than any American actress. Bancroft was occasionally brilliant; I think Ellen would have been consistently unpredictable and fantastic. But I don't think the play was.

"It was a technical, artistic challenge," he says with relish, "to do something that was so stripped down and simple and make a contribution to it without trying to put a stamp on it."

Which is the way critics reacted to the production that opened on December 27, 1981, after twelve previews and closed a short time later.

Once again able to pursue a film project, Friedkin set his sights

---

*Friedkin later separated from *That Championship Season* and sued Jason Miller to recover his expenses on the project. Miller directed the film himself with Robert Mitchum instead of Scott in the role of the basketball coach celebrated by his now-grown star team.

on Los Angeles, but not before a visit to London where, at the invitation of a friend, he attended a dinner and was introduced to actress Lesley-Anne Down.

Born in 1954 to a caretaker from Clapham, England, the stunningly attractive young woman had turned to modeling and then acting in her early teens. At the age of sixteen she began living with writer Bruce Robinson, a man ten years her senior, and appeared in such works as *Upstairs, Downstairs*, *The Pink Panther Strikes Again* and *The Great Train Robbery*. During the ninth year of her relationship with Robinson she was in Egypt starring in *Sphinx* when she met the film's assistant director, Henri Gabriel, and married him in March of 1980. Reportedly Robinson, who would later write *The Killing Fields*, was then working on a script for Down.

In October of 1981 it was reported that Down and Gabriel had separated; later she was linked in the press with designer Bill Gibb; while filming *The Hunchback of Notre Dame* in England in 1982 she met Friedkin.

"I don't believe in marriage any longer," Down told *The Hollywood Reporter* in March of that year. By that time she was carrying Friedkin's child.

After divorcing Gabriel, Lesley-Anne Down married William Friedkin on July 29, 1982. On August 30 Jack was born.

Friedkin moved ahead with his new film: a black comedy about the international arms race, *Deal of the Century*.

It was a troubled film whose problems began before the camera rolled when the Defense Department, which had originally consented to supply military equipment, suddenly backed out. Bud Yorkin, whom Friedkin had asked to produce the picture, was amazed that they had ever agreed in the first place.

"I never thought they would ever do it," Yorkin says. "When I got in, this was supposed to be a *fait accompli*. Warner Brothers had people in Washington, D.C., working on it and I must say I thought, Jesus Christ, these guys pulled off miracles. I proved to be right; why would they [the Defense Department] help this picture be made?"

Stripped of official support, Friedkin fabricated the weapons he needed and obtained props from studio storerooms.

Deal of the Century is an angry film and, like people fueled by anger, it flails wildly at its subject: the aerospace industry. Written by Paul Brickman (who repudiates it), it assumes a level of venality in each of its characters and, as such, becomes a heavy-handed ballet in which everybody tries to screw everybody else, while the public pays the bill.

Three dramatic stories interweave throughout the film. One is the plight of Luckup Industries, headed by militant Frank Stryker (Vince Edwards), a defense contractor burdened by the Peacemaker pilotless bomber. The Peacemaker has two problems: one, it has run $250 million over budget. Two, it doesn't work. And since it doesn't work, the U.S. government is unwilling to buy it. Consequently, Luckup and Stryker have to sell their expensive flying turkey to someone, anyone.

In the Latin American revolutionary country of San Miguel a free-lance used arms dealer, Eddie Muntz (Chevy Chase), is about to close a sale with a guerrilla army seeking the overthrow of General Cardosa (William Marquez). His demonstration goes well—he blows one of the general's jeeps to kingdom come—but at the riverbank exchange of cash for weapons the general's helicopters arrive and scatter the forces. Worse than his bullet wound to the foot, Eddie sees his money fly to the chopper-thrashed winds.

Broke and wounded, Eddie returns to the hotel where he is intercepted by Harold DeVoto (Wallace Shawn), a man so wired he would make a Valium nervous. DeVoto has been in his hotel room for six weeks waiting for a call from Gen. Cardosa. The purpose: to sell the general fifty Peacemaker drones for which Luckup Industries will get $300 million (mostly tax and American foreign aid money).

"They only call once," DeVoto tells Muntz in a fear-tinged tone. Moments after Muntz leaves the room, DeVoto shoots himself. Naturally, the phone then rings. Muntz answers it: it is the general's office. The sale is on.

Muntz meets with the general and his knowledgeable Colonel Salgado (Eduardo Ricard) and the deal is signed—but only if the Peacemaker works. Muntz, not knowing what he's gotten into, assures them that it does. The general gives Muntz a pair of cufflinks as a token of friendship.

It is not friendship that Catherine DeVoto (Sigourney Weaver) has on her mind when she visits Eddie Muntz in his Los Angeles house. She is the mysterious woman Muntz had tried to pick up in San Miguel and when she reveals that she is Harold DeVoto's widow and wants his sales commission, the two struggle and Muntz is shot in his foot—again. With Luckup's blessing, the two conspire to sell Gen. Cardosa the Peacemakers.

The ethics of the sale are starting to disturb Ray Kasternak (Gregory Hines), Eddie's partner in weaponry. A former test pilot known to take planes aloft for unscheduled flights, Ray

has decided to give his life to Jesus Christ and finds the idea of
war repellent, despite Eddie's assurances that it's only a business.

With the annual arms show coming up, Luckup looks forward to a demonstration of its spit-and-wire Peacemaker pro-
totype; Eddie and Catherine can almost taste Gen. Cardosa's
cash; and Ray just seeks peace for Christ even if he has to bomb
the arms show to get it.

After several subplots (involving payoff money for the general, a finessed liaison between the general and Catherine, and
a demonstration that Ray has not exactly converted to passive
resistance) it's time for the Peacemaker to put up or shut up.
When Ray steals a jet and buzzes the arms show, Stryker sees
this as the goldern opportunity to give his Peacemaker a combat test by shooting Ray out of the sky.

Ray, however, manages to shoot down the Peacemaker (after
Eddie disarms it right under Stryker's nose) and sends it crash-
ing and exploding into a quickly evacuated arms show.

Later the racist Stryker goes into public relations for the
NAACP, Ray heads to Africa to do missionary work, and Eddie
and Catherine—still not trusting each other enough to get married—move into a related field, the used car racket.

Like *Dr. Strangelove* (1964), *Deal of the Century* tackles a subject so dark that the only way to address it is with humor. But
a lot has happened to movies and movie audiences over the
twenty years that separated the two films: a war, Watergate,
and the resultant national cynicism about government and what
Dwight D. Eisenhower called the "military-industrial complex." In adapting Peter George's serious novel *Red Alert* into
Dr. Strangelove, Stanley Kubrick, Terry Southern, and George
correctly saw that the enemy was the "bomb" itself, not the
people who were not stupid enough to use it. The intervening
years had convinced a skeptical public that there were, in fact,
people stupid enough to use the bomb. People had even voted
for them. And the entire defense industry was built on that very
real and carefully nurtured fear.

This is at the heart of *Deal of the Century* and it is even articulated by Frank Stryker when he dismisses a cadre of slick advertising consultants and their mom-and-apple-pie soft-sell ad
campaign:

"We're in a battle to sell this plane, gentlemen, and our enemy is not Moscow. Our enemy is Rockwell, Northrup, Lock-
heed, McDonnell-Douglas, Grumman and the rest of our worthy
competitors, foreign and domestic. The corporate well-being

of Luckup is on the line." In other words, better dead than red ink.

In making Stryker such a strident example of aerospace venality, *Deal of the Century*, by comparison, renders Eddie Muntz's bumbling nickel-and-dimer almost likable. It hardly matters that they share the same ethics, or lack of them. The practicality of this tactic—sell to both sides in a war and you'll always have a winning customer—is expressed twice in the film. Its pragmatic presentation is by the wealthy and powerful Kayeem Masaggi (Richard Libertini, who had a small role in *Minsky's*), who informs Eddie Muntz that the more Peacemakers Muntz sells to San Miguel, the more laser guns he, Masaggi, can then sell to neighboring Costa Rica to shoot them down.

The second airing of the argument is an outraged one by Ray who insists that dual sales are immoral since they do nothing more than deprive already-deprived people of the necessities of life in a ruse to buy life-threatening weapons. By then the audience has either caught on, or never will.

As a result of such overkill, *Deal of the Century* is a compliment neither to William Friedkin nor the subject of scandal in the weapons industry. Perhaps, three years into the Reagan era of military expansion, audiences weren't interested in hearing how their tax dollars were being abused. Or perhaps they didn't want to hear it from William Friedkin.

"The aerospace industry is almost a complete fraud perpetrated not only on the American public but on the world," he said just before the film opened in November of 1983. "They build weapons that are obsolete before they go into production. They don't pass any specifications and so, when that happens, they change the specifications.

"And that's what our film is about: the chicanery that goes into the aerospace business. It's not about preserving the world for peace; it's about the making of weapons to make money. And it will never end. There will never be an end to the arms race because it is the life's blood of every nation's economy."

Just as Kubrick *et al.* had determined that *Red Alert* was too serious to take seriously, Paul Brickman had felt that the current arms race had to be mocked. Yet the choice of William Friedkin to direct a straight comedy remains a strange one (Brickman won't discuss the picture). Despite Friedkin's earlier attempts—*Good Times, The Pickle Brothers, The Night They Raided Minsky's* and *The Brink's Job*—no one with an eye on the ledger books could have failed to notice that none of these films had been a financial success. In hindsight Bud Yorkin, producer of *Deal of the Century*, agrees.

"I don't think Billy's forte is comedy and I think he learned that, despite the fact that I think he has a great sense of humor.

"There's a certain kind of discipline to comedy," he feels. "I don't think [in *Deal of the Century*] the comedy was very well done or there was very much of it in the picture. The first couple of scenes started off well and then it sort of wandered and it never did have a focus. But I think one of the problems was that there wasn't enough humor to it and nothing was very good, not as much that was legitimate."

Yorkin is right. Like all satire, *Deal of the Century* presumes a certain level of awareness of the subject from its audience, and this never happens. So what if arms dealers are money-grabbing deathmongers? This is a revelation? As the consultants dismissed by Stryker in the first scene advise, "We're going for the institutional approach to underplay the idea that we're selling weapons of death, even though that *is* the business we're in." With those cards on the table within the first five minutes, there's not much more the film can do to raise the bet.

The film works when it is at its most subtle: Chevy Chase's demonstration of weaponry to his guerrilla customers, the chicken-littered waiting room to Cardosa's office where dealers from all over the world await an audience, and Wallace Shawn's nervous scenes. Unfortunately, as *Deal of the Century* grows more outrageous, its comedy doesn't keep pace. Friedkin is so adept at staging his action sequences (the aerial combat has a genuine sense of menace) that laughter is the last reaction that seems possible.

This follows from the kind of comedy that Friedkin himself likes. Gentle satire is not his humor of choice; a direct assault on someone's dignity is more to his taste. He will use sarcasm to berate a critic, accuse an assistant of incompetence, deride a technician for malingering, or challenge an actor's abilities in front of the whole company. In each case he assumes that the recipient of his remarks is, indeed, worthy and that he is just dispensing some kind of initiation. To be ribbed by him is to be respected, however unpleasant it may be.

But a personal broadside to one's ego is far from the comedy of satire, and this is what *Deal of the Century* required. Instead, Friedkin hammers away at points that would be better expressed subtly. The nuances that reveal the humor in the duplicity of arms merchants who believe they're helping humanity are lost when they are played as ogres. If Friedkin was attempting to duplicate the style of Kubrick in *Dr. Strangelove* it is lost in the tangle of love story, swindle and deception that *Deal* contains.

The combination of Chevy Chase (Friedkin had initially wanted Bill Murray), Sigourney Weaver and Gregory Hines also fails to catch fire, partly because their characters are trying too hard to express themselves. Since each of them is riding his (and her) own agenda, one senses that they are all just double-crossing each other without ever making emotional contact.

Ironically, the credibility of *Deal of the Century* was established in late 1982 when, coincidental with production, President Ronald Reagan announced his support of the MX missile and dubbed it "The Peacekeeper." Then the government withdrew its support of the DIVAD tank, the Bradley troop transport and the B-1 bomber. Prescient as it might have been about real life, *Deal* became an "I-told-you-so" movie and was rejected by critics and public alike. Even the director now discounts it.

"I felt that *Deal of the Century* was a wonderful script about a very important idea," Friedkin says. "I missed a lot of the comedy. At a certain point I realized how sick the whole arms business was and it no longer seemed funny to me. I blew a lot of the jokes that way. People wanted to laugh—[we had] Chevy Chase and people wanted to laugh.

"Still my favorite film is probably *Deal of the Century*," Friedkin insists, enjoying the effect his unexpected appraisal creates. "And when I say favorite [I mean] the one where I had more to say than anything else I've done. I'm not saying it's my best work. I didn't achieve what I was going after, it's plain. But it's probably the most important picture that I've made. You know, the story of my career is sometimes redeemed failure and sometimes unredeemed failure. Sometimes I've failed within a shot or a sequence and was able in some way to redeem the picture, or the audience redeemed it. And other times it's unredeemed. I can't figure out what's wrong with *Deal of the Century*. That's how fucked up I am."

It was on the picture that Friedkin worked with a Los Angeles television newscaster who appeared briefly on a TV set in the background of a scene with Gregory Hines: Kelly Lange, the Emmy-winning anchorwoman for KNBC-TV.

Back in the Friedkin home in Bel Air, however, there was tension that the director—eager to distance himself from a bad *Deal* and proceed with his next film—apparently did not see. Lesley-Anne Down had appeared in the films *The Last Days of Pompeii* and *Arch of Triumph* and, in March of 1985, was in Mississippi, Missouri, Arkansas, and South Carolina shooting the television miniseries *North and South*. Stories started filtering back from the set that Down, then thirty, was having an affair with Don Fauntleroy, a member of the show's camera crew. When the production wrapped in June, Down, rather than return to California, went to England with her and Friedkin's son, Jack, for five weeks.

At that point, acccording to reports, she told Friedkin that she wasn't coming back. Friedkin found out while editing *To Live and Die in L.A.* In his zeal to finish his film he had not noticed that his wife's possessions had been systematically removed from the house.

His reaction was swift and decisive: on August 5 he filed for divorce and full custody of Jack, claiming "a series of incidents in and out of the baby's presence that reflect poor parental judgment on her part, such as alcohol, cocaine and other drug abuse," according to reports. Down, through her attorney, Marvin Mitchelson, rebutted the charges.

"I don't want to see Lesley-Anne punished," Friedkin told *People* magazine. "She needs help for these problems. I feel very concerned because she's forgotten how to be a parent. None of this means I don't love Lesley-Anne, because I do."

On August 11 Down returned to Los Angeles (staying with *North and South* costar Elizabeth Taylor) and prepared for a custody hearing on August 30—ironically, Jack's third birthday. The following March the Friedkins' divorce was granted and in October of 1986 Lesley-Anne married Fauntleroy.

Jack's fate, however, was not to be so easily settled. In arguing for custody, Friedkin contacted Jennifer Nairn-Smith and reestablished contact with their son, Cedric, then nine years old, in an effort to present himself as a fit father. When joint custody was granted by the court, William Friedkin changed his home phone number and withdrew from Nairn-Smith and Cedric. It remains Friedkin's wish to obtain full custody of Jack, who alternates between his mother's and father's homes in the company of his nanny.

CHAPTER 12

REBIRTH IN L.A.

Friedkin and his principal cast of *To Live and Die in L.A.:* (left to right) Willem Dafoe, Friedkin, John Pankow, and William Petersen

IF *DEAL OF THE CENTURY* was a gambit that swung as far afield
of a "William Friedkin film" as it was possible to go, *To Live
and Die in L.A.* offered a retrenchment, even a rebirth for its
fifty-year-old director. The newspaper ads even heralded, "The
director of *The French Connection* is on the streets again," a
blatant sales ploy (and a gnawing reminder) that made Friedkin wince.

"I don't see it as being like *The French Connection* other than
the theme, which is the thin line between the policeman and
the criminal," he repeated during public interviews. Privately,
though, he wasn't kidding himself.

"I think that's fair to say," he admitted, noting that his return to the *policier* was an attempt to recapture the spirit, and
perhaps the triumph, of his fourteen-year-old Oscar winner. But
this time there was also humility. "I've always felt that if a film
of mine doesn't work with an audience, it's not their fault," he
offered. Still, if it was humility, it was tempered:

"But most movie audiences are completely conditioned by
television to expect a happy ending, everything neatly wrapped
up, everybody who's good is all good, there's no evil in the good
characters and no good in any of the bad characters. I mean,
Citizen Kane isn't among the greatest guys who ever lived, but
to me it's the best film I've ever seen."

As a filmmaker who had walked that "thin line between the
policeman and the criminal" as often as any of his characters,
Friedkin felt at home among the Secret Service agents, stool
pigeons, and counterfeiters who peopled Gerald Petievich's novel.
Petievich, himself a former Secret Service man (he resigned from
the agency three weeks before the film's release to devote full
time to writing), had constructed a novel about a T-Man (Treasury agent) whose obsession with catching a brutal counterfeiter leads him to run against every principle he ever knew. Its
insider's view of a secret society grabbed Friedkin's interest the
moment it came across his desk in manuscript form.

"The thing that attracted me was that Petievich created these
characters with feet of clay, and he's one of them," the director says, admiringly. "It isn't like somebody came from the
outside and did a hatchet job. This is *it*. This is what
they *are*."

Friedkin's glee at discovering a milieu as real and complex
as the one he knew through Sonny Grosso, Eddie Egan and
Randy Jurgensen was not echoed by Petievich, who takes a more
cynical view of the law enforcement mindset. After all, he felt
its wrath, especially after writing a book about its dark side.

Just when the film deal was announced, Petievich—who had served fifteen years and was one of the agency's most decorated professionals—found himself the center of an investigation.

"I think there was a lot of resentment against me for making the movie," he reasons. "There was some animosity against me in the Secret Service by, number one, the agent in charge of the Los Angeles field office who, by the way, suddenly resigned a few weeks after initiating the investigation. Another agent, the one assigned to direct the investigation, was my direct rival for an impending office promotion. He was ably assisted by an office sycophant who, by the way, was immediately promoted to the position vacated when I resigned."

It's easy to see why Friedkin was attracted to Petievich's book. He was intrigued by its high-powered exposé of governmental chicken salad and chickenshit and it offered a chance to delve into arcane behavior and hidden secrets, all pushed together into a story of an insider who becomes an outsider merely by doing his job. William Friedkin felt a kinship with Petievich's main character, the aptly named Richard Chance. Hell, he could *be* Richard Chance.

To Live and Die in L.A. would be shot nonunion. Such a move would represent considerable savings over a fully staffed IATSE* crew and streamline the size of the company that Friedkin felt encumbered feature film production.

But respect for a budget was a lesson he had painfully learned, and it was part of the financing plan put together by SLM Productions, a tribunal of financiers comprised of Samuel Schulman, Irving H. Levin and Angelo Marquetti. Their interests were divided between sports and movies, as were Friedkin's; he had known Schulman and Levin since they formed National General Pictures in the late 1960s to distribute *The Boys in the Band.*

Friedkin and SLM intended *To Live and Die in L.A.* to kick off a ten-picture, $100 million deal with Twentieth Century-Fox, for whom he had made *The French Connection* fourteen years earlier. A once-grand studio that had been passed down through a succession of owners who were more interested in its Century City real estate than its filmmaking legacy, the company had recently been purchased by media magnate Rupert Murdoch, primarily for its film library and ability to feed his proposed

---

*International Alliance of Theatrical Stage Employees, Hollywood's main technical union.

Fox TV network. When Murdoch's personnel came aboard, SLM no longer felt comfortable.

"He pulled his whole deal," Friedkin said of Levin, "and he took the whole ten-picture deal to MGM."

But Friedkin remained saddled with a relatively low $8 million budget (for which, according to trade reports, he and SLM were equally responsible), a reality he stoically accepted as the penalty for a decade of less-than-triumphant box offices. Besides, if this first film worked out, he and SLM were ready to embark on a second picture: *Judgment Day,* which columnist Pete Hamill was scripting from the novel by Bob Lancaster and B. C. Hall. Like *To Live and Die in L.A.* it would have to come in at $8 million, but this time Friedkin could have the option of hiring big-name stars—as long as their salaries came out of his half of the possible profits.

Consequently, Friedkin was forced to determine early in its life that *To Live and Die in L.A.* would not be a star vehicle. Or, if there was to be a star, it would be the director.

His actors found validity in such a decision.

"I remember specifically at the beginning of the process, Billy wanted these guys to come out of seemingly nowhere so that he wouldn't have to deal with the baggage of identification with another character," explains Willem Dafoe, who took the role of Eric Masters, the counterfeiter. "I think that was important to him because obviously the casting process was weirdly low profile."

William L. Petersen, a young Chicago actor hired to play Chance, agrees not only with Friedkin's antistar attitude but with Dafoe's recollections about the casting process: acting in Canada, he was asked to fly to New York to meet Friedkin. Half a page into his cold reading, the director told him he had the job.

"I really thought they were nuts," Petersen recalls of Friedkin and his casting director, Bob Weiner. "I thought all the things I'd heard were true and that Billy was sitting in his apartment in New York offering a lead in a movie to everybody that comes in the door. I was gonna walk into a bar in New York and there's gonna be fifteen of us doing the lead in Bill Friedkin's next movie."

On a roll, Petersen called fellow Chicagoan John Pankow and walked him into Friedkin's apartment the next day suggesting him for the role of Vukovich, Chance's partner.

"He took Pankow on the spot," Petersen says, almost giddy. "Pankow and I walked out on the street and I had to get back to the airport, and he and I just looked at each other and said, 'He just cast us both in a movie.' And the last thing we said before he got in a cab to go downtown was, 'Well, this was a riot; if it happens, great. If it doesn't happen, at least we'll have something to tell our children: that we met Friedkin just before he went completely nuts.' "

Nuts or not, it reflected the desire to make a movie as quickly as possible with gut-level impact and the exquisite kind of energy that can only come from working close to the edge.

The story befit its treatment. Richard Chance (William L. Petersen) is a member of the elite Secret Service of the United States Department of the Treasury. In reality, *elite* doesn't describe the job; although best known for their high profile work such as jumping in front of any bullet meant for the President, T-Men are just as readily assigned to cases as gritty as chasing a guy through the slums over a credit card scam.

Chance and his partner, Jim Hart (Michael Greene), have run the gamut and Hart has had his fill. After a harrowing escapade dispatching a bomb-wrapped terrorist atop one of Los Angeles's finer hotels, Hart declares, "I'm gettin' too old for this shit," and vows to take his retirement when it comes up in a few days. He has one job remaining, though—tracking down a lead on Eric Masters, a brilliant but dangerous counterfeiter.

Chance—who has just given his partner a fishing rod as a token of their friendship—wants to go along, but Hart forbids it. The next day, when Hart is shotgunned to death by Masters and a henchman (Jack Hoar), Chance resolves to bring the counterfeiter to justice—any kind of justice will do—and his outrage begins to boil over.

Masters is not a typical criminal. He is careful. He is also an artist—a painter—who compulsively burns every canvas he creates. He is also a businessman, although his method of making cash is not in the national interest. Above all, he is smart; he's beaten prior arrests with a mixture of cunning and a sharp lawyer, Bob Grimes (Dean Stockwell).

Chance and his newly assigned partner, John Vukovich (John Pankow), have no illusions that Masters will be easy to catch. One of their impediments is their office captain, Thomas Bateman (Robert Downey, Sr.), and his bureaucratic aversion to wiretaps, entrapment money, flimsy search warrants, or anything beyond "the book." Chance now must not only avenge his dead partner but break in a new one—Vukovich—who has not yet come to understand the sacred relationship that team-

work demands, even beyond the laws they have sworn to uphold.

Masters, meanwhile, faces his own organizational problems.
His mule, Carl Cody (John Turturro), is busted at the L.A. airport carrying $40,000 in play dough and faces five years in jail.
Because of Hart's death Masters's lawyer cannot win bail for
Cody. Masters brazenly visits Cody in jail and learns that the
bust may have been set up by Max Waxman, a former hippie
lawyer who now moves paper for him, and who probably kept
the $40,000 plus another $560,000 that he said he entrusted to
Cody. Cody is outraged but promises silence; Masters assures
him enigmatically that he will not have to do his entire time
in jail.

Chance now pushes his chief informant (and sometimes girlfriend) Ruthie (Darlanne Fleugel) for a lead to Masters. She
gives him Waxman's name. Chance and Vukovich establish a
stakeout in a seminary across from Waxman's house/law office
hoping to catch Waxman and Masters in a funny-money exchange.

Instead, Masters, believing Cody's assertion that they have
both been stung by Waxman, dispatches his girlfriend, Bianca
Torres (Debra Feuer), to the lawyer's house to test his story.
When Waxman propositions her, Masters suddenly bursts into
the room and shoots him, taking the $560,000 Waxman had
stashed.

Across the street, however, Chance and Vukovich have fallen
asleep. They are awakened by the sound of police cars responding to a call about Waxman's murder. It is obvious that the
police and the T-Men are at odds, but when Chance and Vukovich return to the field office, Chance produces Waxman's appointment book which he had purloined from the murder scene.
Vukovich is horrified at this breach of police procedure but
promises loyalty to his partner.

Chance now makes Masters his career. Every credit card
bust, every interrogation, every lead is checked to compile a
profile of his prey. When Ruthie can offer nothing new, Chance
threatens her with revocation of her parole (only after they
have made love). Desperate, she offers him a tip: a bagman is
about to arrive in town carrying $50,000 to buy stolen dia-
monds. Not enough, Chance tells her; he needs something on
Masters.

Masters meanwhile contracts with Jeff Rice (Steve James),
who moves fake bills for him in the L.A. ghetto, to arrange Cody's
murder behind prison walls. Rice's price is Master's specialty:
counterfeit money.

When Cody's killing is bungled, Chance sees the opportunity to squeeze him into testifying against Masters. Cody refuses—he won't betray *his* partner—but says he will lead Chance to Masters's print shop as long as he doesn't have to face him in open court. Chance agrees.

That night Masters visits Rice to demand return of the advance money for Cody's murder. When Rice tells him he's already spent it and tries to put up a fight, Masters and his henchman demolish him along with his friends. His loot recovered (despite Rice's claims), Masters burns it (as he so often destroyed his paintings) and then makes love to Bianca while his videotape cameras voyeuristically record it all.

The next day Chance, flirting with insubordination, obtains a court order to spring Cody for the purpose of leading him to Masters's shop. Along the way, Cody escapes.

This twist brings the already tense relationship between Chance and Vukovich to a meltdown. Nevertheless, Vukovich bites on an offer from Masters's lawyer, Grimes, to lure Masters into a trap; Grimes insists he's tired of his client pushing him around. Posing as two out-of-town businessmen, Vukovich and Chance meet Masters socially and arrange to buy $30,000 worth of his fake currency. Although he's skeptical of their identities, Masters's arrogance compels him to continue talking with the pair.

The Treasury, however, in the person of Capt. Bateman, will not authorize more than $10,000 for the sting—a bottom line that assures Masters that no T-Man will ever get close to him. Desperate for the entire $30,000, Chance returns to Ruthie for more information on the visiting bagman for the jewelry caper. He then convinces Vukovich to help him intercept the bagman, figuring that no crook is going to run to the police to say he was held up by the wrong guys.

The sting does not go smoothly: although Chance and Vukovich manage to take the cash, their confused bagman is mysteriously shot by a sniper. Chance and Vukovich flee in their unmarked car pursued by an absurd number of gunmen. They escape by driving the wrong way up the Long Beach Freeway but are shaken by the experience. Nevertheless, they now have the money to pay Masters.

The next morning Capt. Bateman announces to his staff that an FBI undercover officer had been killed yesterday and that the two men who robbed him of his sting money have escaped.

Vukovich is now terrified. He visits Grimes for help. Grimes advises him to turn in Chance.

At about the same time, Chance is meeting with Masters to arrange the drop-off. He also follows a lead and recaptures Cody at Cody's girlfriend's apartment. Then he calls Vukovich to tell him that that night they will arrest Masters.

When Vukovich and Chance encounter Masters and his deadly henchman, they pull their guns but the henchman is faster and shoots Chance to death. Masters escapes. Vukovich chases Masters and locates him in a warehouse where he is burning his entire workshop. Masters chides Vukovich for snubbing Grimes's offer of trading Chance's neck for his own—everything had been a fix all along—and knocks Vukovich unconscious, preparing to burn him alive. Vukovich recovers, however, and shoots Masters, who is then swallowed by flames.

The next morning Grimes visits Masters's house and finds Bianca moving out, taking with her not the videotapes she had made with Masters but, instead, a woman named Serena, whom Masters once offered her for sex.

Also that morning Vukovich drives Chance's vehicle to Ruthie's apartment where she, too, is packing. Vukovich stops her and tells her that she now belongs to him, just as she did to Chance. The sun sets on another day of life and death in Los Angeles.

Although the basic plot, characters, and much of the dialogue of *To Live and Die in L.A.* are drawn from Petievich's novel, the film adds such touches as the opening terrorist sequence, the car chase and a much clearer (and earlier) focus on the showdown between Chance and Masters. Friedkin and Petievich differ on the genesis of those changes.

"Billy called me up and said he wanted to collaborate with me on the screenplay," Petievich recalls. "He wrote a good number of scenes. When there was a new scene or the story needed to be changed, he'd have me write that. So we worked together on it."

Friedkin: "I put Gerry Petievich's name on it because he did create create characters and situations. I used a lot of his dialogue and I felt that he was entitled to have his name up there with mine even though I wrote the whole script. He couldn't, because he was back working on the job."

Compared with the tedium of shooting a big-studio release, Friedkin embraced the relative freedom his independent production accorded. William Petersen discovered this looseness early on.

"It was in the first week of shooting that I had ever done in a movie," he recalls. "We were shooting the scene where I come out of the bar with my partner, Michael Greene, and go over to my truck and I give him a fishing pole, and he goes and sits down, and I say some things. Well, that's a one-camera [shot]. We're in the bar and we're gonna rehearse it. We had a second assistant director in the bar, we sorta mapped out where we would walk, we had been miked, and Billy says, 'Let's get a rehearsal in here.' Doors open, blah, blah, blah, I come over, blah, blah, blah, give him the rod, get in the truck, cut. And Billy's talking to [Robbie] Muller [the cinematographer]. He goes, 'Yeah, I got it.' Billy's got the whole crew there. He goes, 'We're done. We're done, we got it.' He looks over to the sound man: 'You got that?' Everybody expected this to be a rehearsal but Billy, just before, said to shoot it. Not Robbie Muller, not Louis [Jean-Louis DuCarme] the sound guy, not us, not anybody thought we wouldn't do another one. I was amazed he shot it, first of all, but it was a first *rehearsal*, not even the first *take*, of a long shot. And we never did another one. He just said, 'Everybody go home.' Everybody's just standing there, and then everybody starts panicking—*did* we get it? Is *this* gonna be in the movie?"

It was. The tentative performance between Petersen and Greene looks like the reluctant affection demonstrated between partners. Friedkin knew that the audience would accept one as the other.

That decisive but unpredictable attitude is a chemistry that few actors can resist, and it drove Friedkin's crew crazy. It was not beyond the director to tell Petersen and Darlanne Fleugel to devise their own blocking, talk to each other, and just let the cameraman worry about keeping them in frame.

"I'm not going to tell these guys where to go," he would tell Muller. "Just shoot them. Try and keep them in the frame. If they're not in the frame, they're not in the movie. That's their problem." The scene happened to be in the sleazy bar when Fleugel (as Ruthie) tells Chance about the visiting bagman. It was a complex dance of mutual deception between the characters.

"Robbie Muller would come over to us before a take," Petersen recalls, "and he'd say, 'I know I'm not supposed to be talking to you or anything, but could you, like, stay by the bar?' That's why [it is good] working with a director like Bill Friedkin, who knows how to push the buttons; all you do is use your instincts."

Having a crew that could think on its feet enabled Friedkin

to thrive in the same atmosphere that had attracted him to the quickness of film in the first place. And as usual, he responded to authority by doing an end run around it.

One of the film's most electric scenes called for Chance and Vukovich to chase Carl Cody through a metal alarm at Los Angeles International Airport and finally collar him in the men's room. Airlines have an aversion even to snapshots being taken around their security areas, but those at LAX had agreed—up to a point, which Friedkin quickly exceeded. He wanted Petersen to set off the alarm and race past the crowd by running on top of the divider between the terminal's moving sidewalks.

"We were not going to be allowed to run on that thing," Petersen recalls with conspiratorial glee. "So we mapped out doing it the other way so all these guys could see it. Then Billy says, 'Action,' and we did it. I run through the crowds, knock people and jump up onto the divider and Robbie had me. Then all these guys come down and Billy goes to me, 'What did you do? We're not allowed to do that! How dare you do that! And later Billy and I were slappin' skin. I guess the guys at LAX were afraid we'd start something, that that's how people would get to the baggage claim from now on."

Behind the glee of stealing shots from strait-laced authority figures, there was a deadly serious conflict going on in *To Live and Die in L.A.*: would Chance live or die?

As American movies move increasingly toward pandering to the expectations of the audience, rather than challenging the audience with something new, more and more pictures are forced to have happy endings, even artifical ones. Writers and directors seeking green lights for their projects know to submit only "upbeat" material with "sympathetic" characters regardless of the contortions that these demands induce.

Although it had been in Friedkin's mind to make Chance a dead man as early as the day he cast Petersen to play him, it was not a *fait accompli* until the actual murder scene was to be filmed.

Bud Smith, the film's editor and second unit director, reports that Vukovich was supposed to be the one who was shot, not Chance.

"Billy came to me and said, 'I just had a thought. What do you think of this?' and we sat down and talked about shooting Petersen and I said, It's your star! If you have people loving this guy, they're really going to destroy you. On the other hand, as a creative filmmaker, why not? That's great! Now you've left this other guy [Vukovich] and what's he going to do? He already fucked up, and he's totally destroyed in his brain and everything is against him; they're doing the wrong thing. He transforms into being this macho guy, which he really wasn't, to go after the killer and take over the girl."

The switch excited both Petersen and Friedkin, who insisted on pulling the trigger himself.

In the actual edited sequence—which is a complex series of moves among Willem Dafoe, Jack Hoar, William Petersen, and John Pankow—Hoar whips out a shotgun and blasts Petersen in the face.

"He shot me with a gun, a real *gun*," says Petersen of Friedkin. "With a paint shell. We wanted it to be real. I didn't want to anticipate, so this guy put together a rifle and I could turn at any time and he nailed me. He stands next to the camera with a paint machine and he tells the actor to turn and he shoots him in the face full of blood. It's simple. It's Filmmaking 101 and most directors get away from it. Billy never does. He's still a kid on the playground."

In January of 1985, after the completion of principal photography, a meeting was called at Irving Levin's Beverly Hills house on a Sunday morning. The room quickly split into two camps: those who now wanted Chance to live (and make the film more commercial, possibly even worthy of a sequel) and those who felt that Chance, having crossed the ethical line, must die.

To pacify SLM Friedkin, Petievich, Smith, Pankow, Petersen, and second unit cinematographer Bob Yeoman shot an alternative ending which satisfied no one (and was probably designed for that purpose). In it, Chance and Vukovich are seen in an office in what Petievich calls "the wilds of Alaska" where, having disgraced the agency, they have been exiled. There, on television, they suffer the ignominy of watching their pencil-pushing boss, Capt. Bateman, taking credit for the case.

"He shot it, we cut it in and dubbed it, and previewed it and then he took it out and threw it away," says Smith economically.

Other gambits weren't so easily dismissed. With the Treasury Department already upset because of Petievich's presence, their concern escalated when they learned that part of the story involved printing counterfeit money on screen.

In the film Masters positions four crisp, new twenty-dollar bills on a copy stand, exposes a lithograph negative, carefully makes color separations into black and green, and blissfully runs off millions on standard office machinery.

"I did learn to print money," Willem Dafoe admits, advising

playfully, "You know, it's not the *making* of the money that's the hard part. The big problem is *passing* the stuff."

Which is just what happened with some of the prop money used in the film when the son of one of the crew members mistook a souvenir twenty-dollar bill for the real thing and tried to buy some candy with it at a local store.

"It was only printed on one side," defends Bud Smith, who shot the sequence in which it was used. "It was pretty obvious. But if that hadn't happened, there wouldn't have been any question about it and the FBI wouldn't have gotten involved."

"They sent three agents in from Washington to screen [the film] while it was still in workprint stage. I refused to give it to them," Friedkin reports. "I told 'em to go and get a subpoena and I reminded them that it was a First Amendment issue. But they interviewed twelve or fifteen members of the crew, including me; I even offered to show the film to the Secretary of the Treasury and if he said there's anything in it that's a danger to the national security, I'd take it out. That was the last I heard of it."

Whatever pressures the government or SLM might apply to Friedkin it was nothing compared to the squeeze he put on himself. Working in the same genre as *The French Connection,* he felt the need to address the most memorable element of that earlier film, the one that drew the most repeat business: the chase.

"I can't remember five memorable chase scenes in the sound era," he states, "and yet I think that people perceive the chase as a cinematic staple. They're very worthwhile for an audience when they work and they're as valid as any other kind of scene in a film because they're drawing on pure cinematic elements. But they're very, very hard to do. I wasn't able to think up a chase for twelve years. Believe me, I thought about it. This one contains elements of stuff that I'd thought about for years; I just haven't been able to put it together."

The scene is Chance's and Vukovich's escape up the Long Beach Freeway. It had its genesis on February 25, 1963, when Friedkin was driving his red Valiant home from Red Quinlan's wedding in Chicago. It was snowing, the wind was whipping off the lake, the wipers were useless in the blizzard and Friedkin nodded off at the wheel only to wake up in the wrong lane with oncoming traffic heading straight for him. He swerved back to his side of the road and thought, for the next twenty years, "How am I going to be able to use this?"

The chase in *To Live and Die in L.A.* took twenty-two days to shoot, a schedule that included three weekends during which sections of the Long Beach Freeway near Wilmington were closed for four hours at a time to enable the crew of over seventy stunt players to stage the planned chaos involving cars, trucks, and semis. It was a permission rarely granted by traffic authorities; not since the cancellation of the *CHiPs* television series had large-scale production been allowed. But because Los Angeles has so many alternate routes, and given Friedkin's stature in the industry, it was approved.

With the delays, *To Live and Die in L.A.* ran a reported one million dollars over budget. With the switch from Fox to MGM (and the residual ill feelings all around) there were rumblings from the exhibition sector that the film was in trouble, but these were dispelled when it premiered in 1,200 theaters—the widest opening ever for a Friedkin picture—on November 1, 1985.

It is easily his most electric and well-realized work since *Sorcerer* and codifies a number of the themes he had explored, to varying degrees, before and has continued to touch upon since. Forsaking the gritty, edge verisimilitude of Owen Roizman's earlier New York camera work, Friedkin chose German cinematographer Robbie Muller's sensual, pastel Los Angeles palette to form the counterpoint for a story of beautiful people who do ugly things. The Friedkin-Muller L.A. (with production designer Lilly Kilvert) is a paradise that devours people and, unlike New York, is all the more vicious because its surface appears so serene.

That duality is embodied in the characters of both Chance and Masters, two men who are moved by a mission whose agenda grows from deep within them. They are not merely doing jobs, they are living a grand scheme.

Masters, particularly, shares much of Friedkin's inner turmoil and ennui. Neither is satisfied with his work and enjoys a certain cynical thrill when others express their appreciation. Unlike Friedkin, Masters's only artistic success comes by copying the work of others (such as the Treasury Department).

In Friedkin's eyes this artistic immorality is as damning as Masters's criminal transgressions; not only will Masters die at the end of the film, but all earthly traces of him and his work will also be utterly destroyed in the same fire—a fitting fate. Contrast this with Chance who, though physically dead, flashes onto the screen as the last image the audience sees before leaving the theater (appropriately, it's from a lovemaking scene).

Within this contest comes the story which starts like a routine "a man's got to avenge his partner" melodrama and quickly escalates. This increasing divergence from formula is unsettling, and Friedkin develops its promise. Chance's vow, "I'm gonna bag Masters and I don't give a shit how I do it," becomes Friedkin's license to constantly challenge the audience. He even forces the viewers to identify passionately with Chance, who ultimately betrays them.

Friedkin's oft-used obsession with betrayal is most profound to *To Live and Die in L.A.* Its double-crosses would fill a corkscrew factory: Grimes, the lawyer, turns against his client, Masters; Rice steals from Masters; Ruthie exposes Ling, the bagman and places Chance in jeopardy; Cody escapes from Chance by lying about his daughter; Max Waxman steals from Masters and hits on Bianca; Bianca switches her sexual preference and Chance ultimately betrays the law in order too uphold it. The only one who survives relatively blameless is Captain Bateman, the pencil-pushing L.A. bureau chief. This is Petievich's assurance that the system continues to function despite the loose cannons within it.

Friedkin's other fascination is with illusion, and that becomes the film's strongest metaphor. It can be as purposely manipulative as a drop of red liquid that hits Masters's metal printing plate—at first assumed to be blood and then revealed to be the photographic developer for the latent image. Or it can be enigmatically misleading, such as when Masters goes backstage after a modern dance performance and kisses one of the male performers; a cut reveals the dancer to be female (in actuality, Friedkin had a slim man stand in for the rear angle and substituted actress Debra Feuer for the front shot).

"It was a practical thing in the respect that he wanted that to happen," Willem Dafoe says of Friedkin's design of that scene. "He wanted the audience to go, 'Oh, my God, he's kissing a man.' A woman's back looks different than a man's back, so they wanted to shoot it that way. The guy wasn't terrifically muscular—he had a slender back—but it was obviously a man's back. You just wonder what's going on. You get ahead of the film and say, 'The guy's gay,' and then, 'Oh, no he isn't.' It's the kind of jogging around that's one of Billy's talents. That one's quite broad because people tend to be so incredibly homophobic and that's titillating, but I kind of like it. And it's also going back to setting his girlfriend up with another woman; there's something about this guy that is beyond the norm."

The constant illusion in the film, of course, is the counterfeit money that is the catalyst for all the characters' actions. But if money is not to be trusted, what is?

Money in civilized society is a tangible representation of worth. When the money becomes fake, the systems society has devised begin to crumble. Unless money has value, something else soon replaces it. In *To Live and Die in L.A.* the new currency is sex.

Sex is what Ruthie is forced to pay to Chance to prevent him from pulling the plug on her parole. Sex is what Masters gives to Bianca as a gift (and it is important that when he has sex with her, he videotapes it, as though illusion is the only reality to him); sex is the commission that Waxman wants from Bianca; it is what delays Cody at his girlfriend's long enough for Chance to find him; it is what first leaps to Ruthie's mind (through flash intercuts) when Vukovich tells her she's now working for him; and it is the price that Masters exacts from Waxman when he shoots him in the genitals.

That particular brand of violence is what reopened the *Cruising* controversy when Clarke Taylor, a writer for the *Los Angeles Times*, published an interview on November 30 with Willem Dafoe shortly after *To Live and Die in L.A.* had opened. Dafoe was quoted by Taylor as saying, "The violence, *per se*, doesn't bother me—it's a violent world. But what does bother me is the kind of latent homosexual violence that Billy Friedkin really grooves on." According to the interview, Dafoe added that he had disagreed with the director's instructions:

"I do get annoyed when you are told to be aggressive or sadistic when the character isn't always required to be. I'd suggest a lighter touch and Billy would say, 'It's inappropriate.' "

Friedkin's reaction to the Taylor interview was swift: he sued the paper for $15 million when the *Times* refused to print a retraction. Said defense attorney Jeffrey Klein, the *Times* "will defend itself against the libel suit with vigor. We believed the article in question was accurate."

Lee A. Casey, Friedkin's attorney, differed, and went so far as to divorce Dafoe from any inclusion in the lawsuit. "It is our client's consideration," Casey said of Friedkin, "that in falsely attributing these statements to Mr. Dafoe, the *Times* and Mr. Taylor have libeled him."

The case was settled quietly three years later; neither side will disclose the agreement.

It shouldn't be surprising that sex is the currency in a film set in Los Angeles; it doesn't even have to be genital sex. Chance, in particular, derives satisfaction of a near sexual level from just doing his job and pushing it to the limits. He is thrilled to be part of a car chase which, at any instant, might cost him his life; he vibrates with nervous (sexual?) energy at the prospect of nailing Masters; he even refers to his base-jumping experience (free-falling from great heights tethered by a slack rope) in sexual terms: "It's the greatest feeling you'll ever have, man. You float out and your balls go up into your throat."

Much has been made of the violent ways in which Chance and, especially, Masters carry out their missions. The film is strewn with ways of killing and injuring people that have seldom been explored in a reputable (that is, non-slasher) film. Realistically speaking, these grow out of the outrages they are used to punish.

"The choice for Rick Masters to shoot Waxman in his groin is understandable," Willem Dafoe defends. "Waxman was trying to shtup his girlfriend."

Adds Petersen matter-of-factly, "That's where people *get* shot! That's how I looked at it. You talk to a cop who's been to see one of his buddies who's been shot and, nine times out of ten, it's their face that's been blown off, or their balls have been blown off in a domestic thing. That doesn't mean that people don't get shot in the hand—just not in Billy's movies. They're not about wounding."

Petievich, though, is pointedly baffled by some of Friedkin's additions, especially those involving sex.

"We had some discussions about that and I still don't really see what it has to do with the story," says the author. "I'm big on anything that's interesting about human behavior but it really had nothing to do with the story. You find that in all of his work. There's a fascination with that, I think, and I don't really understand it."

To Live and Die in L.A. ably reminded the industry that when Friedkin had a subject that intrigued him he could direct it in unmatched style. Ironically, the film was attacked for its use of violence in an age when audiences were flocking to see such fare as *Friday the 13th* and *A Nightmare on Elm Street*, among the most graphic and anatomically explicit gore pictures in the history of the industry. But nobody takes those films seriously. Friedkin, however, was dealing with real characters, and audiences, when confronted with its honesty, were repulsed as much by what they found in themselves as by what they saw on the screen.

The press and the public found the film too violent and cynical; by the end of December it had grossed only $13 million. Although it became hugely successful on home video, its initial failure cannot be ignored. *To Live and Die in L.A.* contains the same elements as any Charles Bronson, Clint Eastwood or Arnold Schwartzenegger blockbuster hit vehicle that pits one rebellious man against vengeful enemies. The difference is that Friedkin gives his characters feet of clay when audiences crave macho, if completely unrealistic, superheroes. *To Live and Die in L.A.* is a tough, complex movie that refuses to provide easy answers. Its deaths are real, its characters' anguish can be shared, and the world it depicts is unquestionably authentic.

All of Friedkin's films had led him to this point but suddenly he was out of place in the very industry he had helped to educate. It was an irony that drove him back to his roots, only this time with the prestige and power to have it his way. William Friedkin returned to television.

CHAPTER 13

TV OR NOT TV

Director Friedkin rehearses Deborah Van Valkenburgh and Steve James before shooting a scene for the television movie *C.A.T. Squad: Python Wolf* in 1987.

WITH RARE EXCEPTIONS, the road that leads from television to feature film is traveled only once. The prestige, time, money, and artistic freedom in feature-length motion pictures are goals to which most television directors aspire, yet are seldom offered. The filmmaker who returns to television does so at great risk to his career, for it is an electronic Rubicon not lightly crossed.

In the spring of 1985 William Friedkin was approached by writer-producer Philip DeGuere, who was then reviving *The Twilight Zone* for CBS television.

"He sent me a letter before they went into production, and a bunch of scripts," Friedkin recalls, "and said, 'I know you won't do anything for television but here are a bunch of scripts. I think they're very good, they're by some of the better writers of the genre: Arthur C. Clarke, Ray Bradbury, Stephen King, Harlan Ellison'—all guys I like. So I started reading the scripts and I read one that he wrote called *Nightcrawlers* and I thought it was great—a twenty-minute film."

Nightcrawlers (from a short story by Robert R. McCammon) is told in the form of a nightmare. A state trooper (James Whitmore, Jr.) visits a roadside diner one stormy night to report that a nearby motel has been shot to pieces and to beware of strangers who may stop by. Almost immediately a haggard-looking young man (Scott Paulin) arrives to request black coffee.

He reveals that he is a Vietnam veteran who was in a combat unit called the Nightcrawlers and, when pressed for a war story, relates one so frightening that the trooper who asked for it is shattered. The soldier, Price, adds that he and others were sprayed with some sort of secret chemical and that they have developed the ability to conjure hallucinations that are so vivid that they actually come alive. When he made the mistake of falling asleep at a local motel, he says, "a little piece of the war came home."

The trooper is now convinced that Price committed the motel massacre and blocks his exit by knocking him unconscious. As Price passes out, combat troops suddenly assault the diner and the people in it. The trooper is killed and the cook is shot by Price's "imaginary" army and the entire structure is leveled before Price himself is executed by his own living nightmare.

The diner's survivors are in terror. They know that there are at least four others with this power out there, somewhere.

Friedkin was impressed enough with DeGuere's script to want to direct it; subsequently, his participation served to legitimize the show in the eyes of other filmmakers and made DeGuere's producing job considerably easier.

Two obstacles immediately presented themselves: first, Oscar-winning directors just don't do TV and, equally sticky, the story was excessively violent.

The first problem solved itself by virtue of Friedkin's reputation for unconventionality. Nobody tells Friedkin what to do and, anyway, short-form television with the kind of budget that *Nightcrawlers* would have (including the construction of an entire exterior set inside a studio) was hardly a step down.

The *Nightcrawlers* violence was another matter. The script called for a virtual war, numerous fiery car explosions, dozens of squib (special effects gunshots) and two instances where people are shot in full camera view. Additionally there was some rough language, graphic descriptions of the horrors of war, and the endangerment of a child. It would be hard to compile a more complete list of how to make a network censor nervous.

"The network, surprisingly enough, recognized from the beginning that it was special material and required special handling," Phil DeGuere remembers with a vestige of astonishment. "It was clear going in that what we wanted to do required a fair degree of integrity and the censors were extremely accommodating. Frankly, I had expected them to be more cantankerous than they were.

"The only thing that bothered them was the actual bullet hit on James Whitmore, Jr.'s back when he was shot," DeGuere continues. "Billy went ahead and shot it anyway. They were very upset when they saw this in dailies and we promised them that we would edit it in such a way that it was extremely difficult to tell whether you were seeing the hits. The way we avoided it was by not putting specific gunshots on the soundtrack."

Friedkin, too, is amazed that the show was permitted to air with so little interference.

"The guy who heads Standards and Practices said it's the most intense television he'd ever seen, and he let it go on," he reports.

Nightcrawlers runs without commercial interruption. Its power comes not only from its sheer drama but also by tapping Americans' lingering doubts about the war in Vietnam, postbattle stress syndrome, Agent Orange and the reasons for the conflict itself. Only a fantasy such as *The Twilight Zone* could attempt such realism.

"It was intense," Friedkin feels. "It really got to what the war had done to a lot of guys and it did so in the context of a nightmare-horror film."

Moreover, he found the television format more invigorating than it was when he left it in 1966.

"What was good," he says like an athlete just back from a workout, "was that I felt the necessary pressure of working faster, pressure that you don't feel on a movie set. And yet they let me work at my own pace; there was nobody who'd come around and say, 'Jeez, we ought to have a few more shots in the can.' "

"With a director of his stature and experience he was afforded a great deal more latitude by the studio than other directors," producer DeGuere explains. "The project went significantly over budget but it was one of those things where nobody complained very much because there was absolutely no evidence that it was any lack of preparation or lack of competency on Billy's part that was causing it."

DeGuere, who had been awed by *Sorcerer*, learned a lot about the creative process in watching Friedkin, editor Bud Smith and the series' supervising producer James Crocker complete the episode.

"I have discovered—in working with over a hundred directors in my television experience—that directors, especially in their first cuts [first edited version before the producer changes it] tend to be apologetic about their own material. Well, let me put it this way: good directors tend to be apologetic; bad directors can't tell the difference.

"When I watched Billy's cut I was amazed. He was doing exactly the same thing that the best television directors would do.

"With most television directors there's an understanding that the producer is the boss and it's a lot easier with creative people if everybody knows the rules going in. Billy had gotten angry with me a couple of times and had threatened to pull his name off the picture. Finally, one time, he told me he was going to take his name off and I had just had it with him and I said, 'Come on, just drop the bullshit with me. There's no way you're going to do that.' And it shut him up."

Nightcrawlers' intensity comes as much from its gothic look as from its technique, which is more like that of a film than a television episode. Long dolly shots, complex blocking, sustained monologues and near expressionistic use of light and shadow distinguish the program's style. Scott Paulin's unbroken speeches reach such a level of clenched power that no reactive cutaways are needed.

The pyrotechnics (gunshots, bazooka rounds, cars being blown apart, flames shooting out, sparks and glassware flying all over) are intensified on the soundtrack and are far above the polite, discreet pops that most TV shows use. The phantom assault on the diner in *Nightcrawlers* comes out of a backlit, smoky darkness as remote from homefront America as Vietnam was from sanity. The impact is complete—and all in twenty continuous minutes.

Enthused with the idea of dragging television into new areas, Friedkin agreed to direct three music videos—ordinarily a way for artists to flex their cinematic muscles without committing to an entire feature project.

For Laura Branigan's "*Self-Control*," he employed sensual images that were far from controlled—whips and chains—and raised eyebrows in a medium where eyebrows are frequently already at half-mast.

"It was like an X-rated video," he says, adding proudly, "It was censored all over the world. A little three-minute video about sexual obsession."

As Laura Branigan sleeps in her bed awaiting sunset a tiny doll sits with its arms outstretched beckoning us into this abstract world where colors shift and lights flash with orgasmic intensity.

"I live among the creatures of the night," Branigan sings, and on screen she begins her rounds through a vinyl nighttown of hustlers, symbols and fantasies. Store windows open to reveal erotic shapes; children flee from her living playground; she walks the wrong way on a street of no return. At last she meets a faceless stranger who beckons her into a netherworld of men and women who paw her, entice her, desire her—and she them, but it is both repulsive and compelling. Eventually the faceless stranger brings her home and they consummate their passion, only to have him vanish with the sunrise. It is then that she turns to her side and sees a man next to her in bed—the man she really did bring home with her—and he, too, has his face covered with the same white mask as the alluring stranger. The toy doll now winks at us "*Self-Control*" fades into the sun.

The video (which runs just over five minutes) is elaborate in its erotic imagery but, on close inspection, is revealed as just that—imagery. Everyone is fully clothed, no untoward caressing actually takes place, and the shot that threatened the video with being banned from MTV—a flash of Branigan's breast—

has been harmlessly excised. But the cumulative effect of Friedkin's twitching forms, vibrating colors, and pulsating music is to conjure a world of such exquisite sensuality that it's often hard to just listen to the music. *"Self-Control"* owes much to modern dance and the pseudo-Freudian imagery of filmmaker Maya Deren's 1940s experimental work. In effect, Branigan has been made a mannequin in her own story, and what better way to portray the paralysis of sexual obsession?

Branigan received a gold record for *"Self-Control,"* a duplicate of which hangs in Friedkin's office.

Friedkin kept his hand in the video pie by crafting the promotional piece for *To Live and Die in L.A.* Rather than construct another fantasy world, he used Todd-AO's Stage One, his favorite mixing facility, as the setting for Wang Chung (musicians Nick Feldman and Jack Hues) to perform their title track for the film. Friedkin and his actual technicians (camera, sound mixing, editing, assistants) share the screen with the musicians who perform their song against scenes from the film on the dubbing stage's mammoth screen. The video is a utilitarian work (edited by Bud Smith) and acts, as was its design, as an extended promotional trailer for the feature film.

On October 29, 1985, just as he was finishing his publicity tour for *To Live and Die in L.A.*, he directed the "Somewhere" (from *West Side Story*) video from Barbra Streisand's *The Broadway Album*. Shot at New York's Apollo Theatre, it was the result of some heartfelt negotiations and not a small amount of creative symbiosis.

Earlier that year, while Friedkin had been in Chicago researching the film that would eventually become *Rampage*, Streisand had proposed that they work together for the first time since the 1976 Oscar show.

"She called me out of the blue," he says. "I have no idea why. She needed a music video but didn't want to do one because the last one had taken her eight days to shoot." Besides, he says, she didn't have a suitable idea.

Streisand sent Friedkin the album and a meeting was arranged. According to Cindy Chvatal, who had assisted Friedkin on *To Live and Die in L.A.* and coproduced the *"Somewhere"* video, the director's advice to his nervous star was a corny-sounding, "Just sing."

"We were having dinner with Barbra Streisand, Billy, and her assistant, Cis Corman," Chvatal reports. "She [Streisand] wanted the point of the video to be—and I think this is why she wanted him—to show people blowing each other up. Mushroom clouds. And she wanted riots in South Africa. Her point of view on how the video should be was, 'If you don't protect it, then it's going to go away.' Billy was completely opposed to that vision for the video, and if you've seen the video it's very sweet—people at Ellis Island, children playing in pools in Africa. But it was the most amazing thing to sit there: Mr. Action-let's-cut-up-your-grandmother talking about avery sweet, nostalgic point of view. And to hear Barbra Streisand, with that very beautiful voice, talking about 'No, that's not what it should be.' He won her over; they were having a charm contest."

As a video, the profundity of "Somewhere" lies in its emotion, not its content. Admittedly, four minutes and twenty-five seconds is not a long time to make a forceful plea for world peace. The song starts in deep space, quickly zooms to earth, flies past the World Trade Center of Manhattan and then shoots through a skylight (in an homage to a famous transition in *Citizen Kane*) into Harlem's Apollo Theatre. There, on a bare stage, Streisand is singing to a thinly spaced audience whose faces reflect the age, ethnic and racial diversity of the world.

Images form a collage: newsreels of immigrants arriving at Ellis Island, black kids swimming in an African pool, dissolves to the black, Hispanic, Jewish, Asian faces in the audience, finally swooping back to show Streisand set off by a spotlight, Christlike, as the camera once again pulls back into space to stress the universality of the song's message.

Unlike typical music videos, "Somewhere" is *about* something and does not detract from either its subject or its performer by flashy cutting or offensive imagery. Yet it is nothing that scores of film school students and underground filmmakers have not done before; the fact that it took two powerful Hollywood people to bring it to MTV and VH–1 may be more significant than the short film itself.

The speed with which television work could be shot and the muscle his feature film reputation accorded him seemed to offer invigorating new avenues for Friedkin. Between the fall of 1985 and the fall of 1987 he shot three feature-length films. One, *Rampage*, was made for theatrical release but the other two were conceived expressly for television.

The C.A.T. Squad was planned as an international intrigue series for NBC that could address a variety of social and political themes while still delivering the goods so important to the action genre. It followed the adventures of a secret, high-tech quartet of U.S. government professionals—the Counter Assault Tactical Squad—which had its origins in a real-life unit organized by Gerald Petievich, the series's co-producer.

"It has a protective function in the Secret Service," Petievich says of the real intelligence unit. "Its mission was to protect the president in certain instances. This," he says of the TV foursome, "is a fictionalized team that strikes before you get hit and handles the problem rather than wait for something to happen."

In the first *The C.A.T. Squad,* which aired on NBC-TV on July 27, 1986, the four team members (Joseph Cortese, Steve James, Jack Youngblood and Patricia Charbonneau) learn that an international terrorist (Eddie Velez) is methodically killing members of a group of scientists trying to perfect a laser weapon technology. Their mission is not only to protect the scientists but intercept and capture "Carlos" (Velez).

Shot mostly in Montreal but with some unit work in Mexicali, Mexico, *The C.A.T. Squad* offered Friedkin certain freedoms, but also the lower prestige of working in television.

The *C.A.T.* budgets are roughly twice what the typical made-for-TV movie is allotted. Most of it goes to lengthier shooting schedules (five six-day weeks plus pick-ups) and the demanding requirements of action films. Unlike most TV dramas where two actors enter a room, sit down, and talk until the scene is over, Friedkin's *C.A.T.*s average between forty and fifty set-ups and often two locations a day.

"The budget's a little over four million dollars," Friedkin offers. "If this was a feature I wouldn't even think of making it for less than seven million. If it was gonna be a Cannon film that would come out and play for two weekends for the action market, you'd be talking about a floor of seven million, and that's with nobody in it. If it was Chuck Norris you'd be talking ten to twelve million."

As with *To Live and Die in L.A.,* the star of *The C.A.T. Squad*s is William Friedkin. The fascination he has for the concept is, once again, its portrayal of secret societies whose rules are, in effect, that there are no rules.

"Global politics is a big game between the big powers," Friedkin states. "It's a self-perpetuating game. This squad was created by the Secret Service to decide who the enemies of the United States were and to go out and deal with them before they become a problem, outside the legal limits. This is nothing they'll ever admit to. One of the stories I used was the terrorist, Carlos, who was executed by the French Secret Service—

they found Carlos in a room, and three or four agents put their pistols to his head and that was the end of Carlos.*

"They pay a heavy price with their own lives," he says of the intelligence operatives, "and sometimes the lives of innocent people who have nothing to do with their game, and that's what fascinates me: how close innocent people come to these games."

*The C.A.T. Squad*s delve into areas seldom explored in action films. Steve James (as Raines), for example, plays an agent who also has a deaf son and the two share a domestic scene in the first feature. In the second installment (*Python Wolf*, aired May 23, 1988) agent Deborah Van Valkenburgh (who replaced Patricia Charbonneau) marries Jack Youngblood and is killed by the enemy. In both programs the various squad members are beaten, put into physical jeopardy and forced to address their own values by the system they are supposedly protecting.

"I'm trying to do something like a John LeCarré novel for television," Friedkin says. "More complex than television usually does, and controversial. But you get into these stories and they seem easy at first and then in trying not to make it stupid, I find I have to keep altering it to make all the parts fit together. I have greater respect for people who write that kind of thing now."

Python Wolf, the second *C.A.T. Squad*, pits the team against two international criminal forces. One is a suave master spy, Kiley (Miguel Ferrer), who procures contraband plutonium to fuel a South African nuclear program for a covert, paramilitary white supremacist group called the Sjambok.

As luck (and television plotting) would have it, this is the same Sjambok that the U.S. government is documenting with its ultrasecret Python Wolf spy plane. When C.A.T. Squad member Jack Youngblood is shot down over South Africa while on a completely separate spy mission, chief C.A.T. Joseph Cortese launches his own rescue operation to fetch his friend from the undeclared enemy.

The allusions to the Iran-contra scandal, Oliver North, Watergate and the litany of outrages that have rocked American democracy over the past twenty years all form an emotional subtext to *Python Wolf*. Yet keeping the plot on course is tricky

---

*In the film Joseph Cortese captures Carlos on an airplane before he can get away. Nevertheless, as the end credits roll, a bus pulls up in front of a Mexican town and a man steps off. The shot is made from such a distance that it is difficult to see that the man is Carlos who has somehow escaped (or been released). Why? "I liked the character and I wanted to bring him back so I could use him again," Friedkin has admitted.

because so much is told by inference. The delicate balance set
Friedkin on edge during the Montreal production schedule in
the fall of 1987; a visit to the set on a typical day revealed
much about his directorial method.

The day is drizzly and Montreal's European character looks
far from romantic this morning. Trucks are parked on a side
street leading up to an anonymous townhouse that is serving a
dual function as "Doc" Burkholder's apartment and, when re-
decorated, a military office later in the film.

The catering lady is the first to act as barometer.

"Billy's upset today," she says with a mixture of concern and
confidentiality as she apprises everybody who passes her truck.
"I just handed him his bagel and said, 'Here,' and then I shut
up. Billy needs his bagels. He also doesn't eat a lot of lunch.
He loves hot dogs, though. Every day for lunch I do two steam-
ies with mustard and onions and send 'em in wrapped in alu-
minum. Then he's happy."

But Friedkin isn't happy this morning. He's tearing apart
the set.

"That's wrong—that goes—*that* goes—that lamp goes—we
bring him in a two-shot here—what kind of lighting do you call
this?"

"Early morning," answers first assistant director Newt Arnold. Arnold has worked off and on with Friedkin since *Sorcerer*, has a suitably loud voice, wears an eyepatch and
communicates with the world outside the location through a
two-way radio into which he snaps, "Be quiet!"

"Is this still plugged in?" Friedkin asks as he plays with a
stereo component system in "Doc" Burkholder's (Cortese) movie
apartment. "See if we can get some light out of it." In this
scene, Doc is awakened at six A.M. by Steve James; this is the
first time the inside of Doc's apartment has been seen. It must
reflect his personality. Friedkin surveys the room.

"What's this? Oh, a *C.A.T. Squad* script!" he jokes, lifting the
bound pages off a small desk where Doc has been sketching
with colored pencils. "There," he says, dumping the pencils out
of their box. "Now he's been working." He drapes a pair of
green corduroy trousers over the desk, covering the pencils.
"Now we know he's got another pair of pants." He scoops up a
paperback copy of William Burroughs's *Naked Lunch* and tosses
it fiercely to crew members waiting in the foyer. "Here's *Naked
Lunch*. Read it."

Friedkin doffs his Stunts Unlimited jacket (the group for which
the late Dar Robinson worked) and is wearing a black, snugly
fitting T-shirt reading, "Sanka Juku North American Tourna-

ment—An Unforgettable Event" pulled over loose khaki trousers and black loafers. He's also wearing a slight scowl as he approaches Doc's closet.

"That's too many records," he announces, grabbing a handful of LPs and tossing them at whoever stands nearby—Arnold, prop man Bill MacSems, anybody. "Make it half. Half of everything, Bill."

While Doc has his records pruned, Friedkin walks over to cinematographer Guy Dufaux.

"Here's what we do," he announces. "He's in bed, he looks at his watch, gets the door, Steve comes in and they go into the kitchen and we're out." He frames the shot with his hands, takes a few script pages out of his pocket and seems to loosen up. Friedkin uses the crew's set-up time to drill Cortese on the mechanics of the shot.

"There's changes in the scene," he tells script supervisor Kelly Snyder (Kelly Lange's daughter) as he breezes past her.

Cortese lies on the bed on his back, his head almost wedged beneath the camera tripod.

"I'll say 'watch,'" Friedkin tells him softly. "Do a two-count on the watch. Then I'll say, 'Go, Joe,' and you do it."

It will be six takes before the timings match.

"Keep it there for at least a two-count, Joe. Don't tilt it toward you so much. *You* can see it, but *we* lose it." In the next room there is a clacking noise; the sound recordist, sitting at the kitchen table, is absent-mindedly playing with some poker chips.

"What's that?" Friedkin asks.

"Keep still. It's a noisy floor," Arnold announces.

"Yeah, but what *is* it," Friedkin persists. The soundman, wearing earphones, has not connected his chips with Friedkin's question. *"What is it?"* Friedkin again demands. "If it's a machine, unplug it." The soundman stops.

After take six, Friedkin calls for a slate and the shot is a keeper. Rather than start each shot with the traditional slate—that black-and-white clapstick that bears identifying scene markings and is used to synchronize sound and picture—Friedkin uses a "tail slate" which slaps the striped sticks together after he has said "cut." This eliminates the loud pop that can break an actor's concentration at the beginning of a shot and also forces the performers to dote on Friedkin's voice for the call of action.

Two hours' effort has gone into capturing this simple ten-second shot which, in the final version of *Python Wolf*, will come after an intense torture scene in the Sjambok prison camp. Unaccountably, the screams of the torture victim will trail over the sound track to haunt Doc Burkholder's dream, a touch of the psychic that seems out of place in this hard-edged story. But what is even more unusual is that none of the bedroom's background detail—artwork, record collection, draped pants, stereo console—will be seen in the tight framing that Friedkin and Dufaux have used.

On a short shooting schedule such doting on detail seems extravagant, but it has served a purpose. By vamping over small matters, Friedkin has gained valuable planning time for the sequences he must complete before the end of the day. The two hours apparently wasted on the ten-second shot of Cortese is earned back quickly in the next scene in which Cortese and James prepare breakfast and discuss what has happened to their C.A.T. Squad buddy, Jack Youngblood. Rather than wait for "inspiration," Friedkin has made use of the traditional early morning lethargy on a movie set to line up his shots for the next ten hours.

Before they shoot the breakfast-making scene, the actors go over it with their director.

"We gotta go for a line about cream cheese here," says Cortese, referring to the action he and James will complete as they talk: one will squeeze orange juice while the other toasts bagels and applies cream cheese.

"This isn't a cream cheese scene," Friedkin insists.

"No," jokes James. "It's a bagel scene."

"It's not that either," Friedkin holds. "C'mon."

While the three men practice slicing bagels and cutting oranges ("You're doing it the wrong way," Friedkin corrects Cortese as he halves yet another orange. "Do it sideways"), gaffers adjust the huge lights just outside the apartment's windows—the ones turning cloudy Montreal into sunny Washington, D.C., for the story—to reflect angles of an hour later in the day.

By now there is a constant stream of toasted, cream-cheesed bagels moving from the kitchen countertop to a plate on the table.

Extra bagels are being toasted in a back room ("props") and another propman constantly smooths and resmooths the surface of a tub of cream cheese into which the actors dip their knives for every take.

At the juicer, Cortese sneaks a long gulp of freshly squeezed O.J. Soon Friedkin does, too. Nobody else dares.

Steve James is having trouble coordinating his dialogue with the props; there's not enough time both to say his lines and spread the cream cheese. He blows four takes before the director tells him, "Steve, why don't you just say the line and carry the bagels over to the table?"

The next take moves along well until the actor flubs his line. "I'll do it again," James offers.

"Slate—you can't," Friedkin tells him. "It's all in one shot. It was goin' real good, too."

Friedkin's voice suggests that too much time has been spent on this piece of business; he himself calls for "quiet" on the set for the next take, ordinarily the assistant director's duty. He gets it.

"The line is, 'The bed was still made,'" Friedkin prompts James. "It doesn't matter if you do four bagels; so you only do two."

James does it flawlessly.

"Slate—that's it for me," the director announces. "That one. Print that one," he next says to Kelly Snyder. "The rest of 'em I don't want to see, I never saw them, we didn't do them."

In such tight quarters Friedkin knows the importance of silence. Although some thirty people crowd all rooms of the tiny apartment, he tries to keep the actors focused on him. Rather than say "action," he calls the person gently by name. When there is need for a camera movement, he softly taps the appropriate crew members on their backs as the signal. And he constantly uses the names of key people as he addresses them.

"You know what'd be nice, Guy?" he says to the director of photography—or, rather, announces rhetorically. "To have the toast pop up into the shot."

All agree that this will make a nice transition from James's entrance to the eating scene with Cortese. The camera is aimed at the toaster and Friedkin pushes a halved bagel into its twin slots.

Is this what it has come to? An Academy Award-winning filmmaker directing breakfast?

"Steve, c'mere," Friedkin calls—with camera turning—a minute into waiting for the toaster to finish. "When it pops up, grab the slices." A new editing scheme has just occurred to him.

By the time the toast and orange juice are filmed to Friedkin's satisfaction, it's time for lunch.

"You said it wasn't about bagels, man," Steve James complains jokingly to Friedkin.

"I lied." He smiles back. "I said it wasn't, but it was."

William Friedkin's day began shortly after six A.M. in his rented apartment in Old Montreal overlooking its waterfront and the ghost of Expo '67. Spacious and decorated in Japanese style— and uncluttered—its multileveled layout includes stairs to a second (bedroom) level, a foyer and long hall, sunken living room with wide, plush white sofas and a large coffee table on which magazines, scripts and an unused ashtray reside. A spotless kitchen is off the living room, its refrigerator stocked with a gourmet's selection of condiments, preserves, vegetables and delicatessen. His driver does his shopping from a list he prepares and cleaning has been arranged by the production office, although Friedkin wipes up as he goes along—brewing a pot of tea from a blend of China black and orange pekoe.

Conspicuous on a lighted shelf above the sink—next to an assortment of vitamins—are three amber-colored prescription bottles, their labels carefully turned toward the wall.

While his crew is eating on location, Friedkin returns a few phone calls from the apartment. On his coffee table is a rough copy of a script that Sylvester Stallone wants him to direct. There is a Federal Express packet of officework that his secretary, Adele Joseph Curcuruto, has shipped him from his Studio City bungalow. There are calls from NBC, with whom William Friedkin Productions is in partnership on *C.A.T. Squad*, about publicity. He takes only the phone call from Newt Arnold that summons him back to the next location, a location at a jazz club in Old Montreal.

On the way, he talks about the freedom he is enjoying on this project.

"As long as we stay within the budget, they don't care what we do," he says. Even though NBC is owned by General Electric and the script criticizes such multinational firms for doing business with South Africa?

"I don't even know if they pay that much attention," he dismisses. "That's why you can often do much more on television than you can in a feature film."

Steve James and Deborah Van Valkenburgh meet him at the jazz club. Special effects people fill the room with mineral oil mist for a close-up of Van Valkenburgh staring off into the distance. In the story, her character of Nikki Pappas has just married Jack Youngblood's John Sommers the night before he leaves for his secret mission. She does not know that he has now been shot down.

Friedkin guides her through the shot from off-camera, telling her where to look. Background noise will be added later, but he wants some ambience to make the actress concentrate more.

"Make some noise," he calls out to the crew. "Christ, before we couldn't keep it quiet, and now that we need the noise, nobody says anything." A few crew members finally mumble at each other.

"You're thinking about him," Friedkin tells Van Valkenburgh. "Nothing, really. There's a lot on your mind. Okay, now, look to your right. Now your left. You're not really looking for anybody, you're looking around."

He walks in front of the camera.

"Hey, anybody wanna be in a movie?" he calls out. "Just walk in front, like you were elbowing your way through a buncha guys in a bar," he says, and shoves a nearby body in front of the lens.

Ten minutes later the crew has moved to the club's brick basement where Van Valkenburgh tells James that she and Sommers are now man and wife.

The hallway is barely five feet wide. The crew must cram into its recesses to get their angles. Friedkin groans as he kneels under the camera.

"Oh, my knees. This is what happens from all that hockey when I was a kid."

The scene plays well in the bare hallway. Friedkin is pleased that there is nothing but a hanging light. "This is great," he tells a beaming Bill MacSems. "Good work. Really good set." Then he adds offhandedly, "Not like the one this morning."

After he calls for a wrap on the day, Friedkin takes Van Valkenburgh aside for some pointers on tomorrow's scene in which she must cajole top secrets out of the evil Kiley while pretending to be his mistress.

"You want him to trust you, but you can't play it too eager," he suggests. As he leaves, Van Valkenburgh asks him, "Hey, how much hockey did you play when you were a kid?"

"Never," he confesses. "I never even *saw* a hockey puck when I was a kid."

While the crew packs the gear away, Friedkin and Newt Arnold hop into the car and tell the driver to head to the airplane hanger where they will inspect a jet fighter cockpit mock-up that has been built. The sun is going down but Friedkin's energy is peaking.

"Are you sure you know where this Goddamned place is supposed to be?" he growls at the driver.

"I've got the instructions right here," the driver says, holding them up to read in the car roof light.

"Are you reading or looking at the road?" Friedkin asks,

checking his seat belt. The driver puts down the instructions and stares ahead.

"We've seen about every island there is around here," Friedkin says rhetorically, but for his driver's benefit. "I thought they said the hangars were right in back of the dome, behind the restaurant.

"That's the restaurant we blew up for the first *C.A.T. Squad*," he offers as it passes into the night. "Hey, look, fuck the instructions. I've got better things to do than drive around in the dark. Let's go back and check it out tomorrow."

"We won't have any time for the rest of the week," Newt Arnold advises. "We'll have to ship it back to Los Angeles and set it up there. You've got to take a look at it now."

"Jesus," Friedkin sighs.

"Wait, here's the way," the driver announces, turning toward a darkened road leading into the night. "It's the only one left."

"I can't spend all this time chasing some cockpit," Friedkin says impatiently. "But what the hell—I mean, we're here, right?"

Half a minute later he stands in front of a lighted hangar, its doors admitting him to check on a camera-ready jet fighter cockpit replete with video screens, flashing lights, movable windows and swivel seats.

"My time is valuable. Every second of it," he says on the way into the hangar.

Friedkin spends the next half hour looking at the mock-up. Built of gray-painted wood, it will be placed on a rooftop in Los Angeles on a clear day. A hand-held camera will film scenes through its removable plastic windows and give the impression of a plane in flight.

Finally Friedkin is delivered to the door of his apartment building at 8 P.M. "I've still got to rewrite the script," he says. "There's a couple things I want to put in. We're shooting the ending and it's not clear enough."

He zips up his Stunts Unlimited jacket and heads for the door.

"I think I'll just grab some dinner at home," he says. "Boy, those were lousy hot dogs today."

Three months later, Friedkin is preparing the sound tracks for *Python Wolf* at Glen Glenn sound studios. While the panel of technicians runs through each ten-minute reel (there are ten) balancing sound and equalization levels for every track of dialogue, music, room ambience or effect (as many as twenty-four elements for every shot), Friedkin sits in the back of the huge mixing theater reading manuscripts, making notes and taking calls. Despite the activity, nothing escapes his attention: he will ask for a line to be made "brighter" (more treble), for a sound effect to be added where the corresponding action is seen ("The guy is writing; somebody put a ballpoint pen in there. Great. Now you can join the Writers Guild"), or to shape the drone of an airplane in the distance in an airport scene.

At the same time he is reading the manuscript for *The Silence of the Lambs*, Thomas Harris's sequel to *Red Dragon*, which was filmed in 1986 as *Manhunter*, starring William Petersen. Friedkin would love to get the rights to this and interrupts his sound crew every now and then with plot updates.

"This is terrific," he says. "Dr. Lektor escapes. He's in a straitjacket and he bites a nurse's eye out." Friedkin recalls that actor Brian Cox played Lektor, the serial killer in *Manhunter*. "But Michael Mann [its director] wanted *me* to play the part originally, you know. I don't know what he saw in me."

A short time later five-and-one-half-year-old Jack is brought for a visit by his nanny and father and son chase each other around the theater for a while, pausing to shoot baskets in a small hoop taped to a doorframe. When Friedkin is called to the mixing console, casting director Rick Montgomery pretends to let Jack tackle him on the room's thickly carpeted floor. Whenever Jack laughs, Friedkin looks up and smiles back.

Prior to the broadcast of *Python Wolf* Friedkin, as was his tradition, did selected interviews with national magazines, key newspapers and local L.A. television and radio stations to hype the show. In each he spoke of government secrecy, the freedom he felt working in TV, the prescience demonstrated by the *C.A.T. Squad* plots and how NBC would love it to become a weekly series despite his protestations that such a schedule would wind up trivializing the situations ("Pretty soon we'd have the C.A.T. Squad going after a guy who stole some lady's purse," he sighed).

Privately he insisted that *Python Wolf* was among the best things he'd ever done and that it touched on a lot of issues he felt were important. He also said that he concentrated on the film's action after NBC excised two domestic scenes from the script, insisting they were "too television."

If Friedkin was accurate in his evaluation of *Python Wolf's* qualities, then its values are to be found in the subtext, not its glossy and unusually violent surface.

What is of special note in this sprawling, not terribly coherent yarn is not its criticism of South Africa, the nuclear industry, government cover-ups, or renegade lieutenant colonels (though all are appropriate), but the vulnerability of the men and women who pursue them.

Of the C.A.T. Squad one dies (Nikki), one is beaten insensate

(Sommers), one is assaulted on several occasions and loses half the time (Raines) and one is shot (Burkholder). These are fallible people whose loyalty is both intense and imperfect (when Sommers flies his secret mission he won't even tell Burkholder). They have the dedication found among the best of cop buddies (two—Nikki and Sommers—even marry) and they also show fear (Burkholder is terrified of surgery and Raines has to comfort him). Unlike the street-smart law enforcers of *The French Connection* or *To Live and Die in L.A.*, the members of the C.A.T. Squad seem torn by the inner doubts of Steve Burns in *Cruising* or Father Karras in *The Exorcist*. Not only do they question their own souls but at times they come to wonder about the job itself. Yet they remain loyal; in Friedkin's world the greatest crime is not weakness, it is betrayal.

Some allusions in *Python Wolf* play from the director's own life. Doc Burkholder is named after a Chicago friend with whom he used to play ball. And Doc's hospital experience—white-hot lights and operating room agony—trace to Friedkin's heart attack.

For all the energy expended on it, *Python Wolf* fared poorly on its network telecast; it was defeated in the ratings by the Miss Universe Pageant and the conclusion of a miniseries about Baby M.

Friedkin used the time between the two *C.A.T. Squad* telefilms to write and direct a feature that may become his most obscure work. *Rampage* was shot in the colorless Northern California winter of 1986 but was never released theatrically in America. It is a startlingly revealing picture for a number of reasons and easily embodies everything in his life that William Friedkin had kept deep inside.

CHAPTER 14

RAMPAGE AND REDIRECTION

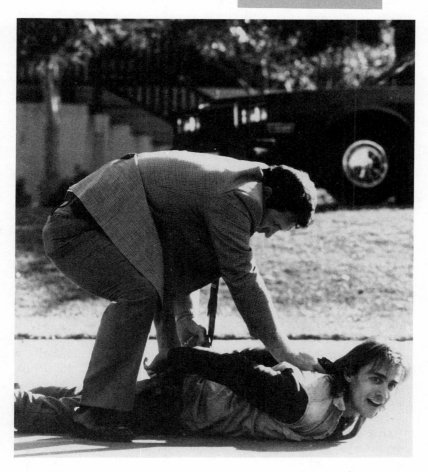

A policeman (Art LaFleur) subdues the crazed—or perhaps not—serial killer (Alex McArthur) in *Rampage*.
COURTESY OF DELAURENTIIS ENTERTAINMENT GROUP; COPYRIGHT © 1987

THREE PEOPLE DIE in the first five minutes of *Rampage*. They are shot, cut up into pieces, stuffed into a plastic garbage bag and their blood is smeared all over their pleasant suburban home in Stockton, California. It is Christmas eve.

The man who did it is Charles Reece. He entered their home on a whim. He does not dispose of his victims completely; he saves some of their vital organs because he believes his blood is being poisoned and he needs their blood to cleanse his. He keeps his trove of body parts in the cellar of his mother's house, where he still lives. The cellar is decorated with Nazi regalia and religious symbols, and blood.

If Charles Reece is insane, then the law says he must be put away in a mental hospital. In twenty or thirty years he might be released.

If he is sane, then he can be executed by the state. But how could a sane man have committed these horrible murders?

And how sane is a state that executes people?

"It's the most passionate film I've ever made," says William Friedkin, who scripted *Rampage* from William Wood's novel, "in terms of the fact that it's about something that I'm deeply concerned about but have no answers for, and that is the imposition of the death penalty. But also the impropriety of psychiatry in the courtroom. The sort of larger impetus for me to make this film is my feeling that psychiatry has played an insidious role in American life. On all levels, specifically in the area of criminal law, but in every other area of the law and in many other walks of life as well. It's getting to a point where people don't seem to be able to make any decisions at all without the advice of a psychiatrist. In business, in personal life, in married life, and then what's happened in the criminal law is that it seems that lawyers and judges have basically abdicated their responsibility to psychiatrists.

"In such things as family law, for example, it's generally a psychiatrist who makes the ultimate decision about the future of a child. Not a judge, not the lawyers, certainly once it gets into court, not the parents themselves."

Speaking in May of 1987 while *Rampage* was in its final sound mixing stage, William Friedkin had every reason to despise psychiatrists. Although he says he has never seen one professionally, he had been forced to be interviewed by at least two in preparation for the custody hearings to be held in August for his son Jack. *Rampage*, a film as angry as *Deal of the Century* but far more personally focused, was his way of exploring the subject and, quite possibly, getting even with the shrinks involved in the custody hearings. But not with a direct frontal assault.

"This film's about the criminal law where it's no longer relevant what somebody did, like committing murder," he says. "The relevant question becomes, 'What was this person's state of mind when he committed the murder?' And in that process the rights of the victim are completely steamrollered. The victim becomes an almost unnecessary appendage to the proceedings, an aberration, "Too bad somebody hadda turn out to be a murder victim.'"

Friedkin's anger, inspired perhaps by his own loss of control in Jack's custody but given direction by the confusion surrounding society's ability to deal with criminal insanity, is given vent in *Rampage*. It summons its textures from a number of influences, notably Ralph Singleton's explosive rape and mutilation of a young woman (for which he was paroled after serving eight years); Dan White's murder of San Francisco supervisor Harvey Milk and Mayor George Moscone; John Wayne Gacy's serial killing of countless young men in Illinois; John Hinkley's attempted assassination of Ronald Reagan and James Brady; his boyhood recollections of the William Heirens case; and even Nazi atrocities in World War Two.

"In a California court, for example, today," Friedkin says, becoming agitated, "the Nazis wouldn't be convicted of anything. The Nazis would be excused because of the insanity plea! What's the difference between the Nazis and a guy who cuts off the arms of an innocent little girl [Singleton]? Qualitatively there's none.

"You take a guy like Dan White [who killed] Mayor Moscone and supervisor Harvey Milk in San Francisco [and later said he'd been compelled to do it by the sugar in the junk food he ate—the "Twinkie defense"]. Here is an absolutely perfect illustration of where psychiatrists have completely befogged the criminal justice system. The same psychiatrist who was in the Hinkley case was also in the case of John Wayne Gacy in Chicago, the man who killed thirty-eight or more boys, and buried them all over his property. In the Hinkley case, this psychiatrist testified in Washington that Hinkley was insane, and that was accepted by the jurors. Now, Hinkley didn't kill anybody; he *attempted* to kill the president. Gacy *killed* those thirty-eight boys; the bodies were found on his property, he confessed . . . *he was found sane!* How can this be?

"There are no absolute standards. Psychiatry is not a finite science, it's not like internal medicine. It's guesswork, especially where they get into the area of predicting future behavior, which they do in these criminal cases. These are some of the things that are brought up and dealt with in *Rampage*."

For Friedkin the issue becomes even more complicated when one remembers that, twenty-five years earlier, it was his effort to gain Paul Crump's release from the electric chair that propelled him into the world of filmmaking. Since then, of course, Crump has admitted his guilt. Friedkin, in dealing with that reality, has now turned almost completely around on capital punishment.

"I believe in capital punishment in the case of rape," he holds. "I think that the brutal traumatization of a woman who's raped by somebody is just unforgivable. I am against abortion other than if it were to save the life of the mother; in the best of all utopian worlds I would prefer a strictly enforced law against abortion, although I am wide open to all of the cogent arguments that are made in favor of abortion, because it's a woman's right to determine what's going to happen to her own body. I honestly feel, after fifty-odd years of life, that I've reached a position where I think life is a gift of God and we really have no control over when or where or how it's given, and in the best of all utopian worlds we should have nothing to say about when it's taken away, either.

"But I can see practical instances where there must be a variance from that. I think in certain cases of euthanasia it is justified to prevent further suffering. Or when somebody goes so far from the code of ordinary decent behavior and commits a brutal, thoughtless murder or murders, that there is no alternative than to take that person's life, if only as an example to the rest of society."

Yet Friedkin admits that his contradictory stands are a way of coming to terms with the issue, which is so complex that no single argument can illustrate it completely. That becomes the conundrum that affects *Rampage* and that makes the film, for all its crisp narrative and electrifying sequences, such a frustrating experience.

Charles Reece (Alex McArthur) murders three members of the Ellis family on Christmas eve: Mrs. Ellis and her parents, the Hendricksons. There is no special reason for this; perhaps it was the bright wreath on their front door that attracted his attention as he walked along the street of the pleasant suburban neighborhood.

A young prosecutor, Anthony Fraser (Michael Biehn), is brought into the case while it is still under investigation. Fraser,

who is against the death penalty, is still haunted by his deci-
sion to euthanize his two-year-old daughter, Molly (Chelsea
Crank), whose coma was deemed by doctors to be irreversible.
The anguish has strained his marriage to Kate (Deborah Van
Valkenburgh).

While Gene Tippetts (Royce D. Applegate) and his son Andy
(Whitby Hertford) are at the dentist, Reece comes to the door.
He walks in on Eileen Tippetts (Brenda Lilly) and her other son
Aaron (Paul Gaddoni), saying "I'm sorry." Then he kills them.

Fraser's superiors are leaning heavily on him to prosecute
the triple Ellis/Hendrickson murder when he is handed the
Tippetts file. From Mr. Tippetts the police have learned that a
quiet young man, Charlie Reece, was suspected of killing their
pet dog; adding that information to clues given by residents in
the area, it seems clear that Reece is the man the authorities
are seeking.

Fraser and Detective Mel Sanderson (Art Lafleur) aren't taking any chances; they obtain the proper warrants and make all
precautions to avoid dismissal of the case on a legal technical-
ity. When they search the house of Reece's mother, Naomi (Grace
Zabriskie), they find their proof: in Reece's basement is a virtual museum of horror—Nazi symbols, church icons, bullets,
S&M devices and a grisly inventory of bloody body parts in
jars and bags.

This cinches it. Sanderson and Detective Nestade (Carlos
Palomino) proceed to the garage where Reece is employed. Reece
tries to elude them but he is subdued and taken into custody.

The more the prosecutors attempt to bring Reece to trial for
murder, the more his psychiatrists become involved in explaining that he was insane at the time of his heinous acts. Yet Reece
is enormously cordial and even manipulative; soon Fraser senses
that his beliefs are on trial as much as Reece's guilt or innocence. Does he believe in the death penalty, or will he risk letting someone like Reece out on the streets after he has served
his time? What is sanity and what is insanity, both morally
and legally?

The trial is more a contest of psychiatric theories than a test
of justice. Reece's seemingly rational behavior belies the insanity alleged during his crimes. One psychiatrist, Dr. Keddie (John
Harkins), even coaches Reece on advice from counsel in how to
explain his illness to the jury.

Meanwhile Gene Tippetts refuses to testify against Reece, despite the killing of his family. He just wants to get himself and
his son away from their recent hell to start a new life.

Dr. Keddie is bent on having his medical opinion believed, even to the point of coercing a hospital physician, Dr. Rudin (Roy London), to cover up a diagnosis he had made that leaned toward Reece's sanity.

By the time the trial concludes in Reece's conviction of murder in the first degree—committed while sane—his guilt or innocence seems moot. Shortly after the jury reaches its verdict, yet another in a series of tests—a P.E.T. scan—shows that Reece's brain chemistry resembles that of an insane man.

Can sanity and insanity be quantified? Fraser—more than ever sensitive to Reece's manipulations—no longer wonders.

When Dr. Keddie and a lawyer visit Reece in jail to tell him that the P.E.T. scan has proved his insanity, they arrive after Reece's mother has departed. They find him dead in his cell, poisoned on the daily medication he had apparently stockpiled instead of taking as prescribed. His lawyer is amazed: "He thought he was butchering people and animals to get blood so he could *cure* his imaginary illness. Why would he kill himself?"

Mrs. Reece, the last person to see her son alive, can provide no insights to police, who suspect that she helped her son die.

At a celebration after his victory, Fraser is told by his wife that she wants to make theirs a permanent separation.

Gene and Andy Tippetts know nothing of the verdict, Reece's death or Fraser's worries. At a traveling carnival somewhere in Northern California they try to forget and, just maybe, find a reason to keep living.

Former Sacramento, California D.A. William Wood based his novel, *Rampage*, on an actual case that resulted in its prosecutor winning appointment to the bench on the heels of his success in court. That was something Friedkin, in adapting the screenplay, had found too reassuring for his plan to show how crime affects a wide swath of people. Although he did shoot a sequence in which Tony and Kate Fraser reconcile their relationship on the night he is made a judge, it was a negative reaction from composer Ennio Morricone that confirmed Friedkin's disdain for the idea and it never made the final cut.

Gone, too, was a scene—present in Wood's novel—of the D.A. actually killing Reece. "I found that a little too fascist for my taste," Friedkin said, and kept it out of his shooting script.

Also deleted was the script's very first sequence in which Reece buys the gun he will use to commit his murders. In it, the young man is asked by the gun shop clerk if he has ever been a mental patient; Reece's personable denial satisfies the salesman.

"It seemed to me to be redundant," the director explains. "So he buys a gun. I edited it, then I took it out. I just kept trying to tighten it up. I never know how much of that can be effective and how much could be harmful."

The scene's presence would have established the premeditated nature of the killings (as well as taking a swipe at how easy it is to buy handguns in America). It is complicated by another device that Friedkin abandoned as he finished his edit: the recurrent voice of a "computer" telling Reece what to do and a number of optical effects taken from his point of view that demonstrate his distorted vision of the world. The effect would have been to force the audience to understand Reece's insanity while throwing allegiance to him at the expense of the legal system.

"That occurred to me," Friedkin says. "I never shot into his mind. Long before I got to making the film I thought, 'Why do I want to go into his mind?' The whole question about the film was that we *don't* know what's in his mind. It looked good in the script but it was self-defeating. That's why I cut the whole fantasy sequence. [You need the] distance."

Friedkin researched *Rampage* at the Isaac Ray Center of the Rush Presbyterian St. Luke's Hospital in Chicago. Run by Dr. Jim Cavanaugh, the fifteen-year-old program selects between twelve and fifteen convicted serial killers for study and treatment, some on nearly an outpatient basis. They are almost entirely male; according to the director's research, no women have become mass murderers. But regardless of their gender, these individuals exhibit hauntingly consistent thought processes.

"Take it down to one word," Friedkin reports. "Repression. In the minds of serial killers, all of the images are of repression: Nazis, the Church—heavy Catholic in most cases—I mean, you don't see Presbyterian symbols or Methodist or Unitarian. Now, these are at wide variance in the computer of most normal people, but in someone's confused circuitry they become constant.

"One of the fellows that I met in this program had, indeed, killed his mother and father and was [now] employed as a security guard at the Field Museum in Chicago," Friedkin relates. "He didn't carry a gun but he was in the program. I sat in on a Rorschach test that he was given and I remember my own responses and his. He saw fields of flowers and beautiful geometric patterns and I saw images of violence and depravity! There is some point there; I'm not sure what it is."

The film was shot in late 1986 and early 1987 in Stockton,

California. Friedkin originally wanted William L. Petersen to play the role of Fraser but Petersen—by then having played another law enforcement official in *Manhunter*—balked at appearing as a third. Subsequently, the friendship between the two Chicagoans cooled. When Michael Biehn (star of *Aliens*) was signed he filled Friedkin's idea of Fraser as a "solidly built, muscular man in his early thirties" who is also tinged with political ambition. Conversely, he asked Alex McArthur (TV's *Desperado*), whom he cast as Reece, to diet down from his already lean 175 pounds to a scrawny 150 ("Lots of dry baked potatoes and coffee," McArthur says with a smile) to play the sickly, insect-like murderer.

The pronounced physical and temperamental differences between the antagonists in *Rampage* also reflect the dichotomy in the film. In commercial terms, audiences lured by the explosive title and the promise of a new release "from the director of *The French Connection*" will be deprived of the emotional catharsis of crime thrillers. Similarly, fans of the "whodunit" genre will be equally distressed when they learn that the *who* is of no interest to writer-director-producer Friedkin; it's the *why* and *how* that fascinate him.

And it is also no accident that the only characters in the entire film who are given any degree of sympathy (even the murder victims are there solely to be killed) are the father and son, Gene and Andy Tippetts, who survive the ordeal by running away from Reece's trial. Just as William and Jack Friedkin desired to be rid of the court system during the custody fight, so director Friedkin separates Gene and Andy from their threatening surroundings.

Regardless of its allusions, *Rampage* is also the ultimate example of Friedkin's need to satisfy his own curiosity to the point of fixating on minutiae. The unresolved nature of the narrative—clearly stated yet endlessly contradicting—shows a Talmudic quest for knowledge even at the expense of dramatic tension.

It might be posed that *Rampage* represents the showdown between the twin sides of William Friedkin. One is the provacateur who is driven by his creative demons to destroy for a cause that is larger than he can explain; the other is the strong and righteous craftsman, sanctioned by the Establishment, yet also goaded by the compulsion to achieve ever higher goals. The Reece-Fraser dynamics in the film are nothing less than the angelic and diabolic temperaments of Friedkin fighting for dominance. It is not accidental that they end in a stalemate and that their bitterness suffuses those around them.

By the end of *Rampage* Reece is dead, his last moments having taken place offscreen. Perhaps significantly, Friedkin's description in the script specifies his death pose as "Christ-like." Just as significantly, the only soul who grieves for him is his mother.

And Fraser, though he has won his trial, knows that he has succeeded only by a caprice of science; inside he still questions not only his ethics but the function of the law in a world where technology is taking hold. Just as Friedkin says he is never fully satisfied with his work, so does the victor in *Rampage* disparage his spoils.

The film was shot quickly—thirty-six days—on a negative pickup arrangement whereby Friedkin's Rampage Productions was responsible for the picture's seven-million-dollar budget until its delivery to the DeLaurentiis Entertainment Group for a fall 1987 release. Working as quickly as he had with the *C.A.T. Squad*s, he and cinematographer Bob Yeoman developed a style that grows increasingly more moody as the film progresses. From the open spaces that show off California's autumn to the coldness of the psychiatric hospitals where insanity is quantified, confined, or both, the picture becomes more and more claustrophobic until, by the time of the trial, the witnesses and jury are all but isolated in spotlighted sections of the courtroom. Just as theatrically, the backgrounds are thrown into darkness; no hoards of spectators can be watching what would be, by definition, a spectacular public trial.

During production, Friedkin was especially open to collaboration, says Alex McArthur, who played Reece, sensing that there may have been some personal exploration going on.

"I think there is a dark side to him," McArthur says with Reecelike charm. "But I think I have a dark side, too. We kind of saw that."

Friedkin allowed McArthur a free hand in decorating the killer's basement chamber of horrors. "We were on the same track," the actor reports.

"In fact, he let me rewrite the scene where I broke down pleading for my life. He gave me a little leeway; actually, after having meetings with him and talking with him before we started filming, I figured he knew what he was doing a lot better than I did."

But Friedkin removed McArthur's breakdown scene after the film's first previews. Also excised was a silent fantasy, from Reece's point of view, in which he walks over and kisses a fe-

male court reporter. The two sequences—one the confession of
a sane man and the other a hallucination of a crazed one—
further complicated the impression of Reece's mental state. The
changes were made by Friedkin at the last moment in a display
of uncertainty.

"I'm very susceptible to the comments," he admitted during
an interview prior to the film's presentation at the 1987 Boston
Film Festival.

That uncertainty may have stemmed from his growing
uneasiness about the financial stability of the DeLaurentiis Entertainment Group, the company that was to distribute the film.
DEG, faced with a string of flops, was finding it hard to secure
bookings for its releases or the funds to market them. *Rampage*,
originally announced for September of 1987, was pushed to
November, then January of 1988, then disappeared from the
schedule entirely.

On June 2, 1988, the European American Bank, which had
underwritten the seven-million-dollar loan to DEG and Rampage Productions, enjoined both parties from "diverting or dis-
sipating funds in which the bank claims an interest." At the
same time, DEG was seeking a major film distributor to take
over its slate of shelved titles in order to generate any revenue
at all. In August DEG filed for reorganization under Chapter 11
of the bankruptcy laws citing liabilities of $199.7 million, as-
sets of $163.1 million (mostly its vast film library and North
Carolina studios) as well as secured and unsecured debts of over
$200 million.

Although *Rampage* has been given European release, it never
hit American screens and is consigned to a future of cable TV
and home video.

The uncertain fate of *Rampage* came at a time when Friedkin
was reassessing his personal life, too. Almost fifty-two, he had
begun to realize that a succession of marriages (and divorces)
was no way to greet the future. On June 7, 1987, he married
Kelly Lange, the KNBC newscaster he had once hired for a small
role in *Deal of the Century*. Los Angeles film critic David Sheehan had introduced them and the relationship grew from shared,
but not conflicting, careers.

Friedkin arranged to buy the house next to Lange's in Los
Angeles. When Jack is staying with his father it is at the Fried-
kin-Lange home; when Jack is with his mother, the Friedkins
live at Friedkin's house.

Friends note with approval and relief how Lange and Friedkin complement each other. They have swapped their awards—

he has her Emmy, she has his Oscar—and, furthermore, they have shared a stability that Friedkin has presumably been seeking since leaving Chicago.

Yet if his personal life was leveling off, his professional life was as turbulent as ever. Despite continual offerings from outside, he insists on generating his own projects, a decision that does not always bring him near the mass-market arena that has come to dominate modern Hollywood. He turned down, after much discussion, *Legion,* William Peter Blatty's *Exorcist* sequel. He spent months languishing at Sylvester Stallone's White Eagle Enterprises offices in Santa Monica unable to develop either of two projects (*The Executioner, Gangster*) on which the two filmmakers had wanted to collaborate, despite the whispers of many in the community who predicted they would soon be at each other's high-priced throats.

"I feel I'm at a point in my own work that is barren," he confessed. "It's like a wasteland and that's a problem for me."

By the spring of 1989, however, a project came to his attention that covered familiar territory, yet did so in subtly different ways that attracted him while it baffled his associates.

On June 19, 1989, he began to shoot *The Guardian* for producer Joe Wizan and Universal Pictures. *The Guardian,* based on *The Nanny* by Dan Greenburg, is a modern gothic horror tale about a sorceress who maintains her immortality by feeding the bodies—and with them the souls—of infants to a large tree. In order to provide her demon with a constant supply of unblemished spirits she has become a nanny and, as the film begins, has moved into the Yuppie age where she holds a young family under emotional ransom until the violent conclusion.

The Guardian (filmed under the title *Carmilla*) deals with the same ideas that popularized *The Exorcist* sixteen years earlier, albeit from a vastly different intellectual direction. Its primal themes of family, a baby's love torn between his real and his surrogate mothers, a father's devotion to his business (the husband is an advertising filmmaker) and his family, and the general use of a child in jeopardy summon elements that run throughout Friedkin's films, particularly his most successful ones.

More deeply, it is an unmistakably revealing story that centers on what may be the most intense and threatening kind of betrayal imaginable: a mother who has abandoned her totally trusting child physically to a surrogate also abandons him spiritually to evil forces.

Yet *The Guardian* also embodies a hopeful note despite its

dark core. In Friedkin's entire body of work it is his only film that portrays a whole family, torn from without, but held together by love. It is as if, at age fifty-five, the Boy Wonder has finally come to terms with the energies and conflicts that he has been trying to resolve through his films. Whether this new direction signals a renewed success at the box office remains to be seen.

This emotional reevaluation has not come easily for Friedkin, and he anguishes over it, particularly when discussing his marriages.

"I feel that I was in a kind of fog when I married those women," he says, sweeping the past aside. "I don't think that either of those two marriages produced any ideas of fruition in terms of the films I have made subsequently. My marriage to Lesley produced a son whom I love very much, but nothing else. And I view the guy that did that as another person.

"I remember some isolated things from each of those marriages, some good things, some bad. I cannot honestly tell you or me why I married either one of them. I think it was a terrible mistake. That's another thing about me: for a guy who's still around at all, I have made some colossal mistakes."

CHAPTER 15

ARTIST IN RESIDENCE

A trim Friedkin posed for this uncharacteristically pensive portrait in 1987.
COURTESY OF WILLIAM FRIEDKIN PRODUCTIONS

"BILLY THRIVES on a fight," insists Gerald Petievich. "I knew cops like that. I knew crooks like that, too. They like the adrenaline rush. They like being right in there." To Petievich, Friedkin sounds like a general who feeds on confrontation but loses purpose during peace.

"He will cause a war over nothing and fight that war and lose his battle but in the end he will be the one that wins," the writer explains. "It's like the guy standing outside of a door on a hundred-degree day while there was a five-mile race going by. Some guy said, 'Hey, I bet you can't run five miles,' and he said, 'The hell I couldn't.' The guy says, 'I'll bet you a beer.'

"So the guy ran five miles in hundred-degree weather and at the end gets handed a one-dollar bottle of beer."

This testing, confrontational attitude permeates Friedkin's relationships in his films and in much of his life, according to those who have worked with him. On screen it is best seen in the almost sensual pleasure that Popeye Doyle, Richard Chance, Tony Pino, and even Eddie Muntz get when they're doing their job and their job is dangerous.

Similarly, Friedkin's pursuit of total control even at the cost of his personal safety is an obsession that energizes all he does.

"Billy is a very dominant personality," reports Ed Gross. "He's a supreme logician so that you really can't fake it too much with him. Since he's interested in stress, he will challenge people intellectually as well. I think that's a favorite sport of his. If you say five sentences to him and one of them isn't right on, that's the one he'll pick up. I find that sort of fun."

If Gross does, others do not. They are the ones whose relationships with Friedkin become abbreviated. Said one writer, "It's been a good week if I've only had three fights with Billy." Offers an actor after a similar falling-out, "It's as though you just disappeared off the face of the earth. You don't exist to him anymore."

Friedkin himself admits to such traits, confessing, "I think that I don't suffer fools gladly. I don't like sloppy work from anybody. It really is a character flaw because it perceives a perfect world, which doesn't exist. As I get older I realize that I have a vision of a world that doesn't exist and perhaps never existed. I don't like to lose my temper and I have on a number of occasions. After all these years I would like to basically correct that need I have to show people my dissatisfaction when they fuck up. Believe me, I'm much harder on myself. Much harder on myself."

Still, the toll is heavy. Says Ed Gross, "Sometimes people

will get hurt by his directness, which is sometimes their problem and sometimes Billy's problem because he can alienate a
lot of people and he is in a business where it sometimes isn't
good to alienate people. If you've just come off *The French Connection* you don't have to worry about alienating anybody. If
you've just come off of *The Exorcist* you don't have to worry
about alienating anybody. People are still going to be very anxious to be around you and to do your next picture. But as time
goes on I don't think that it serves you well to alienate."

Is it arrogance (as Ralph Rosenblum noted) or impatience?
Or is it a combination of the two manifesting itself as control?

"He's obsessed with the idea of control and domination," says
Gerald Petievich. "I don't know what causes this, although
sometimes I've found it in people I've known in my life who
come from emotionally deprived backgrounds. They want to
control the things around them, and Billy wants to control his
environment at all times, more than anyone I've ever met in
my whole life. More than politicians or presidents.

"In a meeting, he will initiate the control from the moment
the meeting begins and he will control it until it ends. It's
something he will explain to somebody later that he did for
purposes of getting his own way because of a business deal, but
it really isn't. He can't stand to be in a room or any environment when he is not in control. I never saw a human situation
in the two years I was working with him when he wasn't."

This control even appears to exist when Friedkin is not in a
room if the charges of surveillance made during his divorce
and custody actions with Lesley-Anne Down are considered. Allegations of his intense desire to keep tabs on his son Jack was
part of the ongoing struggle between him and Down and was
introduced to suggest a need for control that bordered on the
paranoid.

On the other hand, it can be asserted by its absence where,
in the yin and yang of Hollywood, Friedkin dominates a project
by insisting he wants to direct it while refusing to make himself available to do so. Part of it is the standard ploy of keeping
films on various burners; part of it isn't. Still, he is the one who
can pull the plug. Says Ed Gross, "I can't think of a case where
the red-lighting [canceling a project] wasn't at Billy's insistence or wasn't Billy's doing."

Once Friedkin does say yes his control extends into every aspect of the filmmaking process.

"Within forty seconds of stepping onto a Friedkin set there is
no doubt who the director is," says Mark Johnson. "He is bet-

ter prepared than anybody else on the movie and he knows, with a couple of exceptions, how to do everybody's job better than they. So you're afraid of him. You've got to keep pace with him. Billy intimidates, he pushes, and there are certain people who respond very well to that. Other people get all frazzled and start to drop things and they just shouldn't be there."

"He's extraordinary," marvels Bud Yorkin of Friedkin's technical prowess. "He's been around the block so that when we were shooting a picture he can get it done as well as anybody."

But mastering someone else's job also makes Friedkin a stern taskmaster.

"He gives in on nothing," says Jonathan Sanger. "Sure, he will make compromises, but he doesn't show his hand, because he feels it's essential to maintain that control of every aspect of his production, and the moment he lets a little bit of it go, it all seems to slip from his hands. He is very autocratic with a lot of people—he won't explain it and that's the way it is, period, because he doesn't want to take the time unless he feels it's necessary. And there are other cases when he'll be very talkative and he'll discuss your problems and seem very flexible about it, and ultimately you'll come around to want to give him the kind of thing that he wants."

If that fails to happen, of course, there's the door. This explains why Bill Butler, despite being one of his oldest friends, has yet to shoot a film for him since leaving Chicago.

"That's why we're friends," Butler says. "I purposely don't work with him because I like the guy so much. I admire who he is. If we worked together he'd fire me after the first week like he does so many of his DPs [directors of photography] and where do I go from that? I may work with him again some day. I'll set some ground rules and see how it goes; it's a great creative experience. He inspires you; you know instinctively that anything less than one hundred percent just would not be right."

His methods can be sweet or ruthless depending on what the film, and only the film, needs.

"He radiates such enthusiasm that he's a hard sell to turn down," says Red Quinlan. "You either like him very much or you don't like him. I think Bill was a very popular guy in [Chicago]. He may have alienated a lot of people on the West Coast because he can be a tough guy if he doesn't get his way or doesn't keep to production schedules."

Randy Jurgensen admires this assertiveness and pays Friedkin a high compliment. "Billy would make *some* cop," he says. "His energy, everybody around him—you get in an argument with Billy Friedkin, you better know what you're talking about, and I don't mean that as a threat, because by the time he sits down he's ready to argue totally armed with every position and level of his subject." Jurgensen's admiration was formed while researching *The French Connection* when the director accompanied the police on drug busts. "It took a lot of guts to do that," the ex-detective says, "no matter how many detectives he had around."

Eddie Egan agrees. "I thought he was crazy," he chides. "A complete psycho. I mean, anybody that can ride around with me in the car and stay with me the way he did! I did my regular routine as opposed to what I would do for some 'good' guy from Hollywood. And he was right with me, all the way."

But the muscular action that some associates praise is viewed with less affection by others. Robert Weiner thinks, "He does live in a world of fantasy and he plays this big macho guy in everything—macho this and macho that. The language that comes from his mouth is purposely shocking, particularly with women. I don't know what his problem with women is, but he does have a problem."

Given the landscape of his work—male stories about bonding and conflict—the role of women in a Friedkin film is by definition reduced. Yet surely Chris MacNeil in *The Exorcist* is a fully realized character, just as Kate Fraser in *Rampage*—although appearing briefly—is an indication of the director's ability to offer a sensitive female. Even the venal Mrs. DeVoto of *Deal of the Century* is but one scoundrel among others, and achieves a kind of perverse equality.

Yet the real key to understanding Friedkin's women is to note how they relate to the men. From the mercenary Ruthie in *To Live and Die in L.A.* to the Nikki Blake/Nikki Pappas agents in *The C.A.T. Squad*—and even to the cannibalistic nanny Carmilla—Friedkin respects the abilities of women and does not make them into passive victims. Although this tends to make them "one of the guys" (as did Howard Hawks) it also makes them active participants in the stories within which they must function.

What it also does, of course, is to define women in male terms. This recognizes a measure of respect but also reveals a great deal of emotional distance. The braggadocio of the locker room can be shared by men and women alike, but it carries the tinge of vulgarity in doing so. Friedkin's glee in learning that women are repulsed, for example, by the world of *Cruising* is as much a validation of his ability to re-create it as it is a cinematic "no girls allowed" sign. The reaffirmation of a man's world, or forcing women to enter it on a man's terms, is a sign of domination that literally defines Friedkin's screen work, if not his life.

"I think he's much more interested and comfortable with men, just hanging out with them," offers William Petersen. "But the thing about Billy is, if you're weak with Billy, it's a problem. I think he very much likes honesty in a person. But if you get shocked, you're in trouble. I don't know if it's a male-female thing."

In terms of the effect, it is pretty much gender-neutral: if one wants to keep pace with William Friedkin, he or she must do it at William Friedkin's speed. It is, to be sure, a camaraderie shared (even celebrated) with such classically "male" directors as Howard Hawks, Raoul Walsh, Richard Brooks, Henry Hathaway and Victor Fleming, among others.

Friedkin himself courts this reputation. Often he will insist on continuing a walking conversation into a men's lavatory, a clear adult equivalent of a "no girls allowed" clubhouse sign. His on-set dialogue may include a run of permutations on the "cork soaker/coke sacker" dialogue exchanges between the two shakedown cops in *Cruising*. And strolling in public he will casually turn a corner while engaged in a thoughtful discourse on *The Exorcist*, catch sight of two middle-aged women standing at a bus stop, shift into a vulgar detailed description of the film's crucifix scene, then return to more philosophical language once the blushing bystanders are out of earshot.

The question is why an Oscar-winning director still feels compelled to attract attention by talking dirty in public.

"Billy is self-destructive," offers Gerald Petievich. "There are a lot of famous people with self-destructive tendencies. I'm not a psychiatrist; I don't know what causes it. Of course, he doesn't realize it.

"He wants to be able to go into the good restaurants but he doesn't want to wear a tie. And then everybody knows him as the guy who doesn't wear a tie, and he doesn't like that. That's part of his self-destructive bent."

It is most clearly manifested in his films, where he is almost pathologically incapable of offering an uplifting ending. This is his most clearly defined torment: wanting to do what is acceptable but knowing, all the while, that it would be fraudulent to his soul.

"Billy loads his films with the really dark side of human nature and people don't like that," reflects William Petersen. "It has nothing to do with gore. Billy talks to the psyche in you that is dark, which is bad and that we put in our closets. The great thing about Bill Friedkin as a filmmaker, which is why he's heads and tails over most of the people out there, is that we all have a dark side. Billy puts his in his work. People can't get used to Billy in a lot of ways because they end up seeing that switch and have seen him be able to be charming, be light, and then all of a sudden Billy can be dark, and he's not afraid of doing it."

"It has become the nemesis of his films," says Bill Butler. "More than one of his films have been less successful because he cannot help but allow what his view of the truth is to spill over into his films, and people don't want to see those kind of films."

William Peter Blatty agrees. "When it concerns himself, Billy is a one-man *Rashomon*.* He tells himself four different stories about his own personal responses to absolutely anything, and he searches for the truth. But when it comes to his profession—film—Billy is brutally honest, even when that honesty is detrimental to his own reputation."

In many ways the need to push and challenge others has always been present in him; making motion pictures just legitimized it. Friedkin is wide-ranging in his associations and insatiable in gathering new experiences. From his Chicago days he learned the value of seeking the company of those who could expand his world as would a precocious child in selecting a tutor. He often, therefore, found himself in the company of adults rather than peers. From this wealth of writers, lawyers, musicians, civil libertarians, cops and scoundrels he groomed himself into a gadfly, confidant and power broker.

Binding them all together is the single emotion of loyalty. Just as his most powerful motion pictures are about betrayal, so is Friedkin's personal life centered in this most precious commodity. Once it is open to doubt it can never be restored.

"I think that people betray each other constantly," he told interviewer Ric Gentry in a cynical mood when *To Live and Die in L.A.* was released to tepid box office returns in 1985. "I think there is as much betrayal in the world as there are blades of grass. I feel that human relationships are about friendship and

---

*Akira Kurosawa's 1951 classic in which four people describe a crime, each varying it from his point of view, none of them telling the whole truth, but none of them overtly lying.

betrayal and passion and then no passion, just sex. There was a time in my life when I was interested in passion. Both are valid. And you can have one without the other."

Such brooding thoughts, purposely provocative, are offered by the director as much to clarify his own thinking as to unnerve others. He is just as ready to shatter a somber mood with a wisecrack, often at his own expense, as he is to appear confessional and profound. Friends and colleagues quickly learn to navigate his challenging emotional roller coaster rides.

"He's one of the funniest people I know," says Mark Johnson. "He makes me laugh a lot but the humor is very bitter and can be quite hurtful. I used to say that the best laugh he could have would be to reduce somebody *else* to tears."

"If you get shocked, you're in trouble," advises William Petersen, who adds that Friedkin will escalate until he gets a reaction. "Which is why I like to go out to dinner with him. He is one of the greatest dates of all time because you never know what he is going to do. If you deal with his dark side and that's all you see, it can become so huge that that's all you can deal with. But if you deal with that part of him that's lovable and that part of him that's creative and genius, then you can *look* at the black stuff but you can *live* with the white stuff."

"He's such a nice, soft-spoken guy," says Arnold "Red" Auerbach, president of the Boston Celtics, Friedkin's favorite basketball team. "When he popped off doing his thing, the average guy would get amazed. *I* didn't get amazed; I knew he had to be tough when he had to be tough. So he's a tough guy when he has to be tough."

Auerbach, who is no stranger to toughness himself, like Friedkin also inspires intense loyalty; one feeds the other.

"The way you get loyalty," he explains, "is just by taking care of your own. If a guy is straight with him, he'll help the guy for many years to come. That's the way he is, and that's important, because after a while word gets around: Bill Friedkin's straight, his word is his bond, and, Christ, don't cross him, do him straight up, and if he's ever in a position to help you, he'll help you."

It works both ways. Auerbach and Friedkin, although at the top of their respective fields, are savvy enough to maintain a certain professional distance. Has Friedkin ever asserted his coaching advice to Auerbach?

"He better not—I'll break his arm," the Celtic's chief jokes.

And Friedkin's interests are not confined to the parquet floors of the Boston Garden or the soundproofed stages of the Hollywood studios.

"You could talk about almost any subject with Billy and find him responsive and very intelligently so," says film company executive Alan Friedberg. "Billy, in a certain manner of speaking, comes close to being a Renaissance man—any man who was married to Jeanne Moreau has a good leg up to start with!"

How does Friedkin regard himself and his work? Beyond the customary self-deprecation, he gravitates more toward the craft than the art. Craft, after all, is a function of mechanics, is quantifiable and therefore can be controlled. The art—that which lurks below the façade—is more dangerous ground and Friedkin surveys it with off-putting cynicism.

"Ultimately it comes down to *the story* with me," he insists. "Not all fleshed out, but what the subject matter is and whether it is worthwhile. Very often you get down to, Yes it's worthwhile, but the script doesn't work for a variety of reasons: the writer's too lazy or not good enough or my ideas are not sound, or we tried them and it doesn't work."

He decries the movies' reliance on big stars ("The truth is, it's the subject matter and how it's handled that transcend the star. The biggest movies of all time, with one or two exceptions, are all films that did not have stars") and is frustrated that the industry at present seems to feel otherwise. Not that Friedkin cannot get actors to do what he wants—any man who can get Al Pacino to pose tied up on a bed with his pants off as in *Cruising* has to be persuasive—but it is time-consuming.

"That's part of the work process," he declares. "Some actors that I've worked with need a great deal of babysitting, others need none. Some are like Ellen [Burstyn]; Ellen needed constant encouragement, as most of them do, but she always had a feeling herself when she got it right.

"It's hard to get an actor into this artificial process. Where the actor must view past the other actors in a scene and he's seeing lights and technicians standing around picking their nose, often when he's working, it's very distracting. So I do whatever possible to get people off the set who don't need to be there. That's why I'm more drawn to dramatic stories because it's easier to create a dramatic mood than to set up a comic situation that the actor can believe in. But I'm consciously trying to create moods on the set, and it went to an extreme on *The Exorcist* where we were firing shots, scaring the shit out of people, playing music. One of the things I do is that I never say, 'Roll it.' I never tell the actor the film is rolling—I just like them to ease into the scene and not even know when it's over. I don't let them stop until at the end when I think it's gone past the limit, and then I'll say 'okay' and 'slate.' "

The involvement that Friedkin demands from his actors is no less for his crew members, a breed of filmmaking professional known for being jaded about a process that the rest of the world sees as glamorous. This sheds light on his penchant for firing those who do not meet his exacting standards.

"One of my pet peeves is that the people who work on these sets don't give a shit," he says. "They're very irreverent. Very seldom do the people on the crews realize or pay any attention to the fact that the only reason any of us is there is because the actors are here. The actor has the most difficult job in the world and in my experience, on a set, not enough respect is paid to that. On almost every set you go to you find crew members picking their nose or talking or reading a newspaper or something while an actor's doing a big scene. You say, well, these guys, it's so boring once you've hauled a lot of lumber and put it up or fixed a light, you don't want to stand there and watch an actor do it fifteen times. Nevertheless, I've found that actors are very conscious of the mood and attitude of a crew on the set. The actor is always looking for something that proves he's inadequate."

So, in a strange way, is Friedkin. Although he wields a fair amount of power in the Hollywood scheme of things, he is more obsessed with films that probe weakness, not strength. His wildly profitable work was over a decade and a half ago, yet the fact that he enjoyed such success is, in the industry's logic, enough reason to let him keep pursuing it.

But unlike a hack who keeps rehashing the same movie, Friedkin constantly seeks different challenges, albeit within the broad genre of the crime drama. His dealings are mainly with those producers and studio executives who rose with him (and in large measure owe their success to his skills) so there is a loyalty that extends in both directions. Hollywood is about relationships.

But William Friedkin is not going to make the next *E.T.*, even though he admires both the movie and its director. His films don't soothe, they provoke. So does he. This inner turmoil fuels both himself and his motion pictures and he has yet to come to terms with why.

It is as though Friedkin has committed some horrible sin in his life, a sin for which he feels he must atone. In his films he uses betrayal, illusion, commitment and self-deception as themes that can turn in an instant from good into evil, and back, in plots that are a virtual chronicle of human frailties.

But lacking punishment by someone he respects, Friedkin punishes himself. He picks fights, alienates others, conjures the darkest of images and expects people to watch them, shares his love on the most rigid of terms, and frequently wallows in his failures as a means of demonstrating the vulnerability he secretly abhors. He flatly rejects psychiatry, yet his films are the most brutal of self-analyses. He is a man who lives for his craft at whatever the emotional cost.

He can be a great friend to others or a sullen loner when they seek to return the affection. All of these traits comprise (or have created) a man who sets his own agenda which others, for whatever reasons of their own character, follow.

"I don't know if there are people he wants to get even with," muses Ed Gross, who has known Friedkin since his arrival in Los Angeles. "There are some people who are not big fans of his but I don't know of anybody that he really has bad things to say about. You don't hear of it.

"You know what they say: small minds talk about people and big minds talk about things and great minds talk about ideas. He talks about ideas."

But a man who talks about ideas in the vapid world of American commercial movies is courting frustration. And he gets it. William Friedkin constantly decries superficiality, yet has chosen to live and work in the field where it is grown and harvested. In that particular kind of self-hatred which Hollywood nurtures, Friedkin maintains a studied vantage point. He uses it to gain perspective, but also to maintain an escape route. After all, he is the rounder who breaks the rules and then pays a call on the people who made them. It is the kind of a fight a boy wonder can get away with but a grown-up looks foolish continuing. It's a good thing that Hollywood celebrates youth in every form.

They say that by the age of forty a man gets the face he deserves, but that his emotional face is formed a lot earlier. William Friedkin's was formed in Chicago while he was pushing his mail cart through the hallways of a television station, his unspoiled intelligence brightening the lives of those around him who listened to his dreams with paternalistic encouragement.

In television stations there are huge, double windows that seal off the studios from the hallways that connect them. These

windows are built of heavy glass panes layered with air that
serves as soundproofing.

Such a construction creates a curious visual effect, for when
one looks through the double windows a little light always leaks
through to cause a shadowy reflection of the person looking in.
When William Friedkin searched the darkness for his future, he
was doomed forever to see himself staring back.

WILLIAM FRIEDKIN FILMOGRAPHY

The following represents the production credits of the films of William Friedkin as determined by press materials available at the time of their release and an examination of the actual screen credits. Where there is a conflict, the screen credits prevail.

Friedkin's Chicago television work, except as noted, must be presumed lost unless some enterprising coworker or lab gremlin happily proves otherwise. The live and early videotape programs churned out by the tyro director will probably never be known.

Beginnings: The Ulveling Interview (National Educational Television and Radio Center at WTTW-TV, Chicago; produced by *The World Book Encyclopedia*, c. 1960) 30 minutes, B&W kinescope Producer: Don Meier; director: William Friedkin.
Cast: Ken Nordine (host); Prof. Don Federson (interviewer); Dr. Ralph A. Ulveling (guest).

The People Versus Paul Crump (WBKB-TV, Chicago, 1962) 58:45, B&W 16mm.
Producer and director, William Friedkin; cinematographer, Wilmer Butler; editor, Glenn McGowean; sound recording, August H. May; lighting, Jim Wagner; assistant camera, Stan La-

zan; music composed and conducted by Marty Rubenstein.
Cast: John Justin Smith (the reporter); Paul Crump (himself); Mrs. Lonie Crump (herself); Brooks Johnson (Paul, age twenty-two).

Home Again: 77 - Grange of Illinois (WBKB-TV, Chicago, c. 1963) 30 minutes, B&W 16mm.
Executive producer, Dan Schuffman; producer and director, William Friedkin; cinematographer, Wilmer Butler; audio director and associate producer, Robert Strang; editor, Glen McGowean; assistant director, Marlon Partelleau.
Cast: Red Grange (himself), George Halas (himself), Jim Peterson (himself), Bob Rhodes (narrator).

The Bold Men (David L. Wolper in association with ABC News, 1965) 52 minutes, B&W 16mm.
Executive producer, David L. Wolper; presented by the 3-M Corporation; director, William Friedkin; narration written by Don Bresnahan; story by William Friedkin; producer, Julian Ludwig; film editor, Bud Smith; music supervisor, Elmer Bernstein; associate producer, Sam Farnsworth; assistant editor, Fran Kaplan; sound effects editor, Mort Tubor, MPSE; music editor, Jack Tillar; sound supervisor, Jerry Ow Young; sound engineers, James Ow Young, Don Lusby, Jr.; sound recording TV recorder, Dick Olson; cinematographers, Guy Adenis, Angel Bilbatua, Bob Bukor, Wilmer Butler, Miki Carter, Jim Crabe, Doyle Fields, Vilis Lapenieks, Grant Rohloff, Primo Sanchez; business administrator, Harvey Bernhard; film coordinator, Bert Gold; director of research, William Edgar; production assistant, Roberta Goldstein; film processing by Consolidated Film Industries, Inc. We gratefully acknowledge the cooperation of David Chudnow and Thor Brooks, producers of the motion picture *Kwaheri;* Firestone Tire & Rubber Company; Marineland; Jungleland; Cinematografica Ariel, S.A.
Cast: Don Wilson (girder walker), Carlos Roman (reef diver), Red Adair (wild flame control), John Craig (swimming with sharks), Chet Jessyck (lion tamer), Alan Carlton (snake handler), Manuel Benites (matador), Mickey Lukin, Jr. (marksman), Rod Pack and Bob Allen (skydivers), Harry Haynes (pilot), Art Arfons (driver), Van Heflin (narrator).

Pro Football: Mayhem on a Sunday Afternoon (David L. Wolper Productions, 1965) 52 minutes, B&W 16mm.
Executive producer, David L. Wolper; producers Harvey Bernhard and William Friedkin; director, William Friedkin; narration written by Bernard Wiser; story by William Friedkin; editor, David Blewitt; music by Jim Smith; cinematographer, Vilis Lapenieks; second unit cinematographer, John Alonzo; audio director, Nigel Noble; game montage editor, Bud Smith; technical advisors, Gordon Soltau, Dave Bass; additional cinematographers, David Blewitt, Jim Crabe, Erik Daarstad, Steve Lighthill, Stan Troutman; associate producer, Bert Gold; assistant editor, Joe Thornton; assistant to the director, Roberta Gray; production assistant, Allan Folsom; music supervisor, Jack Tillar; sound effects editor, Morton Tubor, MPSE; sound engineers, James Ow Young, Don Lusby, Jr.; supervisory film editor, Larry Neiman; negative cutter, Elva Fraser; assistant negative cutter, Christina Friedgen; opticals and titles, CFI; sound rerecording, Ryder Sound Services; production under the supervision of Mel Stuart. We gratefully acknowledge the cooperation of NFL Films, Inc., Ed Sabol, president; the San Francisco Forty-Niners; the Cleveland Browns; the National Pro Football Hall of Fame, Dick McCann, director.
Cast: Van Heflin (narrator).

The Thin Blue Line (David L. Wolper Productions, a Division of Metromedia, in association with ABC News, 1966) 52 minutes, B&W 16mm.
Executive producer, David L. Wolper; presented by the 3-M Corporation; producer and director, William Friedkin; narration written by Bud Wiser and David Vowell; story by William Friedkin; editors, David Blewitt and Nicholas Clapp; associate producer, Bert Gold; production manager, Sam Farnsworth; audio director, Nigel Noble; sound effects editors, Charles L. Campbell, Colin Mouat; sound engineer, Robert Litt; music supervisor, Jack Tillar; production assistant, Allan Folsom; director of research, William Edgar; film researcher, Jack Goelman; negative supervisor, Elva Fraser; assistant negative cutter, Christina Friedgen; business administrator, Harvey Bernhard; supervising film editor, Lawrence E. Neiman; opticals and titles, Consolidated Film Industries, Inc.; series producer, Mel Stuart. We gratefully acknowledge the cooperation of the California Highway Patrol; the California Bureau of Narcotic Enforcement; UCLA School of Law; WBKB-TV News; Thomas

Lynch, Attorney General of California; the Rochester Police Bureau; the Locust Club and the Dept. of Public Safety of Rochester, New York, and William B. Power.
Cast: Van Heflin (narrator).

Off Season (An Alfred Hitchcock Production, Shanley Productions and Universal City Studios, 1965) 52 minutes, B&W television film.
Producer, Gordon Hessler; director, William Friedkin; writer, Robert Bloch; story by Edward D. Hoch appearing in *Alfred Hitchcock's Mystery Magazine*; cinematographer, John F. Warren, ASC; editor, Douglas Stewart; art director, Andrew Mayer; sound, Lyle Gain.
Cast: John Gavin (Johnny Kendall); Indus Arthur (Sandy Ebbets), Richard Jaeckel (Mily Woodman), Tom Drake (Sheriff Dade), Dodi Heath (Irma Dade), Frederick R. Draper (Dr. Hornbeck), Duncan McCloud (bartender), Jimmy Deutch (Sgt. Grayson). Hosted by Alfred Hitchcock.

Good Times (A Steve Broidy production, a Motion Pictures International production, a Columbia Pictures presentation, 1967) 91 minutes, DeLuxe color.
Executive producer, Steve Broidy; producer, Lindsley Parsons; director, William Friedkin; screenplay, Tony Barrett; story by Nicholas Hyams; cinematographer, Robert Wyckoff; special consultant on musical sequences, Wilmer Butler; production manager, Arthur Broidy; film editor, Melvin Shapiro; art director, Arthur Kramb; assistant film editor, Richard Wahrman; sound effects by Delmore Harris, Carl Lodato; costumes by Leah Rhodes; makeup by Edwin Butterworth, SMA; hair stylist, Hedwig Mjorud; sound recording, Harold Lewis; assistant director, David Salven; script supervisor, Marvin Weldon; choreographer, Andre Tayer; wardrobe by Forrest T. Butler; special photography by Farciot Edouart, ASC; jungle sequences photographed in Africa, USA, Inc.; music composed and conducted by Sonny Bono; music arranged by Harold E. Battiste, Jr.
Cast: Sonny and Cher (themselves), George Sanders (Mordicus), Norman Alden (Warren); Lenny Duran (Smith), Kelly Thorsen (tough hombre), Lenny Weinrib (Leslie Garth), Peter Robbins (Brandon), Edy Williams, China Lee, Diane Haggerty (Mordicus's Girls), James Flavin (lieutenant), Phil Arnold (Solly), Hank Worden (Kid), Morris Buchanan (proprietor), Charles

Smith (telegrapher), John Cliff (gangster), Herk Reardon, Bruce Tegner (wrestlers), Howard Wright (Old Timer), Joe Devlin (bartender), Mike Kopach (deputy), Paul Frees (announcer, unbilled).

Songs: "I Got You, Babe," "It's the Little Things," "Good Times," "Trust Me," "Don't Talk to Strangers," "I'm Gonna Love You," "Just a Name."

The Pickle Brothers (Four Star Television, 1967) 25 minutes, color. Writer-producer-creators, Gerald Gardner and Dee Caruso; director, William Friedkin; music by Quincy Jones; editor (uncredited), Bud Smith.

Cast: Ron Prince (Baxter Pickle), Mike Mislove (Buddy Pickle), Peter Lee (Bobo Pickle), Maureen Arthur (Miss Boom Boom), Carol Veazie (Mrs. DeWitt), George Neise (Tweed), Louis Quinn (Falstaff), Liliane Montevecchi (The Princess).

The Night They Raided Minsky's (Tandem Productions, released through United Artists, 1968) 99 minutes, DeLuxe color. Producer, Norman Lear; director, William Friedkin; screenplay by Arnold Schulman, Sidney Michaels and Norman Lear; based on the book by Rowland Barber; cinematographer, Andrew Laszlo, ASC; music by Charles Strouse; songs: music by Charles Strouse, lyrics by Lee Adams; dances, musical numbers and sketches staged by Danny Daniels; production designers, William and Jean Eckart; art director, John Robert Lloyd; music orchestrated and conducted by Philip J. Lang; production manager, Jim DiGangi; assistant director, Burtt Harris; costume designer, Anna Hill Johnstone; visual consultant and second unit director, Pablo Ferro; associate producer, George Justin; set decorator, John Godfrey; set dresser, Richard Adee; second assistant director, J. Alan Hopkins; camera operator, Richard Kratina; production mixer, Dennis L. Maitland; script supervisor, Margueritte James Powell; assistant to producer, William Giorgio; film editor, Ralph Rosenblum, ACE; sound editor, Jack Fitzstephens; dance arranger and conductor, Richard DeBenedictis; assistant choreographer, Anne Wallace; rerecording mixer, Richard Vorisek; assistant editor, Michael Breddan; assistant cameraman, Vincent Gerardo; still photographer, Josh Weiner; property master, Donald Holtzman; gaffer, William Meyerhoff; technical advisor, Morton Minsky; key grip, Michael Mahoney; set construction, Edward Swanson,

Walter Way; chief scenic artist, Edward Garzen; wardrobe supervisors, George Newman, Florence Transfield; makeup by Irving Bloipian; hairdresser, Robert Grimaldi; casting by Marian Dougherty; extras casting, Bernie Styles; production secretary, Shirley Marcus; costumes by Eaves; opticals by The Optical House, Inc.
Cast: Jason Robards (Raymond Paine), Britt Ekland (Rachel Schpitendavel), Norman Wisdom (Chick Williams), Forrest Tucker (Trim Houlihan), Harry Andrews (Jacob Schpitendavel), Joseph Wiseman (Louis Minsky), Denholm Elliott (Vance Fowler), Elliott Gould (Billy Minsky), Jack Burns (candy butcher), Bert Lahr (Prof. Spats), Gloria LeRoy (Mae Harris), Eddie Lawrence (Scratch), Dexter Maitland (Duffy), Lillian Hayman (singer in speakeasy), Dick Libertini (Pockets), Judith Lowry (Mother Anne), Will B. Able (Clyde), Mike Elias (immigration officer #1), Frank Shaw (immigration officer #2), Chann Hale (Valerie).
The Minsky Girls: Ernestine Barrett, Kelsey Collins, Marilyn C'Monau, Kathryn Doby, JoAnn Lehmann, Dorothea McFarland, Billie Mahoney, Caroline Morris, June Eve Story, Helen Wood. Rudy Vallee (narrator).
Songs/Musical Numbers: "The Night They Raided Minsky's," "A Perfect Gentleman," "Take Ten Terrific Girls (And Only Nine Costumes)," "You Rat, You," "Penny Arcade," "How I Loved Her," "Wait For Me (Love Theme)."

The Birthday Party (Palomar Pictures International, 1968) 124 minutes, Eastman color, processed by Technicolor. MPAA Rating: M.
Executive producer Edgar J. Scherick; produced by Max J. Rosenberg and Milton Subotsky; directed by William Friedkin; screenplay by Harold Pinter; production manager, Teresa Bolland; cinematographer, Denys Coop, BSC; camera operator, Alan Hall; sound recordist, Norman Bolland; sound editors, Jim Roddan, Alan Pattillo; assistant editors, Brian Mann, John Hackney; assistant art director, Martin Atkinson; assistant director, Andrew Grieve; second assistant director, Gerry Harrison; continuity, Kay Rawlings; makeup assistant, Eddie Knight; hairdresser Betty Sherrif; wardrobe supervisor, Dulcie Midwinter; special still photography, Alan Ballard; art director, Edward Marshall; film editor, Anthony Gibbs; assistant editor, Stanley Smith.
Cast: Robert Shaw (Stanley Webber), Sydney Tafler (Nat Gold-

berg), Patrick Magee (McCann), Dandy Nichols (Meg Boles), Moultrie Kelsall (Peter Boles), Helen Fraser (Lulu).

The Boys in the Band (National General Pictures, Cinema Center Films, Leo Productions, Ltd., 1970) 119 minutes, DeLuxe color. MPAA Rating: R.
Executive producers, Dominick Dunne and Robert Jiras; producer-writer, Mart Crowley; director, William Friedkin; director of photography, Arthur J. Ornitz; associate producer, Kenneth Utt; production designer, John Robert Lloyd; costume designer, W. Robert La Vine; set decorator, Phil Smith; assistant director, William C. Gerrity; editors, Carl Lerner, ACE and Gerald Greenberg; production manager, Paul Ganapoler; camera operator, Richard Mingalone; script supervisor, Nancy Tonery; sound, Jack C. Jacobson; assistant art director, Robert Wightman; master scenic artist, Ed Garzero; chief electricians, Willie Meyerhoff, Sal Martorano; key grip, Mike Mahoney; assistant grip, Jim Halligan; head carpenter, Ken Faquette; set dresser, Robert Klatt; property master, Joe Carracholo; makeup supervisor, Robert O'Bradovich; hair stylist, Verne Caruso; wardrobe supervisor, Joseph E. Dehn; assistant cameraman, Felix Trimbali; stills by Muky; assistant editor, Lynn Lewis Lovett; sound editors, John J. Fitzstephens, Sanford Rackow, Vincent Connolly; sound mixer, Al Cramaglia; dubbing editor, Jean Hagley; titles by Everett Alson; unit publicist, Peter Benoit; production secretary, Adeline Leonard; secretary to the producers, Ruth Oberdorfer; production auditor, Lillian Osorowitz; casting by Victor Jay Agency; based on a play as first produced on the stage by Richard Barr and Charles Woodward; filmed at New York City at Production Center; fashion sequences filmed at Waddell Gallery.
Cast: Kenneth Nelson (Michael), Frederick Combs (Donald), Cliff Gorman (Emory), Keith Prentice (Larry), Laurence Luckinbill (Hank), Reuben Greene (Bernard), Peter White (Alan), Robert La Tourneaux (Cowboy), Leonard Frey (Harold).
Songs: "Anything Goes," "The Look of Love," "Love Is Not a Heat Wave," "Funky Broadway," "The Frog," "Take the Fifth Amendment," "Good Lovin' Ain't Easy to Come By."

The French Connection (Philip D'Antoni Productions/Schine-Moore Productions/Twentieth Century-Fox, 1971) 102 minutes, DeLuxe color. MPAA Rating: R.

Executive producer: G. David Schine; producer, Philip D'Antoni; director, William Friedkin; screenplay, Ernest Tidyman, based on the book by Robin Moore; director of photography, Owen Roizman; film editor, Jerry Greenberg; music composed and conducted by Don Ellis; associate producer, Kenneth Utt; art director, Ben Kazaskow; set decorator, Ed Garzero; sound, Chris Newman and Theodore Soderberg; technical consultants, Eddie Egan, Sonny Grosso; chief electrician, Billy Ward; associate editor, Norman Gay; unit production manager, Paul Ganapoler; assistant directors, William C. Gerrity, Terry Donnelly; special effects, Sass Bedig; key grip, Robert Ward; stunt coordinator, Bill Hickman; camera operator, Enrique Bravo; script supervisor, Nick Sgarro; property master, Tom Wright; location consultant, Pat Thomas; makeup artist, Irving Buchman; wardrobe, Joseph W. Dehn, Florence Foy; costumes, Joseph Fretwell III; casting, Robert Weiner.
Cast: Gene Hackman (Jimmy "Popeye" Doyle), Fernando Rey (Alain Charnier), Roy Scheider (Buddy "Cloudy" Russo), Tony Lo Bianco (Sal Boca), Marcel Bozzuffi (Pierre Nicoli), Frederick DePasquale (Henri Devereaux), Bill Hickman (Mulderig), Ann Rebbot (Marie Charnier), Harold Gary (Joel Weinstock), Arlene Farba (Angie Boca), Eddie Egan (Simonson), Andre Ernotte (La Valle), Sonny Grosso (Klein), Benny Marino (Lou Boca), Pat McDermott (chemist), Alan Weeks (pusher), Al Fann (informant), Irving Abrahams (police mechanic), Randy Jurgensen (police sergeant), William Cole (motorman), The Three Degrees (themselves).

The Exorcist (A HOYA Production/Warner Bros., 1973) 121 minutes, Metrocolor. MPAA Rating: R.
Executive producer, Noel Marshall; written for the screen and produced by William Peter Blatty, based on his novel; director, William Friedkin; associate producer, David Salven; director of photography, Owen Roizman; makeup artist, Dick Smith; special effects, Marcel Vercoutere; production design, Bill Malley; first assistant director, Terrence A. Donnelly; set decorator, Jerry Wunderlich; music, Krzysztof Penderecki; additional music, Jack Nitzsche; Iraq sequence director of photography, Billy Williams; production manager, William Kaplan; sound, Jean-Louis Ducarme; film editor, Bud Smith; assistant film editor, Ross Levy; supervising film editor, Jordan Leondopoulos; film editors, Evan Lottman, Norman Gay; assistant film editors, Mikael Goldman, Craig McKay, Jonathan Pontell; sound, Chris

Newman; dubbing mixer, Buzz Knudson; sound effects editors, Fred Browne, Ross Taylor; special sound effects, Ron Nagle, Doc Siegel, Gonzalo Gavira, Bob Fine; sound consultant, Hal Landaker; music editor, Gene Marks; gaffer, Dick Quinlan; key grip, Eddie Quinn; property master, Joe Caracciolo; script supervisor, Nick Sgarro; costume designer, Joe Fretwell; hair stylist, Bill Farley; administrative assistant, Albert Shapiro; casting, Nessa Hyams, Juliet Taylor, Louis DiGiaimo; still photographer, Josh Weiner; second assistant director, Alan Green; ladies' wardrobe, Florence Foy; men's wardrobe, Bill Beattie; production office coordinator, Anne Mooney; master scenic artist, Eddie Garzero; technical advisors, Reverend John Nicola, SJ; Reverend Thomas Bermingham, SJ; Reverend William O'Malley, SJ; Norman E. Chase, MD, Professor of Radiology, New York University Medical Center; Herbert E. Walker, MD; Arthur I. Snyder, MD; optical effects, Marv Ystrom; title design, Dan Perri; color consultant, Robert M. McMillan; photographic equipment by Panavision; jewelry design, Aldo Cipullo for Cartier, N.Y.; furs by Revlon.

Cast: Ellen Burstyn (Chris MacNeil), Max von Sydow (Lancaster Merrin), Lee J. Cobb (William Kinderman), Kitty Winn (Sharon), Jack MacGowran (Burke Dennings), Jason Miller (Damien Karras), Linda Blair (Regan Theresa MacNeil), Peter Masterson (doctor), Reverend William O'Malley, SJ (Father Dyer), Titos Vandis (Karras's uncle), Vasiliki Malliaros (Karras's mother).

With: Barton Heyman, Rudolf Schundler, Gina Petrushka, Robert Symonds, Arthur Storch, Reverend Thomas Bermingham, SJ, Wallace Rooney, Ron Faber, Donna Mitchell, Roy Cooper, Robert Gerringer, William Peter Blatty (unbilled) and Mercedes McCambridge.

Musical Selections: "Kanon for Orchestra and Tape," "Cello Concerto," "String Quartet (1960)," "Polymorphia," "The Devils of London," "Fantasia for Strings," "Threnody 1: Night of the Electric Insects," "Fliessend, Ausserts Zart from Five Pieces for Orchestra, Op. 10," "Beginnings from the Wind Harp," "Tubular Bells," "Study No. 1/Study No. 2."

Sorcerer (Paramount Pictures and Universal Pictures/Film Properties International, 1977) 122 minutes, Technicolor. MPAA Rating: R.

Director and producer, William Friedkin; screenplay by Walon Green, based on the novel by Georges Arnaud; film editor and associate producer, Bud Smith; this film is dedicated to H.G. Clouzot; production designer, John Box; photographed by John M. Stephens and Dick Bush, BSC; sound recording by Jean-Louis Ducarme; original music composed and performed by Tangerine Dream; art director, Roy Walker; set decorator, Bob Laing; draftsman, Leslie W. Tomkins; first assistant director, Newt Arnold; second assistant directors, Al Shapiro, Miguel Gil, Jr., Mark Johnson; production manager, Robert Bakker; unit manager, Gerald Murphy; production secretary, Nanette Siegert; dubbing mixer, Buzz Knudson; rerecording, Bob Glass and Dick Tyler; key grip, Gaylin Schultz; grips, Bernie Schwartz, George Resler, Bill Kenny, Jim Sheppherd; stunt coordinator, Bob Ekins; lighting gaffer, Patrick Blymer; best boy, Mike Weathers; costume designer, Anthony Powell; property master, Barry Bedig; casting director, Lou DiGiaimo; construction, Ken Pattenden, Doug Millett; technical advisor, Marvin Peck; film editor/music editor, Robert K. Lambert, ACE; sound effects editors, Ned Humphreys, Jere Huggins, Cynthia Scheider; musical effects, Ron Nagle, Scott Mathews; makeup, Ben Nye, Jr., Bob Norn, John Norn: assistant property master, Gene Anderson; hairdresser, Verne Caruso; script supervisor, John Franco; transportation coordinator, Whitney Ellison; helicopter pilot, Richard Holley; production accountant, Charles A. Ogle; assistant production accountant, Paul Roedl; assistant to the producer, Luis Llosa; secretary to the director, Toni St. Clair Lilly; optical effects, Marv Ystrom; titles, Jean-Guy Jacques; lenses and Panaflex camera by Panavision (R).

Cast: Roy Scheider (Scanlon/"Dominguez"), Bruno Cremer (Victor Manzon/"Serrano"), Francisco "Paco" Rabal ("Nilo"), Amidou (Kassem/"Martinez"), Ramon Bieri (Corlette), Peter Capell (Lartigue), Karl John ("Marquez"), Frederick Ladebur ("Carlos"), Chico Martinez (Bobby Del Rios), Joe Spinnel (Spider), Rosario Almontes (Agrippa), Richard Holley (Billy White), Anne Marie Descott (Blanche), Jean-Luc Bideau (Pascal), Jacques Francois (Lefevre), Andre Falcon (Guillot), Gerald Murphy (Donnelly), Desmond Crofton (Boyle), Henry Diamond (Murray), Ray Dittrich (Ben), Frank Gio (Marty), Randy Jurgensen (Vinnie), Gus Allegretti (Carlo Ricci).

Music: "Spheres," "I'll Remember April."

The Brink's Job (Dino DeLaurentiis/Universal City Studios, 1978) 118 minutes, Technicolor. MPAA Rating: PG.
Producer, Ralph Serpe; director, William Friedkin; screenplay

by Walon Green based on the book *Big Stick-Up at Brink's* by Noel Behn; director of photography, A. Norman Leigh; production designer, Dean Tavoularis; film editors, Bud Smith, Robert K. Lambert, ACE; music composed by Richard Rodney Bennett; music conducted by Angela Morley; set decorator, George R. Nelson; sound, Jeff Wexler; sound rerecording, Buzz Knudson, Bob Glass, Don MacDougall; music editor, Richard Luckey; sound effects editors, Gordon Eckert, Lou Edemann; special effects, Larry Cavanaugh; production manager, Jonathan Sanger; first assistant director, Terrence A. Donnelly; second assistant director, Mark Johnson; art director, Angelo Graham; casting, Louis DiGiaimo; costume designer, Ruth Morley; cameraman, Enrique Bravo; assistant cameramen, Hank Muller, Jr., Garry Muller, Mike Green; additional photography, James Contner; makeup, Bob Norin; hair stylist, Verne Caruso; costumer, Tony Scarano; assistant costume designer, Gloria Gresham; assistant film editors, Ned Humphreys, Jere Huggins, Scott Smith; script supervisor Catalina Lawrence; dubbing supervisor, Charles L. Campbell; property master, Barry Bedig; second property master, Gene Anderson; rigger gaffer, Lou Tobin; key grip, Gaylin Schultz; construction coordinator, John LaSalandra; production services, Sonny Grosso, Randy Jurgensen; transportation coordinator, William C. Bratton; location manager, Carmine Foresta; electronic department supervisor, John DeBlau; painter, Roger Deitz; boom man, Don Coufal; negative cutting, Donah Bassett; production office coordinator, Nanette Siegert; secretary to the director, Toni St. Clair Lilly; stills, Josh Weiner; color timer, Larry Rovetti; opticals by The Optical House, L.A. With special thanks to Brink's Incorporated for its cooperation: "Since 1859 Nobody Has Ever Lost A Penny Entrusting Their Valuables To Brink's."
Cast: Peter Falk (Tony Pino), Peter Boyle (Joe McGinnis), Allen Goorwitz (Vinnie Costa), Warren Oates ("Specs" O'Keefe), Gena Rowlands (Mary Pino), Paul Sorvino (Jazz Maffie), Sheldon Leonard (J. Edgar Hoover), Gerard Murphy (Sandy Richardson), Kevin O'Connor (Stanley "Gus" Gusciora), Claudia Peluso (Gladys), Patrick Hines (H. H. Rightmire), Malachy McCourt (Mutt Murphy), Walter Klavun (Daniels), Randy Jurgensen (FBI agent), John Brandon (FBI agent), Earl Hindman (FBI agent), John Farrell (FBI agent).

Cruising (Jerry Weintraub/Lorimar/United Artists release, 1980) 106 minutes, in color. MPAA Rating R.

Producer, Jerry Weintraub; written for the screen and directed
by William Friedkin, based upon the novel by Gerald Walker;
director of photography, James Contner; production designer,
Bruce Weintraub; art director, Edward Pisoni; costume designer, Robert deMora; film editor, Bud Smith; music by Jack
Nitzsche; production executive, Mark Johnson; associate pro-
ducer/production manager, Burtt Harris; first assistant director, Alan Hopkins; second assistant director, Robert Warren;
camera operator, Enrique Bravo; assistant cameramen, Hank
Muller, Jr., Gary Muller; property masters, Barry Bedig, James
Raitt; gaffer, Gene Engels; key grip, William Miller; technical
advisors, Randy Jurgensen, Sonny Grosso; sound rerecording,
Robert (Buzz) Knudson, Robert Glass, Christopher Jenkins;
makeup artist, Allan Weisinger; special makeup effects, Robert
Norin; supervising sound editor, Charles L. Campbell; sound
editors, Louis L. Edemann, David A. Pettijohn, Paul Bruce
Richardson; assistant sound editor, Rick Franklin; dialogue editor, Norman Schwartz; casting director, Louis DiGiaimo; assistant film editors, Ned Humphreys, Jere Huggins; music
engineer, Bill Evans; hair stylist, Robert Grimaldi; location
manager, Carmine Foresta; wardrobe supervisors, Michael
Dennison, Dean Jackson; script supervisor, Sidney Gecker; production office coordinator, Jennifer Ogden; stills, Josh Weiner;
auditor, Lucille Cannon; Teamster captain, Edward Iacobelli;
production assistant, Michael Weintraub; secretary to the producer, George Davis; secretary to the director, Toni St. Clair
Lilly; sound mixer, Kim Ornitz; ADR mixer, Athan Gigiakos/
The Sound Shop, New York City; color timer, Larry Rovetti;
negative cutter, Donah Bassett; construction coordinator, Car-
los Quiles, Jr.; scenic artists, Bruno Robotti, Stanley Graham.
Cast: Al Pacino (Steve Burns/"John Forbes"), Paul Sorvino (Capt.
Edelson), Karen Allen (Nancy), Richard Cox (Stuart Richards),
Don Scardino (Ted Bailey), Joe Spinell (Patrolman DiSimone),
Jay Acovone (Skip Lee), Randy Jurgensen (Detective Lefran-
sky), Barton Heyman (Dr. Rifkin), Gene Davis (DaVinci), Ar-
naldo Santana (Loren Lukas), Larry Atlas (Eric Rossman), Allan
Miller (Chief of Detectives), Sonny Grosso (Detective Blasio),
Edward O'Neil (Detective Schreiber), Michael Aronin (Detec-
tive Davis), James Remar (Gregory), William Russ (Paul Gaines),
Mike Starr (Patrolman Desher), Steve Inwood (Martino), Keith
Prentice (Joey), Leland Starnes (Jack Richards), Robert Pope
(DaVinci's friend), Leo Burmester (Water Sport), Bruce Levine
(Dancer), Charles Dunlap (Three Card Monte), Powers Boothe
(hankie salesman), James Sutorius (voice of Jack), Richard Ja-

mieson (Spotter), James Ray Weeks (seller), David Winnie Hayes (bouncer), Carmine Stipo (bartender), James Hayden (Cockpit coke man), Todd Winters (tugboat mate).
And: Robert Carnegie, Dennis Shea, Larry Silvestri, Lawrence Lust, Penny Gumeny, Ray Vitte, Joseph Catucci, Dan Sturkie, Sylvia Gassell, Henry Judd Baker, Kevin Johnson, Louis Grenier, Burr DeBenning, Mike Barbera, Robert Duggan, Linda Gary. Songs performed by The Cripples, Willy DeVille, Germs-G.I., John Hiatt, Mutiny, Rough Trade, Madelyn von Ritz, Egberto Gismonti, Barre Phillips, Ralph Towner, Tom Brown.
Songs: "Three Day Moon," "Batik-Water Wheel," "Herbal Scent."

Deal of the Century (Bud Yorkin Production/Warner Bros., 1983) 99 minutes, Technicolor. MPAA Rating: PG.
Executive producers, Jon Avnet, Steve Tisch, Paul Brickman; producer, Bud Yorkin; director, William Friedkin; written by Paul Brickman; director of photography, Richard Kline, ASC; production designer, Bill Malley; supervising film editor, Bud Smith; film editors, Ned Humphreys, Jere Huggins; associate producer, David Salven; music by Arthur B. Rubenstein; casting, Nancy Klopper; unit production manager, David Salven; first assistant director, Terrence A. Donnelly; second assistant director, James Freitag; costumes, Rita Riggs; set decorator, Richard Goddard; supervising sound effects editor, Stephen Hunter Flick; supervising dialogue editor, J. Paul Huntsman; sound effects editors, Warren Hamilton, Jr., Mark Mangini; dialogue editor, Andrew Patterson; music editor, Abby Treloggen; production mixer, Willie Burton; rerecording mixers, Robert "Buzz" Knudson, Christopher Jenkins, Robert Glass, Don Digirolamo; script supervisor, Betty Abbott Griffin; location managers, Bill Bowling, David Salven, Jr.; camera operator, Al Bettcher; Panaglide (R) operator, Dan Lerner; assistant cameraman, Jud Kehl; second assistant cameraman, Kevin Jewison; property master, Barry Bedig; assistant property master, Stan Cockerell; assistant film editors, Craig Bassett, Seth Flaum; video coordinator, Rick Whitfield; negative cutter, Donah Bassett; color timer, Aubrey Head; orchestrator, Mark Hoder; special effects, Chuck Gaspar, Joe Day; DGA trainee, Linda Rockstroh; production associate, Tim Chisholm; production secretary, Nanette Siegert; assistant to the producer, Dolores Hyams; men's costumer, Liza Stewart; makeup artist, Frank Griffin; hairstylist, Kaye Powell; second unit in charge of optical effects, Bruce Logan; motion control photography, Dream

Quest Images; motion control supervisors, Scott Squires, Hoyt Yeatman; motion control technicians, David Hardberger, Thomas Hollister, Robert Hollister, Fred Iguchi, Bess Wiley; motion control assistant, William Reilly; computer operator, Michael Bigelow; motion control gaffer, Robert Thomas; motion control grip, Eric Stoner; production coordinator, Keith Shartle; front projection system, Zoptic, Inc.; consultant, Zoran Perisic; Zoptic operator, Allen Blaisdell; Zoptic projectionist, Norman Markowitz; rear projection coordinator, Bill Hansard; visual effects assistant editor, Jerry Colonna; special miniature effects by Coast Special Effects; matte paintings by Dream Quest Images; matte artist, Rocco Gioffre; titles, Pacific Title.
Cast: Chevy Chase (Eddie Muntz), Sigourney Weaver (Mrs. DeVoto), Gregory Hines (Ray Kasternak), Vince Edwards (Frank Stryker), William Marquez (Gen. Cordosa), Eduardo Richard (Colonel Salgado), Richard Herd (Lyle), Graham Jarvis (Babers), Wallace Shawn (Harold DeVoto), Randi Brooks (Ms. Della Rosa), Ebbe Roe Smith (Bob), Richard Libertini (Masaggi), J. W. Smith (Will), Carmen Moreno (woman singer), Charles Levin (Dr. Rechtin), Pepe Serna (Vardis), Wilfredo Hernandez (Rojas), John Davey (pilot on screen), Miguel Pinero (Molino), Maurice Marsac (Frenchman), Joe Ross (Russian translator), Jonathan Terry (Gaylord), Robert Cornthwaite (Huddleston), Gwil Richards (Reverend Borman), Kelly Lange (newscaster), Ken Letner (Senator Bryce), Jomarie Payton (Baptist #1), Tony Plana (Chicano man), Betty Cole (Baptist #2), John Hancock (Baptist minister), Helen Martin (Baptist #3), Eddie Hice (bagman), David Haskell (Rockwell official), Ray Manzarek (Charlie Simbo), David Hall (Rick Penido), Alex Colon (street robber), John Reilly (Swain), James Staley (JWT associate), Stephen Keep (promoter), Louis Giambalvo (Freddie Muntz), Robert Alan Browne (man from Grumman), Brad English (man from McDonnell-Douglas), Jim Ishida (Masaggi's aide #1), Michael Yama (Masaggi's aide #2), Judy Baldwin (Luckup hostess #1), Ian McGill (Luckup hostess #2), Frank Lugo (station wagon driver), Loyda Ramos (Chicano woman), Wendy Solomon (Freddy's wife), John Stinson (helicopter reporter), Janet Louise Smith (woman in commercial); Jesus Carmona (accordionist).
Songs: "Someone to Watch Over Me," "Shine."

To Live and Die in L.A. (MGM/UA/New Century Productions, Ltd. and SLM, Inc., 1985) 116 minutes, prints by Technicolor. MPAA Rating: R.

Executive producer, Samuel Schulman; producer, Irving H. Levin; director, William Friedkin; screenplay by William Friedkin and Gerald Petievich, based upon the novel by Gerald Petievich; production designer, Lilly Kilvert; supervising film editor, Bud Smith; film editor, Scott Smith; casting, Bob Weiner; consultants, Pablo Ferro, Barry Bedig; music composed and performed by Wang Chung; co-produced by Bud Smith; director of photography, Robby Muller; second unit director, Bud Smith; unit production manager, John J. Smith; first assistant director, Charles Myers; second assistant director, Bob Roe; stunt coordinator (fight sequences), Pat E. Johnson; stunt coordinator (driving and chase sequences), Buddy Joe Hooker; second unit photography, Robert Yeoman; rerecording mixers, Christopher Jenkins, Robert Glass, Gary Alexander; rerecorded by TODD-AO; sound effects editors, Louis L. Edemann, Michael Dobie, Jeff Bushelman; dialogue editor, J. Paul Huntsman; additional editing, Jere Huggins; assistant film editors, Sonny Baskin, Joseph Mosca, Jill Smith; special effects, Phil Corey; art director, Buddy Cone; set decorator, Cricket Rowland; production coordinator, Dianne Lisa Cheek; head makeup artist, Jefferson Dawn; costume designer, Linda Bass; casting associate, Gary M. Zuckerbrod; sound recordists, Jean-Louis DuCarme, Roger Pardee; script supervisor, Julie Saunders; assistant set decorators, Richard Hummel, Portia Iverson; set dressers, John Stadelman, Jon Hutman; still photographer, Jane O'Neal; location manager, Michael Healy; assistant location manager, Michael Helfand; printer, Amanda Flick; assistant art director, Dins Danielson; construction coordinator, Frank Viviano; captains, Raymond Camaioni, Dennis Hoerter, William Jones, Gavin McCune; costume supervisor, Susie DeSanto; hair stylist, Peter Tothpal; negative cutter, Donah Bassett; chief lighting technician, Greg Gardiner; best boy electric, Scott Guthrie; electricians, Robert Field, Kevin Galbraith; key grip, Robert Feldman; best boy grip, Lesley Percy; grips Bill Guerre, Timothy Moore; transportation coordinator, Jeffrey Renfro; transportation captains, Richard Brasic, Olivia Varnado; production secretary, Betsy Oliver Luhrsen; assistants to William Friedkin, Adele Joseph, Cindy Chvatal; assistant to the producer, Michele Troxell; prison institutional coordinator, Gil Miller; prison technical advisor, Woody Wilcoxan; extra casting, The Atmosphere Agency; post production auditor, Diana Gold; completion guarantee provided by Film Finance, Inc.; insurance provided by Bob Jellen/Albert G. Rubin & Co., Inc.; mainservice provided by Rick Pollack, Sherman Oaks, Ca.; Christian Dior bed linens

by Wamsutta; Masters's paintings by Rainer Fetting; payroll
services, TPI/EPPI; optical effects, Movie Magic; dialogue re-
corded by The Sound Shop; lab consultant, Larry Rovetti; color
timers, Dick Ritchie, Aubrey Head; Dolby consultant, Jim Fitz-
patrick; choreographer, Lesli Linka Glatter.

Cast: William L. Petersen (Richard Chance), Willem Dafoe (Eric
Masters), John Pankow (John Vukovich), Debra Feuer (Bianca
Torres), John Turturro (Carl Cody), Darlanne Fleugel (Ruthie
Laurice), Dean Stockwell (Bob Grimes), Steve James (Jeff Rice),
Robert Downey (Thomas Bateman), Michael Greene (Jim Hart),
Christopher Allport (Max Waxman), Jack Hoar (Jack), Val
DeVargas (Judge Codillis), Dwier Brown (doctor), Michael Chong
(Thomas Ling), Jackey Giroux (Claudia Leith), Michael Zand
(terrorist), Bobby Bass, Dar Allen Robinson (FBI agents), Anne
Betancourt (nurse), Kathering M. Loure (ticket agent), Edward
Harrell (airport guard), Gilbert Espinoza (bartender), John Pet-
ievich, Zarkow Petievich, Rick, Dalton, Richard I. Lane, Jack
Costa (agents), Shirley J. White (airline passenger), Gerald H.
Brownlee (visiting prison guard), David M. DuFriend (tower
guard), Ruben Garcie (Ruben), Joe Duran (prison guard), Bu-
ford McClerkins, Gregg Dandridge (prison assassins), Donny
Williams, Earnest Hart, Jr. (Rice's friends), Thomas Duffy (sec-
ond suspect), Gerry Petievich (special agent), Mark Gash (Mark
Gash), Pat McGroarty (criminal), Brian Bradley (toilet visitor),
Jane Leaves (Serena).

Dancers: Jane Leaves, Cherise Bate, Michael W. Higgins, Chris
Lattanzi, Shaun Earl.

Stunt Players: Jeb Adams, Carl L. Anderson, Bobby Bass, Joph-
rey Brown, Bobby Andrew Burns, Bill Burton, Dave Carlton,
John Casino, Phil Chong, Carl Ciarfalio, Ray Gilbert, Clarke
Coleman, Jim Connors, Wally Crowder, Tim Culbertson, Jay C.
Currin, Jeffrey J. Dashnaw, Steve M. Davison, Tim A. Davison,
Justin DeRosa, Eddie Donno, Doc Duhame, David R. Ellis,
Richard M. Ellis, Kenny Endoso, Tony Epper, Eric Felix, Glo-
ria Fioramanti; Pat Green, James M. Halty, Orwin C. Harvey,
Steve Halladay, Larry E. Holt, Bill (Hank) Hooker, Buddy
Joe Hooker, Hugh M. Hooker, Richard Hooker, Thomas J. Huff,
Gary Hymes, Loren Janes, Matt Johnson, Donna McKeegan,
Henry Kingi, Billy D. Lucas, Pat McGroarty, Gary McCarty,
Pat McNamara, John C. Meier, Charly Marie Morgan, Jimmy
Nickerson, Manuel Perry, Jon Pochran, Chad Rondell, Cyn-
thia Lee Rice, Jean Riddid, Vernon Rieta, Dar Allen Robin-
son, Danny Rogers, Patrick Romano, R. A. Rondell, Ronald
Rondell, Debby Lynn Ross, Mike Runyard, Ray Saniger, Den-

nis R. Scott, Keith Tellez, David H. Welch, Scott Wilder, Dick Ziker.

To Live and Die in L.A. (music video, 1985) 3:58, in color.
Director, William Friedkin; editor, Bud Smith; with Wang Chung (musicians Nick Feldman and Jack Hues) and sound technicians playing themselves. With scenes from the film. Shot at TODD-AO studios.

Self-Control (music video; Atlantic Records/Atco-Cotillion Records, 1985) 5:05, in color.
Director, William Friedkin. With Laura Branigan.

Nightcrawlers (CBS-TV; *The Twilight Zone*, 1985) 20 minutes, color.
Executive producer, Philip DeGuere; supervising producer, James Crocker; director, William Friedkin; teleplay by Philip DeGuere, based on short story by Robert S. McCammon; producer, Harvey Frand; executive story consultant, Alan Brennert; story editor, Rockne S. O'Bannon; creative consultant, Harlan Ellison; associate producer, James Heinz.
Cast: Scott Paulin (Price), James Whitmore, Jr. (Trooper Dennis), Robert Swan (Bobby the chef), Exene Cervenka (waitress).
Airdate: October 16, 1985.

Somewhere (music video, Columbia Records, 1986) 4:25, in color.
Executive producer, Barbra Streisand; producers Cindy Chvatal, Glenn Goodwin; director, William Friedkin; director of photography, Andrzej Bartowiak; editor, Bud Smith; assistant editor, Scott Smith; music by Leonard Bernstein; lyrics by Stephen Sondheim; from *West Side Story*; produced and arranged by David Foster; engineered by Humberto Gatica; additional engineering by Magic Moreno; assistant engineers, Woody Woodruff, Randy Waldman.

The C.A.T. Squad (NBC-TV, 1986) 100 minutes, in color.
Executive producer, William Friedkin; supervising producer, Gerald Petievich; producer, David Salven; director, William Friedkin; co-producer, Bud Smith; co-producer, Cindy Chvatal;

teleplay by Gerald Petievich; director of photography, Robert D. Yeoman; music by Ennio Morricone; film edited by Bud Smith and Scott Smith; production designer, Douglas Higgins; second unit director, Bud Smith; stunt coordinator, Pat Johnson; production designer (Mexico), Buddy Cone; casting (New York), Bob Weiner; (Montreal) Rosina Bucci; (Mexicali), Rick Montgomery, Gary Zuckerbrod; production manager, David Salven; first assistant director, Charles A. Myers; second assistant director, Michael Healy; costume supervisor, Barry Delaney; property master, Sam Moore; special effects, Bob Dawson; production controller, Paul Marquez; production secretary, Nanette Siegert; assistant to Mr. Friedkin, Adele Joseph; animal trainer, Alvin Mears; assistant to executive producer, Kelly Snyder; Canadian staff: production manager, Wendy Grean; second assistant director, Anne Murphy; costume supervisor, France Lachadelle; location manager, Carole Mondello; first assistant camera, Yves Drapeau; sound mixer, Don Cohen; gaffer, Don Saari; key grip, Serge Grenier; second unit cameraman, Bert Touges; film editors, Walt Mulconery, Jere Huggins; sound effects editor, Mike Dobie; ADR editor, Carl L. Lewis; rerecording mixer, Chris Jenkins; assistant editors (US), Seth Flaum, Richard Alderette, Mike Mulconery; assistant editors (Canada), Jackie Carmody, Josceline Genest.

Cast: Joe Cortese (Doc Burkholder), Jack Youngblood (John Sommers), Steve W. James (Bud Raines), Patricia Charbonneau (Nikki Blake), Barry Corbin (the Director), Eddie Velez (Carlos), Sam Gray (Dr. Henry Spivak), Al Shannon (Irish Johnny), Frank Military (Willie Darby), Anna Maria Horsford (Mrs. Raines), Anne Curry (Janet), Hans Bogild (Dieter Porzig), Tom Hauff (Ernie Nolan), Michael Sinelnikoff (Sir Cyril Sharpe), John Novak (Jack Connery), Reg Hanson (Dr. John Woodhouse), Pamela Collyer (Janice Brown), Umas Rasberry (Buddy, Jr.).

With: Vlasta Vrana, Nanette Workman, Guy Provost, Nick Ramus, Rick Garcia, Roberto Jimenez. Broadcast: July 27, 1986.

Rampage (DeLaurentiis Entertainment Group, Rampage Productions, 1987) 97 minutes, color. MPAA Rating: R.
Producer, David Salven; director, William Friedkin; screenplay by William Friedkin, based on the novel by William P. Wood; director of photography, Robert D. Yeoman; edited by Jere Huggins; original music by Ennio Morricone; production designer, Buddy Cone; casting, Rick Montgomery; first assistant

director, Michael Daves; second assistant director, Regina Gordon; special visual effects, Pablo Ferro; camera operator, Robert D. Yeoman; first assistant cameraman, Brian Sweeney; second assistant cameraman, John Boccaccio; camera loader, Kelly Snyder; stills, Francois Duhamel; script supervisor, Trudy Ramirez; production coordinator, Patty Raya; location manager, Brian Brosnan; sound mixer, David MacMillan; boom operator, Steve Bowerman; property master, Barry Bedig; assistant property, Tony Maccario; art director, Carol Clements; set decorator, Nancy Nye; assistant set decorator, Joni Indursky; costume supervisor, Barbara Siebert Bolticoff; men's costumer, Gene Deardorff; women's costumer, Victoria Snow; makeup artist, Teresa Austin; hair stylist, Steven Frank; casting associate, Maureen Arata; extras casting, Keith Hirabayashi; gaffer, Patrick Melly; best boy, Steve Flood; key grip, Tim Moore; best boy, Les Percy; dolly grip, Mike Moad; transportation coordinator, Tommy Tancharoen; transportation captain, Lee Garibaldi; construction coordinator, Dean Brown; assistant to Mr. Friedkin, Adele Joseph; assistant to Mr. Salven, Christine Baer; production secretary, Mickie Cecchini; production accountant, Ken Ryan; assistant auditor, Mayda Renizzi-Holt; assistant editors, Seth Flaum, Kelly Snyder; apprentice editor, Craig Kitson; supervising sound editor, Mike Dobie; sound editors, Don Warner, James J. Isaacs, Jayme S. Parker; assistant sound editor, Kim Nolan; ADR editor, Cari Lewis; rerecording mixer, Chris Jenkins; mixers, Gary Alexander, Doug Hemphill; negative cutter, Donah Bassett; lab consultant, Larry Rovetti; color timer, Terri Haggar; production assistants, Shane Ryan, Jaime Camarena, Larry Felix, Terry Garcia; caterer, Stageside Service; postproduction services, TODD-AO/Glen Glenn; opticals by Pacific Title; camera and lenses by Panavision.
Cast: Michael Biehn (Anthony Fraser), Alex McArthur (Charles Reece), Nicholas Campbell (Albert Morse), Deborah Van Valkenburgh (Kate Fraser), John Harkins (Dr. Keddie), Art Lafleur (Mel Sanderson), Billy Greenbush (Judge McKinsey), Royce D. Applegate (Gene Tippetts), Grace Zabriskie (Naomi Reece), Carlos Palomino (Nestade), Roy London (Dr. Paul Rudin), Donald Hotton (Dr. Leon Gables), Andy Romano (Spencer Whalen), Patrick Cronin (Harry Bellenger), Roger Nolan (Dr. Ray Blair), Chris Mulkey (salesman), Rosalyn Marshall (Sally Ann), Whitby Hertford (Andrew Tippetts), David A. Kimball (doctor in flashbacks), Brenda Lilly (Eileen Tippetts), Joseph Whipp (Dr. George Mahon), Chip Heller (guard #1), Rodney Cornelius (guard #2), Dave Alan Johnson (Del Cameron), Robert Broyles (Joe Kauf-

man), Edith Fields (Rose Gurgan), Art Frankel (John Malone), Neal Hahn (Mr. Hendricksen), Gale Beeman (Mrs. Hendricksen), Marni Webb (Mrs. Ellis), Paul Gaddoni (Aaron Tippetts), Bernard Zanck (priest), Noreen Farley (waitress), Charlie Holliday (narc #1), Ken Jackson (narc #2), Miguel Najera (Cardenas), John Petievich (jury foreman), Miriam Gray, Tara O'Leary, Dorothy D. Johnson, George Johnson, Edward Ivory (jurors), Violet Yip (court clerk), Juliette Dienum (Wendy), Robert Gonzales (guard #1), Steven A. Jones (guard #2), Dr. Javad Jamshidi (Dr. Jamshidi), Robert Knudsen, Marina Valtierra, Gaetano Comporato (ID techs), Clifford Milton (evidence tech), Pamela Tarver (woman in car), Chelsea Crank (Molly Fraser), Margaret Rose Ott (Mrs. Cardenas), S. Richard Goldman, Robert Wright, Colleen Casby-Rohde, Susan Thomas, Laura Moreno-Orrison, Leonard Neuman (ER techs), Richard J. Baskin (attorney), Tino R. Enebradj, Jr. (officer), Robert Louis Raballo (patient), Angelo M. Vitale (assistant D.A.), Richard Markel (bailiff), Mack Haywood Flanders (sheriff), Erin Hazlett-Oakes, Nancy L. Sicotte, Elizabeth J. Prager (technologists), Michael Tamburro (helicopter pilot), Peter McKiernan, Jr. (co-pilot). Stunts by Bobby Bass.

The C.A.T. Squad: Python Wolf (NBC/TV/William Friedkin Productions, 1988) 98 minutes, color (television version); 99 minutes (home video version).
Executive producer, William Friedkin; producer, David Salven; director, William Friedkin; created by Gerald Petievich and William Friedkin; teleplay by Robert Ward; story by Gerald Petievich & William Friedkin and Robert Ward; music by Ennio Morricone; edited by Jere Huggins; production designer, Richard Sawyer; director of photography, Guy Dufaux; casting, Rick Montgomery; stunt coordinator, Pat Johnson; first assistant director, Newt Arnold; costume supervisor, Ray Summers; special effects, Bob Dawson; property master, Bill MacSems; production executive, Nanette Siegert; production manager (Canada), Mychelle Boudrias; script supervisor, Kelly Snyder; location managers, Carole Mondello, Jennifer Jonas; key grip, Serge Grenier; special makeup, Charles Carter; jazz consultant, Charles Ellison; technical advisor, Wilbert Cox; sound effects by Blue Light Sound, Inc.; ADR editor, Paul Huntsman; rerecorded at TODD-AO; assistant film editor, David Dresher; postproduction supervisor, Dorothy J. Bailey; video graphics, Homer & Associates/Peter Conn; miniatures by Chuck

Comiskey; computer equipment furnished by Honeywell Bull (Canada); location sites furnished by Banque de Montreal; Via Rail Canada, Inc.; Canadian Armed Forces and Department of Defense; executive in charge of production, William F. Phillips. Cast: Joe Cortese (Richard Earl "Doc" Burkholder), Jack Youngblood (John Summers), Steve James (Bud Raines), Deborah Van Valkenburgh (Nikki Pappas), Miguel Ferrer (Kiley), Alan Scarfe (Bekker), Alan Coates (Cellier), Michael Fletcher (Van Crewe), Chris Loomis (General Highsmith), William Mooney (Curtin), Peter Neptune (Reeves), Abdoulaye N'Gom (Bothezi), George Seremba (Gafsha), Seth Sibanda (Motlono), William Bell Sullivan (Anderson), Chris Walker (Fox).
With: Brian Delate, Neil Hunt, Ted Dillon, Russell Wong, James Saito, Vlasta Vrana, David O'Brian, Ron Frazier, Ron Parady, Bruce Young. Broadcast May 23, 1988.

It's hard to know who's doing more acting: Friedkin with the pipe and outstretched hand or Peter Falk enraptured with the "direction" he's receiving during the filming of *The Brink's Job*.
COURTESY OF *THE BOSTON HERALD*

BIBLIOGRAPHY

The material in this book has been drawn from interviews conducted with William Friedkin since 1974, first for publicity in connection with his films and then specifically for this work. In no instance was he given, nor did he request, the right to approve any part of it.

Other information has been drawn from interviews arranged for the book or held in connection with the various films at the time of their release, plus published and unpublished accounts in all media.

The author would like to make a special note of thanks to the Margaret Herrick Library of the Academy of Motion Picture Arts and Sciences and its personnel for their extraordinary devotion to chronicling the reality of Hollywood fantasy.

American Film Institute, The. *Dialogue on Film*, Vol. 3, No. 4, Feb.–Mar. 1974, William Friedkin. California: The American Film Institute, 1974.

Applebaum, Ralph. "Tense Situations." *Films and Filmmaking*, Vol. 25, Number 6, March 1979.

Archerd, Army. "New Wrinkle." *Variety*, May 18, 1977.

Associated Press (unsigned), item on Friedkin vs. Warner Bros., April 1, 1975.

Barrett, Gerald R. "William Friedkin Interview." *Film Quarterly*, Vol. 4, No. 4 (Fall 1975).

Beck, Marilyn. "Friedkin Prepares *L.A.* for Europe." Wire services, December 2, 1985.

Behn, Noel. *Big Stick-Up At Brink's*. New York: G. P. Putnam's Sons, 1977.

Bell, Arthur. "Bell Tells." *The Village Voice*, July 1, 1979.

Bevilacour, Richard and Earl Marchand. "Director Denies 'Brink's

Job' Movie Paid Off Mob." *Boston Herald-American,* December 16, 1978.

Blatty, William Peter. *William Peter Blatty on The Exorcist From Novel to Film.* New York: Bantam Books, 1974.

Blatty, William Peter. *The Exorcist.* New York: Harper & Row, 1971.

Blatty, William Peter. *Legion.* New York: Simon & Schuster, 1983.

Blowen, Michael. "The Brains Behind the Big Brink's Job." *Boston Globe,* August 6, 1978.

Boston Globe (unsigned). "There'll Be No Ransom for Stolen Brink's Film." August 8, 1978.

Boston Globe (unsigned). "Filming of Brink's is Probed." December 14, 1978.

Boston Globe (unsigned). "Brink's Producer Going Before Jury." January 3, 1979.

Boston Herald-American (unsigned). "Brink's Producer Testifies." February 7, 1979.

Bowles, Stephen E. "The Exorcist and Jaws." *Film Quarterly,* Vol. 4, No. 3, Summer 1979.

Bradbury, Ray and Hal Kanter. "Forty-Ninth Academy Awards Show." Academy of Motion Picture Arts and Sciences television script (unpublished). California: A.M.P.A.S., 1977.

Brass, Sally K. "Director Gets 'Birthday' Wish." *Los Angeles Times,* May 19, 1968.

Caplan, Lincoln. *The Insanity Defense and the Trial of John W. Hinkley, Jr.* Boston: David R. Godine, 1984.

Claffey, Charles E. "Probe Widens into Brink's Filmmaker Payoffs." *Boston Globe,* December 15, 1978.

Connolly, James. "Four Indicted in Hub Extortion of Film Makers." *Boston Herald-American,* June 13, 1981.

Consumer Guide. *Movie Trivia Mania.* New York: Beekman House, 1984.

Crowley, Mart. *The Boys in the Band.* New York: Farrar, Straus & Giroux, 1968.

Daniels, Dennis. "Getting Down." *The Boston Herald,* July 9, 1987.

Dineen, Joe. "Brink's Holdup, the Way It Was." *The Boston Globe,* December 17, 1978.

Eller, Claudia. "DEG Wards Off Bankruptcy in Fight for Financial Survival." *The Hollywood Reporter,* July 5, 1988.

Eller, Claudia. "DEG Story Nears Final Chapter as TWE Closes in on Takeover." *The Hollywood Reporter,* December 20, 1988.

Eller, Claudia. "Gangster on Ice: Friedkin Exits Film." *The Hollywood Reporter,* October 20, 1988.

Ellison, Bob. "Top of the World: Billy (*French Connection*) Friedkin Films *The Exorcist.*" *Today's Film Maker,* 1973.

Finler, Joel W. *The Movie Director's Story.* New York: Crescent Books, 1985.

Friedkin, William. "Anatomy of a Chase: The French Connection." *Di-*

rectors in "Action": Selections From "Action," The Official Magazine of the Directors Guild of America. Bob Thomas, ed. Indianapolis:
Bobbs Merrill Co., 1973.

Friedkin, William. The Making of The Exorcist. Unpublished manuscript, 1974.

Friedkin, William. Rampage. Unpublished screenplay, September 10,
1986.

Friedkin, William. Letter to the Editor. The New York Times, February
24, 1974.

Garrett, Bob. "Exorcist Director Making a Big Run at $ Gross Re-
cord." Boston Herald-American, January 24, 1974.

Gentry, Ric. "William Friedkin: An Interview." Post Script, 1985.

Ginsberg, Steven. "Friedkin and Weintraub Defend 'Cruising' Against
MPAA's Rating Charges." Variety, June 18, 1980.

Haber, Joyce. Feature. Los Angeles Herald-Examiner, January 17,
1972.

Haber, Joyce. Column item. Los Angeles Times, February 5, 1974.

Hart, Richard. "Brink's Movie Hit By Scene-Stealers." The Boston Globe,
July 29, 1978.

Hirschberg, Lynn. "William Petersen: Wanted Man." Us magazine.
September 8, 1986.

Hollywood Reporter (unsigned). Exorcist lawsuit. November 6, 1973.

Hollywood Reporter (unsigned). Item. February 21, 1980.

Kelly, Kevin. "What Happened to the Lad Who Wrote 'Boys in the
Band'?" The Boston Globe, May 27, 1973.

Key, Wilson Bryan. Media Sexploitation. New York: The New American Library, 1976.

Kilday, Gregg. "Friedkin vs. Taylor." Los Angeles Herald-Examiner,
February 19, 1980.

Kilday, Gregg. "Predicting Which Movie William Friedkin Will Direct." Los Angeles Times, October 29, 1977.

Kimmel, Daniel M. "Rampage" (review). Variety, September 30,
1987.

King, Andrea. "SLM Goes Fox Hunting With Multimillion-Dollar
Lawsuit." The Hollywood Reporter, December 7, 1988.

Klein, Norma. "William Friedkin Sued." Los Angeles Herald-Examiner,
March 29, 1978.

Knoedelseder, William K., Jr. "Dino: King of Movie Flops." New York
Post, September 22, 1987.

Kroll, Jack. "Duet for One." Newsweek, December 26, 1981.

Lamere, Richard. "Teamsters Absolved by Two Film Men." Boston
Herald-American, January 20, 1982.

Lane, Lydia. Interview with Jennifer Nairn-Smith. Los Angeles Times,
October 5, 1978.

Leyda, Jay, ed. "Ellen Burstyn, interviewed for Show Magazine." Film
Makers Speak. New York: Da Capo Press, 1977.

Loeb, Anthony. Filmmakers in Conversation. Chicago: Columbia College, 1982.

Los Angeles Herald-Examiner (unsigned). Item. February 19, 1986.

Los Angeles Magazine. "The Lange/Friedkin Solution." Unsigned. September 1987.

"Mack." "Oscar Awards 1977 Review." *Variety,* March 29, 1977.

Mahoney, John C. "Norman Twain Sets William Friedkin to Direct." *Los Angeles Times,* September 22, 1977.

Marchand, Earl. "Brink's Film 'Payoff' Probed." *Boston Herald-American,* December 14, 1978.

Maslin, Janet. "Friedkin Completes 'Cruising' . . . Intact." *The New York Times,* September 21, 1979.

McCarthy, John and Brian Kelleher. *Alfred Hitchcock Presents: An Illustrated Guide to the Ten-Year Career of the Master of Suspense.* New York: St. Martin's Press, 1985.

McMillan, Nancy Pomerene. "Brink's Is Robbed in Boston Again." *The New York Times,* July 2, 1978.

McMillan, Nancy Pomerene. "FBI in Inquiry in Brink's Film Case." *The New York Times,* August 7, 1978.

Minahan, John. Interview. *Los Angeles Magazine,* December 1978.

Monaco, James. *American Film Now.* New York: The New American Library, 1979.

Moore, Robin. *The French Connection.* Boston: Little, Brown & Co., 1969.

Murphy, A. D. "Friedkin Suit Seen as Direct Challenge to Longtime Film Industry Practices." *Variety,* April 2, 1975.

New York Times. Remarks, film and stage directors. June 12, 1981.

New York Times. "Four Gunmen Steal Reels of Film About $2 Million Brink's Robbery." July 29, 1978.

Newman, Howard. *The Exorcist: The Strange Story Behind the Film.* New York: Pinnacle Books, 1974.

Newsweek. "Directors Company." September 25, 1972.

Newsweek. "William Friedkin Files for Divorce from Jeanne Moreau." June 25, 1979.

Nolan, William F. "Log of a Screen Writer." *The World of Books: Writers and Writing.* Matthew J. Bruccoli, editorial director. Michigan: Gale Research Co., 1976.

O'Brien, Greg. "Brink's Job Strong-Arm Trial Opens." *Boston Herald-American,* January 18, 1982.

O'Neill, John and Bob Creamer. "Brink's Reel-Life Reel Heist Not Part of the Script." *Boston Herald-American,* July 29, 1978.

Orenstein, Bill. "Bill Friedkin Sees Plotted Picture on Way Out; Youth Wants Abstract." *The Hollywood Reporter,* April 6, 1967.

Pave, Marvin. "Brink's Film Extortionists Get a Negative Reply." *The Boston Globe,* August 7, 1978.

People Magazine. "Moreau and Mate." February 13, 1978.

Petievich, Gerald. *To Live and Die in L.A.* New York: Pinnacle Books, 1984.

Pinter, Harold. *The Birthday Party.* New York: Grove Press, 1959.

Pollack, Dale. "Cruising." *Los Angeles Times,* February 4, 1980.

Reed, Rochelle. "Morning After the Oscar." *The Hollywood Reporter,* April 12, 1972.

HURRICANE BILLY** **309**

Rosenbaum, David. "What Makes Billy Friedkin Yell?" *Boston Herald-American*, December 20, 1978.
Rosenblum, Ralph and Robert Karen, *When The Shooting Stops . . . The Cutting Begins*. New York: The Viking Press, 1979.
Rothenberg, Fred. "The Plot Sounds Familiar." *New York Post*, May 13, 1988.
Rothschild, Donald S., Nancy J. Tapella and Elmer Gertz, Esq. *Brief and Argument for Plaintiff-Appellant Paul O. Crump*. Unpublished. Illinois: Seventh Circuit Court of Appeals, 1986.
Russo, Vito. *The Celluloid Closet: Homosexuality and the Movies*. New York: Harper & Row, 1981, 1987.
Ryweck, Charles. "Duet for One." *The Hollywood Reporter*, December 21, 1981.
Sanders, Richard and Jackie Savaino. "Director Billy Friedkin and Lesley-Anne Down Make a Home Movie—Divorce Hollywood Style." *People* magazine, September 2, 1985.
School of Performing Arts, University of Southern California. *First Distinguished Alumni Award to David L. Wolper* program booklet. Los Angeles: University of Southern California, 1979.
Shedlin, Michael. "Police Oscar: The French Connection and an Interview with William Friedkin." *Film Quarterly*, Vol. 25, No. 4, Summer 1972.
Sherman, Eric for The American Film Institute. *Directing the Film: Directors on Their Art*. Boston: Little, Brown & Co., 1976.
Stack, James and Charles Claffey. "Attorney Seen Movie Tie to Mob." *The Boston Globe*, December 15, 1978.
Stack, James. "Director Denies Mob Was Paid Off for Brink's Movie." *The Boston Globe*, December 18, 1978.
Taylor, Clarke. Willem Dafoe interview. *Los Angeles Times*, November 30, 1985.
Taylor, Maureen. "Film 'Boys in the Band' Faithful to Hit Legit Version." *The Boston Sunday Advertiser*, March 15, 1970.
Thomas, Bob. "$10m 'Exorcist' Tab Doesn't Faze Director Friedkin." Associated Press, January 8, 1974.
Thomas, Bob. "Gene Hackman: Big Talent." Associated Press, June 11, 1972.
Tidyman, Ernest and William Friedkin, *The French Connection*. Unpublished screenplay, April 26, 1971.
"Tone." "C.A.T. Squad: Python Wolf." *Variety*, June 8, 1988.
Travers, Peter and Stephanie Reiff. *The Story Behind The Exorcist*. New York: Crown Publishers, Inc., 1974.
Tusher, Will. "William Friedkin Says DGA Award Went to Wrong Man." *The Hollywood Reporter*, March 21, 1972.
Tusher, Will. "Friedkin 'Exorcist' Version." *The Hollywood Reporter*, November 6, 1975.
Tusher, Will. "Judgement Day Is Second SLM Prod'n Deal for Friedkin." *Variety*, November 20, 1985.
Tusher, Will. "To Live and Die in L.A. $8 M Budget." *Variety*, July 25, 1985.

United Press International (unsigned). "Friedkin Files $15 Million Libel Suit Against L.A. Times." February 19, 1986.

United Press International (unsigned). Item. July 8, 1987.

Variety (unsigned). "A Minsky Burlesque Theme Needs N.Y." August 2, 1967.

Variety (unsigned). "Non-Camp Homosexual Slant Favored by Friedkin in Filming 'Boys in Band.' " August 13, 1969.

Variety (unsigned). "In Paris" item. December 17, 1976.

Variety (unsigned). "William Friedkin Drops Out of Neil Diamond Special." February 4, 1977.

Variety (unsigned). "N.Y. Gays Try to Stop Filming of 'Cruising'." July 5, 1979.

Variety (unsigned). Item. September 22, 1977.

Variety (unsigned). "William Friedkin Out of 'Streamers.' " October 27, 1977.

Variety (unsigned). "Multi-Deal at Warner Bros." December 6, 1978.

Variety (unsigned). "Friedkin vs. Taylor." February 20, 1986.

Variety (unsigned). Correction. February 27, 1986.

Variety (unsigned). Item. September 2, 1982.

Variety (unsigned). "The Directors Company." August 20, 1972.

Variety (unsigned). "Bank Receives an Injunction vs. DEG." June 8, 1988.

Walker, Gerald. *Cruising*. New York: Stein and Day, 1970.

Walstad, David. "Down: Steamy On and Off Screen." *Boston Herald-American*, November 4, 1985.

Ward, Robert. *C.A.T. Squad: Python Wolf*. Unpublished screenplay, September 22, 1987.

Weil, Fran. "Meet William Friedkin, Entertainer." *Boston Record-American*, June 13, 1972.

Weil, Fran. "Friedkin Already Planning His Next Film." *Boston Herald-American*, May 26, 1978.

Wiley, Mason and Daniel Bona. *Inside Oscar: The Unofficial History of the Academy Awards*. Gail MacColl, ed. New York: Ballantine Books, 1986, 1987.

Wolf, William. "Surefooted Friedkin Riding Tide of Success." *Los Angeles Times*, October 15, 1972.

Wood, Robin. *Hollywood from Vietnam to Reagan*. New York: The Columbia University Press, 1986.

Wood, William P. *Rampage*. New York: St. Martin's Press, 1985.

INDEX